13⁵⁰

977

The Division of Labour

MARXIST THEORY AND CONTEMPORARY CAPITALISM
General Editor: John Mepham

This is a new series of texts, of new British books and of translations, committed to:

the development of Marxist theory

the analysis of contemporary capitalism, its tendencies and contradictions

the record of struggles to which they give rise .

Also in this series:

Charles Bettelheim
The Transition to Socialist Economy

Michel Bosquet
Capitalism in Crisis and Everyday Life

Claudie Broyelle
Women's Liberation in China

Lucien Sève
Man in Marxist Theory: Towards a Marxist Theory of Personality

The Division of Labour:

The Labour Process and Class-Struggle in Modern Capitalism

edited by André Gorz

Humanities Press

This edition first published in the USA
in 1976 by the Humanities Press Inc.,
Atlantic Highlands, N.J. 07716

© 1976 The Harvester Press Limited
'What do bosses do?' © 1976 S. A. Marglin
First published in France as
Critique de la division du travail
copyright © Editions du Seuil 1973

Library of Congress Cataloging in Publication Data

Gorz, André, comp.
    The division of labour.

    (Marxist theory and contemporary capitalism)
    Translation of Critique de la division du travail.
    Includes bibliographical references and index.
    1.   Division of labor – Addresses, essays, lectures.
2.   Industrial sociology – Addresses, essays, lectures.
I.   Title.   II.   Series.
HD51.G67913   1976   301.5'5   76-5847
ISBN 0-391-00591-X

Set by Input Typesetting Ltd., London
and printed in Great Britain by
Redwood Burn Ltd., Trowbridge, Wiltshire

Contents

Contents

ANDRÉ GORZ
Preface

The capitalist division of labour is the source of all alienation. 'It converts the labourer into a crippled monstrosity, by forcing his detail dexterity at the expense of a world of productive capabilities. The knowledge, the judgement, and the will, which, though in ever so small degree, are practised by the independent peasant or handicraftsman . . .' are taken away from the workers and confiscated by capital, which concentrates them in its machines, its organization of labour, its technology. Furthermore, '. . . the labourer is brought face to face with the intellectual potencies of the material process of production, as the property of another, and as ruling power.' This separation of manual and intellectual labour '. . . cuts down the labourer into a detail labourer . . .'. And it '. . . makes science a productive force distinct from labour and presses it into the service of capital.'[1]

In short, 'To subdivide a man is . . . to assassinate him. . . . The subdivision of labour is the assassination of a people.'[2] And communism is nothing other than the movement that suppresses this division of labour; that '. . . overturns the basis of all earlier relations of production and intercourse', that replaces the capitalist hierarchization of functions and jobs by the voluntary collaboration of individuals; and that '. . . subjugates them to the power of the united individuals'.[3]

In Europe the traditional organizations of the labour movement were in the process of forgetting all that when, beginning in 1967, the capitalist division of labour found itself once again at the centre of the class struggle throughout the world; in France and Italy a new generation of workers of rural origin, driven towards the assembly line by the capitalist concentration in agriculture, rebelled against the fragmentation of work, the hierarchy, work speeds, the supervisors, the piece-rates, while in the United States absenteeism, silent rebellion against work speeds and outright sabotage of the product were cutting into anticipated profit margins.

Elsewhere the war in Vietnam and the Chinese Cultural Revolution were at the same time overthrowing accepted ideas of the superiority of western technology and the neutrality of science. We were discovering that there was a Vietnamese and Chinese type of medicine that, though much less unwieldly, less expensive and less 'learned' (that is to say incomprehensible to the masses) than ours, was no less effective. The same thing was happening in matters concerning agricultural or industrial technology: the vast and complex machines dominating the hundreds of unskilled workers who are at their service are not necessarily more efficient than teams of men and women collaborating in the use of simpler and smaller machines that have been perfected by the workers themselves. Thus we began to learn that peasant peoples could defeat the 'technotronic' world; and that the separation of intellectual and manual forces, of theory and practice, of the producers from their tools and their products, does not even make capitalist technology more efficient.

It does not matter much through which subterranean processes the two movements came together in the minds of the workers. The fact is that the impulse of 'Asian communism' and the rebellion of assembly-line workers in Europe suddenly put paid to a myth on which the mandarins of our society had based their powers and privileges – the myth that science and technology are 'neutral', that they have neither class-content nor class-imprint, and that the division of labour that they establish results from 'objective necessities' rather than from the requirement of capitalist accumulation.

Later in this book it is argued that the fragmentation and specialization of jobs, the divorce between intellectual and manual labour, the monopolization of science by élites, the gigantism of industrial plant and the centralization of power that results – that none of this is a necessary prerequisite for efficient production.[4] It is necessary only for the perpetuation of capitalist domination. For capital, all organization of work must be inextricably a technique of production and a technique of dominating those who are producing, because the goal of capitalist production can only be the growth of capital itself, and this goal, alien to the workers, can be realized through them only by constraint (direct or disguised).[5]

To produce and to dominate; to dominate those who are made to produce and who are enslaved to goals that are alien to them, to tools that must be used in a minutely predetermined way: the will to dominate is inherent in the nature of the machines, in the organization of production, in the division of labour in which it is put into practice: capital, its representatives and functionaries on the one hand, and the direct producers on the other.[6] Organization, production technology, division of labour form the material matrix that invariably reproduces through inertia hierarchical work relations, the capitalist relations of production. Marx had already seen this clearly, but he did not always draw the necessary conclusions: 'The technical subordination of the workman to the uniform motion of the instruments of labour, and the peculiar composition of the body of workpeople, consisting as it does of individuals of both sexes and of all ages, give rise to a barrack discipline, which is elaborated into a complete system in the factory, and which fully develops the before mentioned labour of overlooking, thereby dividing the workpeople into operatives and overlookers, into private soldiers and sergeants of an industrial army.'[7]

In this passage it is the technology of the factory that imposes a certain technical division of labour, which in turn requires a certain type of subordination, hierarchy and despotism. Thus technology is apparently the matrix and ultimate cause of everything and it is difficult to see how 'collective appropriation' of the means of production carrying the imprint of this technology would be able to change anything in the order of the factory, in the mutilation and oppression of the workers. It is certainly not by becoming collective 'owners' of these factories that the proletariat will be able to develop a 'totality of abilities' [8] in working there. As long as the material matrix remains unchanged, the 'collective appropriation' of factories can be only a completely abstract transfer of legal ownership, a transfer that can never put an end to the oppression and subordination of the workers.[9]

If it leaves the organization and techniques of production intact, such a transfer will also leave intact the matrix of hierarchical relations of domination and authority along with the old division of labour – in other words the capitalist relations of production. Power will remain with capital; only those who represent it will be different. Private management will be replaced by state management, capitalist bureaucracy by a 'political' bureaucracy, equally divorced from the people, and so on. The roles and 'expertise' required by the old division of labour will justify the preservation of the old oppressive, hierarchizing, selective educational system and the bourgeois educational system will continue to propagate bourgeois values and to select a new bourgeoisie (or 'state bourgeoisie'), who will no longer own property but who will have the powers of disposition and decision that were once linked to property. [10]

If the transition to communism is to take place, if there is to be collective (and not state) appropriation *by the producers* of the means of production and if voluntary collaboration is to supersede the hierarchical division of tasks, the direct producers must themselves take over and radically transform production technology, the way work is organized and machines are used, the relationship between work and knowledge and work and institutions (i.e. schools and colleges) transmitting knowledge. It must always be remembered that the 'means of production' are not only plant and machines; they are also the technology and the science incorporated in machines and installations, which *dominate* [11] the workers as a 'productive force distinct from labour'. Science and technology must be revolutionized and taken over by the proletariat, and reappropriated collectively as a common power by means of a reunification of manual and intellectual labour and a complete rebuilding of the organization of both labour and education.[12]

In no case can the working class, once in power, restrict itself to making workloads lighter, to cutting down the working week and to increasing pay, for the work process as shaped by capitalism represents, besides its unacceptable production goals, the destruction of the worker, the negation of his freedom, in other words his alienation. Marx stated this admirably in those sections of *Capital* from which extracts are included in this book:

At the same time that factory work exhausts the nervous system to the uttermost, it does away with the many-sided play of the muscles, and confiscates every atom of freedom, both in bodily and intellectual activity. The lightening of labour, even, becomes a sort of torture, since the machine does not free the labourer from work, but deprives the work of all interest. Every kind of capitalist production . . . has this in common, that it is not the workman that employs the instruments of labour, but the instruments of labour that employ the workman. [13]

That is why the emancipation of the working class, its power, begins through the struggle to recover its physical, psychic, intellectual and cultural integrity at work, that is to say in the struggle to impose the power of self-determination of the labour process. 'Indeed how could the working class exercise its power . . . if it had only a narrow, fragmented knowledge of production and was "dominated by technology"?' asks Claudie Broyelle.[14] And in the same book:

The Soviet system can no longer satisfy anybody: 'Here is a State factory, and the State is the Party, and the Party is the masses, thus this factory belongs to you, worker. QED.' No, this is no good any more. If someone says to me: 'This factory is yours, it belongs to the people', but I blindly obey the orders of the directors, I understand nothing of my machine and still less of the rest of the factory, if I do not know what becomes of my product when it is finished nor *why* it was produced, if I work fast, very fast for a bonus, and if I am bored to death, waiting all day for work to stop and longing every day for the weekend, if I am even more ignorant after years of work than at the beginning – in that case this factory is not mine, it does not belong to the people!

And it does not belong to the people either if work, even while enabling physical and intellectual faculties to develop, has goals that cannot be shared by everyone and produces wealth reserved for a minority.[15] Furthermore it does not belong to the people if by reason of their enormous size the units of production can be managed only centrally, can only be a techno-bureaucracy, and if the rigidity of their imperatives of operation take away all initiative and all choice from the people in defining the goals of production (and therefore of consumption). Thus the giant industrial (or administrative) concentrations that doom whole cities, or even regions, to monoproduction (Turin, Belfort, Coventry, Detroit to a particular industry; Paris, Rome, The Hague to bureaucratic activities) make whole populations incapable of producing – and consuming – according to their own needs, or even of defining these needs in an autonomous manner. Compelled to consume the *marketable* goods and services that the institutional monopolies offer them, they are the compulsory producers of other marketable goods and services within monopolistic institutions.

The monopolization of production and administration by giant institutions – industrial corporations, bureaucracies, specialized professions (doctors, teachers, civil servants) – means that everyone is compelled to produce what he does not consume, to consume what he does not produce, and is unable to produce or consume according to his own individual or collective desires. There is no longer any place where the unity of socially divided labour can correspond to an experience of cooperation, of exchange, of production in common of an overall result. This unity is assured only by the market on the one hand, and by private and state bureaucracies on the other. Hence it is imposed on individuals as an external unity, as 'an alien force existing outside them, of which they are ignorant of the origin and goal . . .'. In short, the link between social production and individual consumption, between individual work and social consumption, between the individual and society, is destroyed at the level of lived experience. The individual is not 'at home' anywhere. He encounters the implements and results of social production as an 'alien power', over which 'he has no control' and which 'enslave him instead of being controlled by him'.[16]

Here again a simple transfer of the ownership and legal status of industrial and commercial monopolies will not change anything. To speak of 'collective ownership' of a national or even a multinational monopoly is an abstraction and as devoid of meaning as speaking of the incarnation of the 'sovereignty of the people' in Parliament. The simple fact is that the institutional apparatuses of production and exchange do not lend themselves, given their present structure, to control and ownership by the associated producers within real living and working communities. They lend themselves solely to institutional control and ownership by state apparatuses that perpetuate, along with the social division of jobs, the stratification of society into classes and, in particular, the existence of a bureaucracy that keeps the proletariat in a state of dependence and subordination as total as under capitalism.

There is no such thing as communism without a communist life-style or 'culture'; but a communist life-style cannot be based on the technology, institutions and division of labour which derive from capitalism. The power of the proletariat and collective proletarian ownership can be realized only if the proletariat, as individuals, groups, teams, communities, have the power to unite and decide together, at their place of work and in the districts in which they live, what they want to produce and, how, when and where. In the absence of this power, the class power of the proletariat (its dictatorship, its state) will be completely nominal and abstract. It will cease to be nominal and abstract only if the means and organization of production, by virtue of their size, technology, location and so on, permit – indeed promote – a real autonomy of real communities producing and sharing a reasonable proportion of the necessities of life and creating most of the superfluous commodities of their own sweet will. Ivan Illich has put it better than anyone else:

> Tools fitting a convivial society must be simply designed so that their use can be learned with ease; they must be small enough to be used by individuals or ad hoc groups of laymen. Most important is that one can freely decide what to do with a tool – and that one can abstain from its use altogether. . . . It is obvious that not every means of production

would ever fit these criteria. Steel or electricity[17] cannot be commonly
produced in the backyard. But large-scale production is not excluded in
a convivial society. What is fundamental to such an economy is the
overall balance between the input of human and mechanical energy on
one side, and between the per capita mechanical energy available and
the amount used by the median person.

The collective ownership of tools, Illich continues, can have

... two opposite effects: it could subordinate social relations to tools
even more effectively than than private ownership could; that is,
socialism can become the totally efficient use of people at the service of
the tools they own. This is the essence of Stalinism. Or the public
ownership of tools could subordinate their use to the overreaching
commitment of the community to shape its social relations according to
a convivial life-style. This, of course, requires a commitment on the part
of the community to *renounce* – at whatever cost and whenever possible
– the benefits of efficient large-scale production whenever such
efficiency would destroy conviviality; that is, the socialization of tools
can be used to proscribe the existence of tools of a nature, size and
power which do not fit a convivial life style.

This by no means implies a regression to primitive tools and to a pastoral
life-style: 'During the last hundred and fifty years, the more effective use of
science seemed to demand an increasing specialization and division of
labour. This is no longer so. Science has now made possible the
development of more tools which increase individual autonomy. . . .'[18]

NOTES

1 Karl Marx, *Capital*, I, trans. Moore and Aveling (London: Lawrence & Wishart 1961),
pp. 360–1.
2 D. Urquhart, *Familiar Words* (London 1855), cited in Marx, *op. cit.*, p. 363.
3 Karl Marx and Frederick Engels, *The German Ideology* (London: Lawrence Wishart
1965), pp. 86–7. Cf. also the following passage:

The transformation through the division of labour, of personal powers (relationships)
into material powers, cannot be dispelled by dismissing the general idea of it from one's
mind, but can only be abolished by the individuals again subjecting these material
powers to themselves and abolishing the division of labour ... The illusory community,
in which individuals have up till now combined, always took on an independent
existence in relation to them, and was at the same time, since it was the combination of
one class over against another, not only a completely illusory community, but a new
fetter as well. In the real community the individuals obtain their freedom in and
through their association [p. 91].

4 This argument is developed in this book in the article by Dominique Pignon and Jean
Querzola, and also in my own article 'Technology, technicians and class struggle'.
5 The unity of techniques of production and of domination is discussed in this book in my
articles and also in the article by the *Il Manifesto* group.
6 In 'Technology, technicians and class struggle' I discuss the problem of under what
circumstances and to what extent engineers and technicians are members of the working
class, and to what extent they are, on the contrary representatives and functionaries of

capital (in particular of fixed capital), i.e. both functionally and ideologically bourgeois. On the problem of revolutionizing the division of labour see Marco Macció's well-documented analysis in this book.

7 Marx, *op. cit.*, Ch. xv, sec. 4, p. 423.

8 Marx speaks moreover of 'the appropriation of productive forces', and not only of the means of production; and the term 'appropriation' is for him much broader than its mere legal meaning. Cf. for example, *The German Ideology*,

> Thus things have now come to such a pass, that the individuals must appropriate the existing totality of productive forces, not only to achieve self-activity, but, also, merely to safeguard their very existence. This appropriation is first determined by the object to be appropriated, the productive forces, which have been developed to a totality and which only exist within a universal intercourse . . . the appropriation of these forces is itself nothing more than the development of the individual capacities corresponding to the material instruments of production. The appropriation of a totality of instruments of production is, for this very reason, the development of a totality of capacities in the individuals themselves. This appropriation is further determined by the persons appropriating. Only the proletarians of the present day, who are completely shut off from all self-activity, are in a position to achieve a complete and no longer restricted self-activity, which consists in the appropriation of a totality of productive forces and in the thus postulated development of a totality of capacities [Marx and Engels, *op. cit.*, p. 83].

This passage, which defines the idea (or essence) or the proletariat, implies a dialectical reversal that is dearly Hegelian (and Christian) in origin. Only those who are nothing can become everything. In fact, this postulate is totally abstract: the fact of being totally negated by everything will not automatically engender in the proletariat the *ability* or the *possibility* of totally regaining themselves while appropriating the totality that negates them. How can they be enabled to do this? Surely not from the conditions of oppression and 'crippling' in which they are held. It can come to them only through *the struggle against* these conditions, a struggle through which the proletariat revolutionizes everything, including itself. On this point see André Gorz, *La Morale de l'Histoire*, ch. III (Paris éd. du Seuil 1959).

9 This is, moreover, what Marx and Engels note a little further on in *The German Ideology*, 'In all expropriations up to now, a mass of individuals remained subservient to a single instrument of production; in the appropriation by the proletarians, *a mass of instruments of production must be made subject to each individual*, and property to all' (*op. cit.*, p. 84; (my italics).

10 Cf. Charles Bettelheim, *Economic Calculation and Forms of Property* (London: Routledge & Kegan Paul, forthcoming).

11 Marx, *op. cit.*, ch. xiv, sec. 5, p. 361. In a footnote Marx quotes from W. Thompson *An Inquiry into the Principles of the Distribution of Wealth* (London: 1824); 'The man of knowledge and the productive labourer come to be widely divided from each other, and knowledge, instead of remaining the handmaid of labour in the hand of the labourer to increase his productive powers . . . has almost everywhere arrayed itself against labour . . . systematically deluding and leading them [the labourers] astray in order to render their muscular powers entirely mechanical and obedient'.

12 See the essays in this book by Marco Macció and Antonio Lettieri.

13 Marx, *op. cit.*, ch. xv, sec. 4, p. 422.

14 Claudie Broyelle, *La Moitié du Ciel* (Paris: Denoël Gonthier 1973), pp. 39 and 27. To be published as *Women's Liberation in China* by The Harvester Press, Hassocks, and The Humanities Press, N.J., 1976.

15 Capitalist development in fact progresses by modernizing privileges (Concorde, colour television, flats with swimming pools) as well as poverty. Thus as the masses have access to goods previously reserved for the élite, so the élite obtain access to 'better' goods, which devalue their former privileges. The capitalist model of consumption is based on the principle that what is good enough for everybody is not good enough for *you*. The communist model of consumption is based on the inverse principle: only that which is good for everybody is good enough for me.

16 Marx and Engels, *op. cit.*, pp. 44–6. The passage deserves to be quoted in full:

... as long, therefore, as activity is not voluntarily, but naturally, divided, man's own deed becomes an alien power opposed to him which enslaves him instead of being controlled by him. For as soon as the distribution of labour comes into being, each man has a particular, exclusive sphere of activity, which is forced upon him and from which he cannot escape. He is a hunter, a fisherman, a shepherd, or a critical critic, and must remain so if he does not want to lose his means of livelihood; while in communist society, where nobody has one exclusive sphere of activity but each can become accomplished in any branch he wishes, society regulates the general production and thus makes it possible for me to do one thing today and another tomorrow, to hunt in the morning, fish in the afternoon, rear cattle in the evening, criticize after dinner, just as I have a mind, without ever becoming hunter, fisherman, shepherd or critic. This fixation of social activity, this consolidation of what we ourselves produce into an objective power above us, growing out of our control, thwarting our expectations, bringing to naught our calculations, is one of the chief factors in historical development up till now ...

The social power, i.e., the multiplied productive force, which arises through the cooperation of different individuals as it is determined by the division of labour, appears to these individuals, since their cooperation is not voluntary but has come about naturally, not as their own united power, but as an alien force existing outside them, of the origin and goal of which they are ignorant, which they thus cannot control, which on the contrary passes through a peculiar series of phases and stages independent of the will and the action of man, nay even being the prime governor of these.

In this passage Marx gives a definition and a description of alienation that are totally free of the 'anthropological essentialism' for which the Althusserians reproach him. Not that this conception of alienation coincides with the one developed by Sartre in the *Critique de la Raison Dialectique* in terms of serialized activities unified through the material field of the practico-inert and coming back against each individual as his negation by others.

17 The production of solar and wind-generated electricity in fact poses no insurmountable problems, even (or especially) on a small scale.

18 See Ivan Illich, *Tools for conviviality* (London: Calder & Boyers 1973).

Part One
DEVELOPMENT AND CRISIS OF THE CAPITALIST DIVISION OF LABOUR

KARL MARX

From Manufacture to Modern Industry

'The subdivision of labour is the assassination of a people'
D. Urquhart, *Familiar Words*, (London 1855), quoted in Marx, *Capital*, I, p. 363.

1 MANUFACTURE*

The collective labourer, formed by the combination of a number of detail labourers, is the machinery specially characteristic of the manufacturing period. The various operations that are performed in turns by the producer of a commodity, and coalesce one with another during the progress of production, lay claim to him in various ways. In one operation he must exert more strength, in another more skill, in another more attention; and the same individual does not possess all these qualities in an equal degree. After Manufacture has once separated, made independent, and isolated the various operations, the labourers are divided, classified, and grouped according to their predominating qualities. If their natural endowments are, on the one hand, the foundation on which the division of labour is built up, on the other hand, Manufacture, once introduced, develops in them new powers that are by nature fitted only for limited and special functions. The collective labourer now possesses, in an equal degree of excellence, all the qualities requisite for production, and expends them in the most economical manner, by exclusively employing all his organs, consisting of particular labourers, or groups of labourers, in performing their special functions.[1] The one-sidedness and the deficiencies of the detail labourer become perfections when he is a part of the collective labourer.[2] The habit of doing only one thing converts him into a never-failing instrument, while his connection with the whole mechanism compels him to work with the regularity of the parts of a machine.[3]

Since the collective labourer has functions, both simple and complex, both high and low, his members, the individual labour-powers, require different degrees of training, and must therefore have different values. Manufacture, therefore, develops a hierarchy of labour-powers, to which there corresponds a scale of wages. If, on the one hand, the individual labourers are appropriated and annexed for life by a limited function; on the other hand, the various operations of the hierarchy are parcelled out

* From Karl Marx, *Capital*, I, transl. Moore and Aveling (London: Lawrence & Wishart 1961), ch. 14, sects 3 and 5, pp. 348–350, 360–364.

among the labourers according to both their natural and their acquired capabilities.[4] Every process of production, however, requires certain simple manipulations, which every man is capable of doing. They too are now severed from their connection with the more pregnant moments of activity, and ossified into exclusive functions of specially appointed labourers. Hence, Manufacture begets, in every handicraft that it seizes upon, a class of so-called unskilled labourers, a class that handicraft industry strictly excluded. If it develops a one-sided speciality into a perfection, at the expense of the whole of a man's working capacity, it also begins to make a speciality of the absence of all development. Alongside the hierarchic gradation there steps the simple separation of the labourers into skilled and unskilled. For the latter, the cost of apprenticeship vanishes; for the former, it diminishes, compared with that of artificers, in consequence of the functions being simplified. In both cases the value of labour-power falls.[5] An exception to this law holds good whenever the decomposition of the labour-process begets new and comprehensive functions, that either had no place at all, or only a very modest one, in handicrafts. The fall in the value of labour-power, caused by the disappearance or diminution of the expenses of apprenticeship, implies a direct increase of surplus-value for the benefit of captial; for everything that shortens the necessary labour-time required for the reproduction of labour-power extends the domain of surplus-labour. . . .

In manufacture, as well as in simple co-operation, the collective working organism is a form of existence of capital. The mechanism that is made up of numerous individual detail labourers belongs to the capitalist. Hence, the productive power resulting from a combination of labours appears to be the productive power of capital. Manufacture proper not only subjects the previously independent workman to the discipline and command of capital, but, in addition, creates a hierarchic gradation of the workmen themselves. While simple co-operation leaves the mode of working by the individual for the most part unchanged, manufacture thoroughly revolutionizes it, and seizes labour-power by its very roots. It converts the labourer into a crippled monstrosity, by forcing his detail dexterity at the expense of a world of productive capabilities and instincts, just as in the States of La Plata they butcher a whole beast for the sake of his hide or his tallow. Not only is the detail work distributed to the different individuals, but the individual himself is made the automatic motor of a fractional operation,[6] and the absurd fable of Menenius Agrippa, which makes man a mere fragment of his own body, becomes realized.[7] If, at first, the workman sells his labour-power to capital, because the material means of producing a commodity fail him, now his very labour-power refuses its services unless it has been sold to capital. Its functions can be exercised only in an environment that exists in the workshop of the capitalist after the sale. By nature unfitted to make anything independently, the manufacturing labourer develops productive activity as a mere appendage of the capitalist's workshop.[8] As the chosen people bore in their features the sign manual of Jehovah, so division of labour brands the manufacturing workman as the property of capital.

The knowledge, the judgement and the will that, though in ever so small a degree, are practised by the independent peasant or handicraftsman, in the same way as the savage makes the whole art of war consist in the exercise of his personal cunning – these faculties are now required only for the workshop as a whole. Intelligence in production expends in one direction, because it vanishes in many others. What is lost by the detail labourers is concentrated in the capital that employs them. [9] It is a result of the division of labour in manufactures that the labourer is brought face to face with the intellectual potencies of the material process of production, as the property of another, and as a ruling power. This separation begins in simple co-operation, where the capitalist represents to the single workman the oneness and the will of the associated labour. It is developed in manufacture that cuts down the labourer into a detail labourer. It is completed in modern industry, which makes science a productive force distinct from labour and presses it into the service of capital. [10]

In manufacture, in order to make the collective labourer, and through him capital, rich in social productive power, each labourer must be made poor in individual productive powers. 'Ignorance is the mother of industry as well as of superstition. Reflection and fancy are subject to err; but a habit of moving the hand or the foot is independent of either. Manufactures, accordingly, prosper most where the mind is least consulted, and where the workshop may . . . be considered as an engine, the parts of which are men.'[11] As a matter of fact, some few manufacturers in the middle of the eighteenth century preferred, for certain operations that were trade secrets, to employ half-idiotic persons. [12]

'The understandings of the greater part of men,' says Adam Smith, 'are necessarily formed by their ordinary employments. The man whose whole life is spent in performing a few simple operations . . . has no occasion to exert his understanding . . . He generally becomes as stupid and ignorant as it is possible for a human creature to become.' After describing the stupidity of the detail labourer he goes on:

> The uniformity of his stationary life naturally corrupts the courage of his mind . . . It corrupts even the activity of his body and renders him incapable of exerting his strength with vigour and perseverance in any other employments than that to which he has been bred. His dexterity at his own particular trade seems in this manner to be acquired at the expense of his intellectual, social, and martial virtues. But in every improved and civilized society, this is the state into which the labouring poor, that is, the great body of the people, must necessarily fall. [13]

For preventing the complete deterioration of the great mass of the people by division of labour, Smith recommends education of the people by the State, but prudently, and in homeopathic doses. G. Garnier, his French translator and commentator, who under the first French Empire quite naturally developed into a senator, quite as naturally opposes him on this point. Education of the masses, he urges, violates the first law of the division of labour, and with it 'our whole social system would be proscribed'.

Like all other divisions of labour [he says], that between hand labour and head labour[14] is more pronounced and decided in proportion as society [he rightly uses this word, for capital, landed property and their State] become richer. This division of labour, like every other, is an effect of past, and a cause of future progress . . . ought the government then to work in opposition to this division of labour, and to hinder its natural course? Ought it to expend a part of the public money in the attempt to confound and blend together two classes of labour, which are striving after division and separation?[15]

Some crippling of body and mind is inseparable even from division of labour in society as a whole. Since, however, manufacture carries this social separation of branches of labour much further, and also, by its peculiar division, attacks the individual at the very roots of his life, it is the first to afford the materials for, and to give a start to, industrial pathology.[16]

'To subdivide a man is to execute him, if he deserves the sentence, to assassinate him if he does not . . . . The subdivision of labour is the assassination of a people.'[17]

Co-operation based on division of labour, in other words, manufacture, commences as a spontaneous formation. As soon as it attains some consistence and extension, it becomes the recognized methodical and systematic form of capitalist production. History shows how the division of labour peculiar to manufacture, strictly so called, acquires the best adapted form at first by experience, as it were behind the backs of the actors, and then, like the guild handicrafts, strives to hold fast that form when once found, and here and there succeeds in keeping it for centuries. Any alteration in this form, except in trivial matters, is solely owing to a revolution in the instruments of labour. Modern manufacture wherever it arises – I do not here allude to modern industry based on machinery – either finds the *disjecta membra poetae* ready to hand, and only waiting to be collected together, as is the case in the manufacture of clothes in large towns, or it can easily apply the principle of division, simply by exclusively assigning the various operations of a handicraft (such as book-binding) to particular men. In such cases a week's experience is enough to determine the proportion between the numbers of the hands necessary for the various functions.[18]

By decomposition of handicrafts, by specialization of the instruments of labour, by the formation of detail labourers, and by grouping and combining the latter into a single mechanism, division of labour in manufacture creates a qualitative gradation, and a quantitative proportion in the social process of production; it consequently creates a definite organization of the labour of society, and thereby develops at the same time new productive forces in the society. In its specific capitalist form –

and under the given conditions, it could take no other form than a capitalistic one – manufacture is but a particular method of begetting relative surplus-value, or of augmenting at the expense of the labourer the self-expansion of capital – usually called social wealth, 'Wealth of Nations' and so on. It increases the social productive power of labour, not only for the benefit of the capitalist instead of for that of the labourer, but by crippling the individual labourers. It creates new conditions for the lordship of capital over labour. If, therefore, on the one hand it presents itself historically as a progress and as a necessary phase in the economic development of society, on the other hand, it is a refined and civilized method of exploitation. . .

2 THE FACTORY*

. . . To work at a machine, the workman should be taught from childhood, in order that he may learn to adapt his own movements to the uniform and unceasing motion of an automaton. When the machinery as a whole forms a system of manifold machines, working simultaneously and in concert, the co-operation based upon it requires the distribution of various groups of workmen among the different kinds of machines. But the employment of machinery does away with the necessity of crystallizing this distribution after the manner of Manufacture, by the constant annexation of a particular man to a particular function.[19] Since the motion of the whole system does not proceed from the workman, but from the machinery, a change of persons can take place at any time without an interruption of the work. The most striking proof of this is afforded by the *relays system,* put into operation by the manufacturers during their revolt from 1848 to 1850. Lastly, the quickness with which machine work is learnt by young people does away with the necessity of bringing up for exclusive employment by machinery a special class of operatives.[20] With regard to the work of the mere attendants, it can to some extent be replaced in the mill by machines,[21] and owing to its extreme simplicity, it allows a rapid and constant change of the individuals burdened with this drudgery.

Although then, technically speaking, the old system of division of labour is thrown overboard by machinery, it hangs on in the factory, as a traditional habit handed down from Manufacture, and is afterwards systematically remoulded and established in a more hideous form by capital, as a means of exploiting labour-power. The life-long speciality of handling one and the same tool now becomes the life-long speciality of serving one and the same machine. Machinery is put to a wrong use, with the object of transforming the workman, from his very childhood, into a part of a detail-machine.[22] In this way not only are the expenses of his reproduction considerably lessened, but at the same time his helpless dependence upon the factory as a whole, and therefore upon the capitalist, is rendered complete. Here, as everywhere else, we must distinguish

* From Marx, *op. cit.*, ch. 15, sect. 4, pp. 421–427.

between the increased productiveness due to the development of the social process of production and that due to the capitalist exploitation of that process. In handicrafts and manufacture the workman makes use of a tool; in the factory, the machine makes use of him. There the movements of the instrument of labour proceed from him, here it is the movement of the machine that he must follow. In manufacture the workmen are parts of a living mechanism. In the factory we have a lifeless mechanism independent of the workman, who becomes its mere living appendage. 'The miserable routine of endless drudgery and toil in which the same mechanical process is gone through over and over again is like the labour of Sisyphus. The burden of labour, like the rock, keeps ever falling back on the worn-out labourer.' [23] At the same time as factory work exhausts the nervous system to the uttermost, it does away with the many-sided play of the muscles, and confiscates every atom of freedom, both in bodily and in intellectual activity.[24] Even the lightening of the labour becomes a sort of torture, since the machine does not free the labourer from work, but deprives the work of all interest. Every kind of capitalist production, in so far as it is not only a labour-process but also a process of creating surplus-value, has this in common, that it is not the workman that employs the instruments of labour, but the instruments of labour that employ the workman. But it is only in the factory system that this inversion acquires for the first time technical and palpable reality. By means of its conversion into an automaton, the instrument of labour confronts the labourer, during the labour-process, in the shape of capital, of dead labour, that dominates and pumps dry living labour-power. The separation of the intellectual powers of production from the manual labour and the conversion of those powers into the might of capital over labour is, as we have already shown, finally completed by modern industry erected on the foundation of machinery. The special skill of each individual insignificant factory operative vanishes as an infinitesimal quantity before the science, the gigantic physical forces and the mass of labour that are embodied in the factory mechanism and, together with that mechanism, constitute the power of the 'master'. This 'master', therefore, in whose brain the machinery and his monopoly of it are inseparably united, whenever he falls out with his 'hands' contemptuously tells them:

> The factory operatives should keep in wholesome remembrance the fact that theirs is really a low species of skilled labour; and that there is none which is more easily acquired, or of its quality more amply remunerated, or which by a short training of the least expert can be more quickly, as well as abundantly, acquired. ... The master's machinery really plays a far more important part in the business of production than the labour and the skill of the operative, which six months' education can teach, and a common labourer can learn. [25]

The technical subordination of the workman to the uniform motion of the instruments of labour and the peculiar composition of the body of workpeople, consisting as it does of individuals of both sexes and of all ages, give rise to a barrack discipline, which is elaborated into a complete system in the factory, and which fully develops the labour of overlooking, thereby dividing the workpeople into operatives and overlookers, into private soldiers and sergeants of an industrial army.

The main difficulty [in the automatic factory] ... lay ... above all in training human beings to renounce their desultory habits of work and to identify themselves with the unvarying regularity of the complex automaton. To devise and administer a successful code of factory discipline, suited to the necessities of factory diligence, was the Herculean enterprise, the noble achievement of Arkwright! Even at the present day, when the system is perfectly organized and its labour lightened to the utmost, it is found nearly impossible to convert persons past the age of puberty, into factory hands.[26]

The factory code in which capital formulates, like a private legislator, and at his own good will, his autocracy over his workpeople, unaccompanied by that division of responsibility, in other matters so much approved of by the bourgeoisie, and unaccompanied by the still more approved representative system, this code is but the capitalistic caricature of that social regulation of the labour-process which becomes requisite in co-operation on a great scale, and in the employment in common of instruments of labour and especially of machinery. The place of the slave-driver's lash is taken by the overlooker's book of penalties. All punishments naturally resolve themselves into fines and deductions from wages, and the law-giving talent of the factory Lycurgus so arranges matters that a violation of his laws is, if possible, more profitable to him than the keeping of them.[27]

We shall here merely allude to the material conditions under which factory labour is carried on. Every sense organ is injured to an equal degree by artificial elevation of the temperature, by the dust-laden atmosphere, by the deafening noise, not to mention the danger to life and limb among the thickly crowded machinery, which, with the regularity of the seasons, issues its list of the killed and wounded in the industrial battle.[28] Economy of the social means of production, matured and forced as in a hothouse by the factory system, is turned, in the hands of capital, into systematic robbery of what is necessary for the life of the workman while he is at work, robbery of space, light, air and of protection of his person against the dangerous and unwholesome accompaniments of the productive process, not to mention the robbery of appliances for the comfort of the workman.[29] Is Fourier wrong when he calls factories 'tempered bagnos'?[30]

NOTES

1 'The master manufacturer, by dividing the work to be executed into different processes, each requiring different degrees of skill or of force, can purchase exactly that precise quantity of both which is necessary for each process; whereas, if the whole work were executed by one workman, that person must possess sufficient skill to perform the most

difficult, and sufficient strength to execute the most laborious of the operations into which the article is divided' (C. Babbage, *On the Economy of Machinery* London 1832., ch. xix).

2 For instance abnormal development of some muscles, curvature of the bones and so on.

3 The question put by one of the Inquiry Commissioners, How the young persons are kept steadily to their work, is very correctly answered by Mr W. Marshall, the general manager of a glass manufactory: 'They cannot well neglect their work; when they once begin, they must go on; they are just the same as parts of a machine' (*Children's Empl. Comm., 4th Rep.*, [1865] p. 247).

4 Dr Ure, in his apotheosis of Modern Mechanical Industry, brings out the peculiar character of manufacture more sharply than previous economists, who had not his polemical interest in the matter, and more sharply even than his contemporaries – Babbage, for instance, who, though much his superior as a mathematician and mechanician, treated mechanical industry from the standpoint of manufacture alone. Ure says, 'This appropriation . . . to each, a workman of appropriate value and cost was naturally assigned, forms the very essence of division of labour.' On the other hand he describes this division as 'adaptation of labour to the different talents of men', and lastly, characterises the whole manufacturing system as 'a system for the division or gradation of labour', as 'the division of labour into degrees of skill' (Ure, *The Philosophy of Manufacturers* pp. 19–23).

5 'Each handicraftsman being . . . enabled to perfect himself by practice in one point, became . . . a cheaper workman' (*Ibid.*, p. 19.)

6 Dugald Stewart calls manufacturing labourers 'living automatons . . . employed in the details of the work'. (*Lectures on Political Economy*, p. 318).

7 In corals each individual is, in fact, the stomach of the whole group; but it supplies the group with nourishment, instead of, like the Roman patrician, withdrawing it.

8 'L'ouvrier qui porte dans ses bras tout un métier, peut aller partout exercer son industrie et trouver des moyens de subsister: l'autre [the manufacturing labourer] n'est qu'un accessoire qui, séparé de ses confrères, n'a plus ni capacité, ni indépendance, et qui se trouve forcé d'accepter la loi qu'on juge à propos de lui imposer' H. Storch *Cours d'Economie Politique* Petersb. ed. [1815] Vol. I., p. 204.)

9 A. Ferguson, *An Essay on the History of Civil Society*, Edinburgh 1767, p. 281: 'The former may have gained what the other has lost.'

10 'The man of knowledge and the productive labourer come to be widely divided from each other, and knowledge, instead of remaining the handmaid of labour in the hand of the labourer to increase his productive powers . . . has almost everywhere arrayed itself against labour . . . systematically deluding and leading [the labourers] astray in order to render their muscular powers entirely mechanical and obedient' (W. Thompson, *An Inquiry into the Principles of the Distribution of Wealth* [London 1824], p. 274.)

11 Ferguson, *op. cit.*, p. 280.

12 J. D. Tuckett, *A History of the Past and Present State of the Labouring Population.* (London, 1846).

13 A. Smith, *Wealth of Nations*, Bk. v., ch. i, art. ii. Being a pupil of A. Ferguson, who showed the disadvantageous effects of division of labour, Adam Smith was perfectly clear on this point. In the introduction to his work, where he *ex professo* praises division of labour, he indicates only in a cursory manner that it is the source of social inequalities. It is not until the 5th Book, on the Revenue of the State, that he reproduces Ferguson. In my *Misère de la Philosophie*, I have sufficiently explained the historical connection between Ferguson, A. Smith, Lemontey and Say, as regards their criticisms of Division of Labour, and have shown, for the first time, that Division of Labour as practised in manufactures, is a specific form of the capitalist mode of production.

14 Ferguson had already said, 'And thinking itself, in this age of separations, may become

a peculiar craft' (*op. cit.*, p. 281).

15 G. Garnier, Vol. v of his translation of A. Smith, pp. 4–5.

16 Ramazzini, Professor of Practical Medicine at Padua, published in 1713 his work *De morbis artificum*, which was translated into French in 1781, reprinted in 1841 in the *Encyclopédie des Sciences Médicales, 7me Dis. Auteurs Classiques.* The period of Modern Mechanical Industry has, of course, very much enlarged his catalogue of labour's diseases. See *Hygiène physique et morale de l'ouvrier dans les grandes villes en général et dans la ville de Lyon en particulier. Par le Dr. A. L. Fonteret* (Paris 1858) and *Die Krankheiten, welche verschiedenen Ständen, Altern und Geschlechtern eigenthümlich sind,* 6 vols (Ulm 1860) and others. In 1854 the Society of Arts appointed a Commission of Inquiry into industrial pathology. The list of documents collected by this commission is to be seen in the catalogue of the Twickenham Economic Museum. Very important are the official *Reports on Public Health.* See also Eduard Reich MD, *Ueber die Entartung des Menschen* (Erlangen 1868).

17 D. Urquhart, *Familiar Words* (London 1855), p. 119. Hegel held very heretical views on division of labour. In his *Rechtsphilosophie* he says: 'By well educated men we understand in the first instance, those who can do everything that others do.'

18 The simple belief in the inventive genius exercised *a priori* by the individual capitalist in division of labour exists nowadays only among German professors, of the stamp of Herr Roscher, who, to recompense the capitalist from whose Jovian head division of labour sprang ready formed, dedicates to him 'various wages' (*diverse Arbeitslöhne*). The more or less extensive application of division of labour depends on length of purse, not on greatness of genius.

19 Ure grants this. He says that 'in case of need' the workmen can be moved at the will of the manager from one machine to another, and he triumphantly exclaims: 'Such a change is in flat contradiction with the old routine, that divides the labour, and to one workman assigns the task of fashioning the head of a needle, to another the sharpening of the point.' He had much better have asked himself why this 'old routine' is departed from in the automatic factory, only 'in case of need'.

20 When distress is very great, as for instance during the American Civil War, the factory operative is now and then set by the bourgeois to do the roughest of work, such as road-making. The English *ateliers nationaux* of 1862 and the following years, established for the benefit of the destitute cotton operatives, differ from the French of 1848 in that in the latter the workmen had to do unproductive work at the expense of the State, while in the former they had to do productive municipal work to the advantage of the bourgeois, and that, too, cheaper than the regular workmen, with whom they were thus thrown into competition. 'The physical appearance of the cotton operatives is unquestionably improved. This I attribute . . . as to the men, to outdoor labour on public works' (*Rep. of Insp. of Fact,* [31 October 1863], p. 59). The writer here alludes to the Preston factory operatives, who were employed on Preston Moor.

21 An example: the various mechanical apparatus introduced since the Act of 1844 into woollen mills, for replacing the labour of children. As soon as it shall happen that the children of the manufacturers themselves have to go through a course of schooling as helpers in the mill, this almost unexplored territory of mechanics will soon make remarkable progress.

Of machinery, perhaps self-acting mules are as dangerous as any other kind. Most of the accidents from them happen to little children, from their creeping under the mules to sweep the floor whilst the mules are in motion. Several 'minders' have been fined for this offence, but without much general benefit. If machine makers would only invent a self-sweeper, by whose use the necessity for these little children to creep under the machinery might be prevented, it would be a happy addition to our protective measures. [*Reports of Insp. of Fact. for 31st. Oct., 1866*, p. 63].

22 So much then for Proudhon's wonderful idea: he construes machinery not as a synthesis of instruments of labour, but as a synthesis of detail operations for the benefit of the labourer himself.

23 F. Engels, *Die Lage der Arbeitenden Klasse in England*, Leipzig 1845, p. 217. Even an ordinary and optimistic Free-trader, like Mr Molinari, goes so far as to say, 'Un homme s'use plus vite en surveillant, quinze heures par jour, l'évolution uniforme d'un mécanisme, qu'en exerçant, dans le même espace de temps, sa force physique. Ce travail de surveillance qui servirait peut-être d'utile gymnastique à l'intelligence, s'il n'était pas trop prolongé, détruit à la longue, par son excès, et l'intelligence, et le corps même' (G. de Molinari, *Études Économiques* [Paris 1846].

24 Engels, *op. cit.*, p. 216.

25 *The Master Spinners' and Manufacturers' Defence Fund, Report of the Committee*, (Manchester 1854), p. 17. We shall see hereafter that the 'master' can sing quite another song, when he is threatened with the loss of his 'living' automaton.

26 Ure, p. 15. Whoever knows the life history of Arkwright will never dub this barber-genius 'noble'. Of all the great inventors of the eighteenth century, he was incontestably the greatest thiever of other people's inventions and the meanest fellow.

27 The slavery in which the bourgeoisie has bound the proletariat, comes nowhere more plainly into daylight than in the factory system. In it all freedom comes to an end both at law and in fact. The workman must be in the factory at half past five. If he come a few minutes late, he is punished; if he come 10 minutes late, he is not allowed to enter until after breakfast, and thus loses a quarter of a day's wage. He must eat, drink and sleep at word of command. . . . The despotic bell calls him from his bed, calls him from breakfast and dinner. And how does he fare in the mill? There the master is the absolute law-giver. He makes what regulations he pleases; he alters and makes additions to his code at pleasure; and if he insert the veriest nonsense, the courts say to the workman: Since you have entered into this contract voluntarily, you must now carry it out. . . . These workmen are condemned to live, from their ninth year till their death, under this mental and bodily torture [Engels, *op. cit.*, pp. 217 ff.].

What, 'the courts say' I will illustrate by two examples. One occurs at Sheffield at the end of 1866. In that town a workman had engaged himself for two years in a steelworks. In consequence of a quarrel with his employer he left the works, and declared that under no circumstances would he work for that master any more. He was prosecuted for breach of contract and condemned to two months' imprisonment. (If the master break the contract, he can be proceeded against only in a civil action, and risks nothing but money damages.) After the workman has served his two months the master invites him to return to the works, pursuant to the contract. Workman says: No, he has already been punished for the breach. The master prosecutes again, the court condemns again, although one of the judges, Mr Shee, publicly denounces this as a legal monstrosity, by which a man can periodically, as long as he lives, be punished over and over again for the same offence or crime. This judgement was given not by the 'Great Unpaid', the provincial Dogberries, but by one of the highest courts of justice in London. [*Added in the 4th German edn.* This has now been done away with. With few exceptions, e.g., when public gas-works are involved, the worker in England is now put on an equal footing with the employer in case of breach of contract and can be sued only civilly – FE.] The second case occurs in Wiltshire at the end of November 1863. About 30 power-loom weavers, in the employment of one Harrup, a cloth manufacturer at Leower's Mill, Westbury Leigh, struck work because master Harrup indulged in the agreeable habit of making deductions from their wages for being late in the morning; 6d for 2 minutes; 1s for 3 minutes, and 1s 6d for 10 minutes. This is at the rate of 9s per hour, and £4 10s 0d *per diem;* while the wages of the weavers on the average of a year never exceeded 10s to 12s weekly. Harrup also appointed a boy to announce the starting time by a whistle, which he often did before six o'clock in the morning: and if the hands were not all there at the moment the whistle ceased, the doors were closed, and those hands who were outside were fined: and as there was no clock on the premises, the unfortunate hands were at the mercy of the young Harrup-inspired time-keeper. The hands on strike, mothers of families as well as girls, offered to resume work if the time-keeper were replaced by a clock, and a more reasonable scale of fines were introduced. Harrup summoned 19 women and girls before the magistrates for breach of contract. To the utter indignation of all present, they were each mulcted in a fine of 6d and 2s 6d for costs. Harrup was followed from the court by a crowd of people who hissed him.

A favourite operation with manufacturers is to punish the workpeople by deductions made from their wages on account of faults in the material worked on. This method gave rise in 1866 to a general strike in the English pottery districts. The reports of the *Ch. Empl. Com.* (1863–6) give cases where the worker not only receives no wages, but becomes, by means of his labour, and of the penal regulations, the debtor to boot of his worthy master. The late cotton crisis also furnished edifying examples of the sagacity shown by the factory autocrats in making deductions from wages. Mr R. Baker, the Inspector of Factories, says:

> I have myself had lately to direct prosecutions against one cotton mill occupier for having in these pinching and painful times deducted 10d a piece from some of the young workers employed by him, for the surgeon's certificate [for which he himself had only paid 6d], when only allowed by the law to deduct 3d, and by custom nothing at all. . . . And I have been informed of another, who, in order to keep without the law, but to attain the same object, charges the poor children who work for him a shilling each, as a fee for learning them the art and mystery of cotton spinning, so soon as they are declared by the surgeon fit and proper persons for that occupation. There may therefore be undercurrent causes for such extraordinary exhibitions as strikes, not only wherever they arise, but particularly at such times as the present, which without explanation, render them inexplicable to the public understanding.

[He alludes here to a strike of power-loom weavers at Darwen, June, 1863] [*Reports of Insp. of Fact. for 30 April, 1863*, pp. 50–1]. The reports always go beyond their official dates.

28 The protection afforded by the Factory Acts against dangerous machinery has had a beneficial effect.

> But . . . there are other sources of accident which did not exist twenty years since; one especially, viz., the increased speed of the machinery. Wheels, rollers, spindles and shuttles are now propelled at increased and increasing rates; fingers must be quicker and defter in their movements to take up the broken thread, for, if placed with hesitation or carelessness, they are sacrificed. . . . A large number of accidents are caused by the eagerness of the workpeople to get through their work expeditiously. It must be remembered that it is of the highest importance to manufacturers that their machinery should be in motion, i.e., producing yarns and goods. Every minute's stoppage is not only a loss of power, but of production, and the workpeople are urged by the overlookers, who are interested in the quantity of work turned off, to keep the machinery in motion; and it is no less important to those of the operatives who are paid by the weight or piece, that the machines should be kept in motion. Consequently, although it is strictly forbidden in many, nay in most factories, that machinery should be cleaned while in motion, it is nevertheless the constant practice in most if not in all, that the workpeople do, unreproved, pick out waste, wipe rollers and wheels, &c., while their frames are in motion. Thus from this cause only, 906 accidents have occurred

during the six months. . . . Although a great deal of cleaning is constantly going on day by day, yet Saturday is generally the day set apart for the thorough cleaning of the machinery, and a great deal of this is done while the machinery is in motion.

Since cleaning is not paid for, the workpeople seek to get done with it as speedily as possible. Hence 'the number of accidents which occur on Fridays, and especially on Saturdays, is much larger than on any other day. On the former day the excess is nearly 12 per cent over the average number of the four first days of the week, and on the latter day the excess is 25 per cent over the average of the preceding five days; or, if the number of working-hours on Saturday being taken into account – $7\frac{1}{2}$ hours on Saturday as compared with $10\frac{1}{4}$ on other days – there is an excess of 65 per cent on Saturdays over the average of the other five days.' (*Rep. of Insp. of Fact., 31st Oct., 1866*, pp. 9, 15, 16, 17).

29 In Part i of Book iii I shall give an account of a recent campaign by the English manufacturers against the clauses in the Factory Acts that protect the 'hands' against dangerous machinery. For the present, let this one quotation from the official report of Leonard Horner suffice:

I have heard some mill-owners speak with inexcusable levity of some of the accidents; such, for instance, as the loss of a finger being a trifling matter. A working-man's living and prospects depend so much upon his fingers, that any loss of them is a very serious matter to him. When I have heard such inconsiderate remarks made, I have usually put this question: Suppose you were in want of an additional workman, and two were to apply, both equally well qualified in other respects, but one had lost a thumb or a forefinger, which would you engage? There never was a hesitation as to the answer. . . . [The manufacturers have] mistaken prejudices against what they have heard represented as a pseudo-philanthropic legislation [*Rep. of Insp. of Fact., 31st Oct., 1855*].

These manufacturers are clever folk, and not without reason were they enthusiastic for the slave-holders' rebellion.

30 In those factories that have been longest subject to the Factory Acts, with their compulsory limitation of the hours of labour and other regulations, many of the older abuses have vanished. The very improvement of the machinery demands to a certain extent 'improved construction of the buildings', and this is an advantage to the workpeople. (See *Rep. of Insp. of Fact. for 31st Oct., 1863*, p. 109)

STEPHEN A. MARGLIN

What do bosses do?

The origins and functions of Hierarchy in Capitalist Production*

1 INTRODUCTION: DOES TECHNOLOGY SHAPE SOCIAL AND ECONOMIC ORGANIZATION OR DOES SOCIAL AND ECONOMIC ORGANIZATION SHAPE TECHNOLOGY?

Is it possible for work to contribute positively to individual development in a complex industrial society, or is alienating work the price that must be paid for material prosperity? Discussions of the possibilities for meaningful revolution generally come down, sooner or later, to this question. If hierarchical authority is essential to high productivity, then self-expression in work must at best be a luxury reserved for the very few regardless of social and economic organization. And even the satisfactions of society's élite must be perverted by their dependence, with rare exception, on the denial of self-expression to others. But is work organization determined by technology or by society? Is hierarchical authority really necessary to high levels of production, or is material prosperity compatible with nonhierarchical organization of production?

Defenders of the capitalist faith are quite sure that hierarchy is inescapable. Indeed their ultimate line of defence is that the plurality of capitalist hierarchies is preferable to a single socialist hierarchy. To seal the argument the apologist may call on as unlikely a source of support as Friedrich Engels. Perhaps it was a momentary aberration, but at one point in his career at least Engels saw authority as technologically rather than socially determined:

> If man, by dint of his knowledge and inventive genius, has subdued the forces of nature, the latter avenge themselves upon him by subjecting him, in so far as he employs them, to a veritable despotism, *independent of all social organization*. Wanting to abolish authority in large-scale industry is tantamount to wanting to abolish industry itself, to destroy the power loom in order to return to the spinning wheel. [1]

Going back to the spinning wheel is obviously absurd, and if the producer must typically take orders, it is difficult to see how work could in the main

* The research on which this paper reports is still in progress. It is published in its present form to stimulate discussion and comment. This paper represents my initial and in parts preliminary thinking on this subject, and no attempt has been made to reflect the many helpful criticisms and suggestions I have received. Copyright by Stephen Marglin, 1974.

be anything but alienating.

Were the social sciences experimental, the methodology for deciding whether or not hierarchical work organization is inseparable from high material productivity would be obvious. One would design technologies appropriate to an egalitarian work organization, and test the designs in actual operation. Experience would tell whether or not egalitarian work organization is utopian. But social science is not experimental. None of us has the requisite knowledge of steel-making or cloth-making to design a new technology, much less to design one so radically different from the present norm as a serious attempt to change work organization would dictate. Besides in a society whose basic institutions − from schools to factories − are geared to hierarchy, the attempt to change one small component is probably doomed to failure. For all its shortcomings, neoclassical economics is undoubtedly right in emphasising *general* equilibrium over *partial* equilibrium.

Instead of seeking alternative designs, we must take a more roundabout tack. In this paper it is asked why, in the course of capitalist development, the actual producer lost control of production. What circumstances gave rise to the boss-worker pyramid that characterizes capitalist production? And what social function does the capitalist hierarchy serve? If it turns out that the origin and function of capitalist hierarchy has relatively little to do with efficiency, then it becomes at least an open question whether or not hierarchical production is essential to a high material standard of living. And workers − manual, technical, and intellectual − may take the possibility of egalitarian work organization sufficiently seriously to examine their environment with a view to changing the economic, social, and political institutions that relegate all but a fortunate few to an existence in which work is the means to life, not part of life itself.

It is the contention of this paper that neither of the two decisive steps in depriving the workers of control of product and process − (1) the development of the minute division of labour that characterized the putting-out system and (2) the development of the centralized organization that characterizes the factory system − took place primarily for reasons of technical superiority. Rather than providing more output for the same inputs, these innovations in work organization were introduced so that the capitalist got himself a larger share of the pie at the expense of the worker, and it is only the *subsequent* growth in the size of the pie that has obscured the class interest which was at the root of these innovations. The social function of hierarchical work organization is not technical efficiency, but accumulation. By mediating between producer and consumer, the capitalist organization sets aside much more for expanding and improving plant and equipment than individuals would if they could control the pace of capital accumulation. These ideas, which are developed in the body of this paper, can be conveniently divided into four specific propositions.

1 The capitalist division of labour, typified by Adam Smith's famous example of pin manufacture, was the result of a search not for a

technologically superior organization of work, but for an organization which guaranteed to the entrepreneur an essential role in the production process, as integrator of the separate efforts of his workers into a marketable product.

2 Likewise, the origin and success of the factory lay not in technological superiority, but in the substitution of the capitalist's for the worker's control of the work process and the quantity of output, in the change in the workman's choice from one of how much to work and produce, based on his relative preferences for leisure and goods, to one of whether or not to work at all, which of course is hardly much of a choice.

3 The social function of hierarchical control of production is to provide for the accumulation of capital. The individual, by and large and on the average, does not save by a conscious and deliberate choice. The pressures to spend are simply too great. Such individual (household) savings as do occur are the consequence of a lag in adjusting spending to a rise in income, for spending, like any other activity, must be learned, and learning takes time. Thus individual savings is the consequence of growth, and not an independent cause. Acquisitive societies – precapitalist, capitalist or socialist – develop institutions whereby collectivities determine the rate of accumulation. In modern capitalist society the pre-eminent collectivity for accumulation is the corporation. It is an essential social function of the corporation that its hierarchy mediate between the individual producer (and shareholder) and the market proceeds of the corporation's product, assigning a portion of these proceeds to enlarging the means of production. In the absence of hierarchical control of production, society would either have to fashion egalitarian institutions for accumulating capital or content itself with the level of capital already accumulated.

4 The emphasis on accumulation accounts in large part for the failure of Soviet-style socialism to 'overtake and surpass' the capitalist world in developing egalitarian forms of work organization. In according first priority to the accumulation of capital, the Soviet Union repeated the history of capitalism, at least as regards the relationship of men and women to their work. Theirs has not been the failure described by Santayana of those who, not knowing history, unwittingly repeat it. The Soviets consciously and deliberately embraced the capitalist mode of production. And defenders of the Soviet path to economic development would offer no apology: after all, they would probably argue, egalitarian institutions and an egalitarian (and community oriented) man could not have been created over night, and the Soviet Union rightly felt itself too poor to contemplate an indefinite end to accumulation. Now, alas, the Soviets have the 'catch-up-with-and-surpass-the-U.S.A.' tiger by the tail, for it would probably take as much of a revolution to transform work organization in that society as in ours.

The following sections of this paper take these propositions one by one, in the hope of filling in sufficient detail to give them credibility.

2 DIVIDE AND CONQUER

Hierarchy was of course not invented by capitalists. More to the point, neither was hierarchical production. In precapitalist societies, industrial production was organized according to a rigid master-journeyman-apprentice hierarchy, which survives today in anything like its pure form only in the graduate departments of our universities. What distinguished precapitalist from capitalist hierarchy was first that the man at the top was, like the man at the bottom, a producer. The master worked along with his apprentice rather than simply telling him what to do. Second, the hierarchy was linear rather than pyramidal. The apprentice would one day become a journeyman and likely a master. Under capitalism it is a rare worker who becomes even a foreman, not to mention independent entrepreneur or corporate president. Third, and perhaps most important, the guild workman had no intermediary between himself and the market. He generally sold a product, not his labour, and therefore controlled both product and work process.

Just as hierarchy did not orginate with capitalism, neither did the division of labour. The *social* division of labour, the specialization of occupation and function, *is* a characteristic of all complex societies, rather than a peculiar feature of industrialized or economically advanced ones. Nothing, after all, could be more elaborate than the caste society of labour and its accompanying hierarchy in traditional Hindu society. Nor is the *technical* division of labour peculiar to capitalism or modern industry. Cloth production, for example, even under the guild system was divided into separate tasks, each controlled by specialists. But, as we have said, the guild workman controlled product and process. What we have to account for is why the guild division of labour evolved into the capitalist division of labour, in which the workman's task typically became so specialized and minute that he had no product to sell, or at least none for which there was a wide market, and had therefore to make use of the capitalist as intermediary to integrate his labour with the labour of others and transform the whole into a marketable product.

Adam Smith argues that the capitalist division of labour came about because if its technological superiority; in his view, the superiority of dividing work into ever more minutely specialized tasks was limited only by the size of the market.[2] To understand the limitations of this explanation requires clarity and precision on the meaning of 'technological superiority,' and the related ideas of technological efficiency and inefficiency; indeed, these ideas are central to the whole story told in this paper. We shall say, in accordance with accepted usage, that a method of production is technologically superior to another if it produces more output with the same inputs. It is not enough that a new method of production yield more output per day to be technologically superior. Even if labour is the only input, a new method of production might require more hours of labour, or more intensive effort, or more unpleasant working conditions, in which case it would be providing more output for more input, not for the same amount. It will be argued here that – contrary to neoclassical logic – a new method of production does not have to be technologically superior to be adopted; innovation depends as much on economic and social institutions – on who is in control of production and under what constraints control is exercised.

The terms 'technological efficiency' and 'technological inefficiency,' as used by economists, have meanings that are slightly at variance with the ordinary, every-day ideas of better and worse that they evoke. A method of production is technologically efficient if no technologically superior alternative exists. It is inefficient if a superior alternative does exist. Thus more than one method of production may be – and generally is – technologically efficient if one looks only at a single product. Wheat, for example, can be efficiently produced with a lot of land and relatively little fertilizer, as in Kansas, or with a lot of fertilizer and relatively little land, as in Holland.

But if one views technological superiority and efficiency from the point of view of the whole economy, these concepts reduce, under certain circumstances, to *economic* superiority and efficiency. Under text-book assumptions of perfect and universal competition, the technologically efficient method of production is the one that costs least, and cost reduction is an index of technological superiority.[3] The relationship between minimum cost and technological efficiency is a purely logical one and does not depend at all on whether or not the world exhibits the assumptions of the model. On the other hand, the relevance of the identification of technological with economic efficiency depends absolutely on the applicability of the assumptions of the competitive model to the development of capitalism. In critical respects the development of capitalism necessarily required denial, not fulfilment, of the assumptions of perfect competition.

In a way it is surprising that the development of capitalist methods of work organization contradicts essential assumptions of perfect competition, since perfect competition has virtually nothing to say about the organization of production! Indeed, even the firm itself, a central economic institution under capitalism, plays no essential role in models of the competitive economy;[4] it is merely a convenient abstraction for the household in its role as producer and does nothing that households could not equally well do for themselves. Defenders of the faith from Wicksell to Samuelson have grandly proclaimed the perfect neutrality of perfect competition – as far as the model goes, workers could as well hire capital as capitalist workers![5] Alas, the failure of the competitive model to account for one of the most distinctive features of capitalism (and of socialism imitating capitalism – the pyramidal work order – is for neoclassical economists a great virtue rather than a shortcoming; it is supposed to show the great generality of the theory. Generality indeed: neoclassical theory says only that hierarchy must be technologically efficient to persist, but denies the superiority of capitalist hierachy (workers can just as well hire capital, remember!) This is to say very little, and that little, it will be argued, quite wrong.

To return to Adam Smith, *The Wealth of Nations* advances three arguments for the technological superiority of dividing labour as finely as the market will allow.

(This) great increase of the quantity of work, which, in consequence of the division of labour, the same number of people are capable of performing, is owing to three different circumstances; first, to the increse of dexterity in every particular workman; secondly, to the saving of the time which is commonly lost in passing from one species of work to another; and lastly, to the invention of a great number of machines which facilitate labour and abridge labour, and enable one man to do the work of many.[6]

Of the three arguments, one – the saving of time – is undoubtedly important. But this argument has little or nothing to do with the minute specialization that characterizes the capitalist division of labour. A peasant, for example, will generally plough a whole field before harrowing it rather than alternating plough and harrow, furrow by furrow – in order to economize on the set-up time. But peasant agriculture is the antithesis of capitalist specialization; the individual peasant normally undertakes all the activities necessary to bring a crop from seed to marketable product. In respect of set-up time, there is nothing to differentiate agriculture from industry. To save 'the time that is commonly lost in passing from one species of work to another' it is necessary only to continue in a single activity long enough that the set-up becomes an insignificant proportion of total work time. The saving of time would require at most only that each worker continue in a single activity for days at a time, not for a whole life time. Saving of time implies *separation* of tasks and *duration* of activity, not *specialization*.

Smith's third argument – the propensity to invention – is not terribly persuasive. Indeed, the most devastating criticism was voiced by Smith himself in a later chapter of *The Wealth of Nations*:

In the progress of the division of labour, the employment of the far greater part of those who have by labour, that is, of the great body of the people, come to be confined to a few very simple operations, frequently to one or two. But the understandings of the greater part of men are formed by their ordinary employments. The man whose life is spent in performing a few simple operations, of which the effects too are, perhaps, always the same, or very nearly the same, has no occasion to exert his understanding, or to exercise his invention in finding out expedients for difficulties which never occur. He naturally loses, therefore, the habit of such exertion and generally becomes as stupid and ignorant as it is possible for a human creature to become ..

It is otherwise in the barbarous societies, as they are commonly called, of hunters, of shepherds, and even of husbandman in that crude state of husbandry which precedes the improvement of manufactures. In such societies the varied occupations of every man oblige every man to exert his capacity, and to invent expedients for removing difficulties which are continually occurring. Invention is kept alive, and the mind is not suffered to fall into tht drowsy stupidity, which, in a civilized society, seems to benumb the understanding of almost all the inferior ranks of people.[7]

The choice does not, however, seem really to lie between stupidity and barbarity, but between the workman whose span of control is wide enough that he sees how each operation fits into the whole and the workman confined to a small number of repetitive tasks. It would be surprising indeed if the workman's propensity to invent has not been diminished by the extreme specialization that characterizes the capitalist division of labour.

This leaves 'the increase of dexterity in every particular workman' as the basis of carrying specialization to the limits permitted by the size of the market. Now if Adam Smith were talking about musicians or dancers or surgeons, or even if he were speaking of the division of labour between pin-making and cloth-making, his argument would be difficult to counter. But he is speaking not of esoteric specializations, nor of the social division of labour, but of the minute division of ordinary, run-of-the-mill, industrial activities into separate skills. Take his favourite example of pin manufacture:

... in the way in which this business is now carried on, not only the whole work is a peculiar trade, but it is divided into a number of branches, of which the greater part are likewise peculiar trades. One man draws out the wire, another straightens it, a third cuts it, a fourth points it, a fifth grinds it at the top for receiving the head; to make the head requires two or three distinct operations; to put it on, is a peculiar business, to whiten the pins is another; it is even a trade by itself to put them into the paper; and the important business of making a pin is, in this manner, divided into about eighteen distinct operations, which in some manufactories, are all performed by distinct hands, though in others the same man will sometimes perform two or three of them. I have seen a small manufactory of this kind where ten men only were employed, and where some of them consequently performed two or three distinct operations. But though they were very poor, and therefore but indifferently accommodated with the necessary equipment, they could, when they exerted themselves, make among them about twelve pounds of pins in a day. There are in a pound upwards of four thousand pins of a middling size. Those ten persons, therefore could make among them upwards of forty-eight thousand pins in a day. Each person, therefore, making a tenth part of forty-eight thousand pins, might be considered as making four thousand eight hundred pins in a day. But if they had all wrought separately and independently, and without any of them having been educated to this peculiar business, they certainly could not each of them have made twenty, perhaps not one pin in a day . . .[8]

To the extent that the skills at issue are difficult to acquire, specialization is essential to the division of production into separate operations. But, judging from the earnings of the various specialists engaged in pin-making, these were no special skills. At least there were none that commanded premium wages. In a pin manufactory for which fairly detailed records survive from the early part of the nineteenth century, T. S. Ashton reported wages for adult males of approximately 20 shillings per week, irrespective of the particular branch in which they were engaged.[9] Women and children, as was customary, earned less, but again there appear to be no great discrepancies among the various branches of pin production. It would appear to be the case that the mysteries of pin-making were relatively quickly learned, and that the potential increase in dexterity afforded by minute division of tasks was exhausted. Certainly it is hard to make a case for specialization of workmen to particular tasks on the basis of the pin industry.[10]

The dichotomy between specialization and the separate crafting of each individual pin seems to be a false one. It appears to have been technologically possible to obtain the economics of reducing set-up time *without* specialization. A workman, with his wife and children, could have proceeded from task to task, first drawing out enough wire for hundreds or thousands of pins, then straightening it, then cutting it, and so on with each successive operation, thus realizing the advantages of dividing the overall production process into separate tasks.

Why, then, did the division of labour under the putting-out system entail specialization as well as separation of tasks? In my view the reason lies in the fact that without specialization, the capitalist had no essential role to play in the production process. If each producer could himself integrate the component tasks of pin manufacture into a marketable product, he would soon discover that he had no need to deal with the market for pins through the intermediation of the putter-outer. He could sell directly and appropriate to himself the profit that the capitalist derived from mediating between the producer and the market. Separating the tasks assigned to each workman was the sole means by which the capitalist could, in the days preceding costly machinery, ensure that he would remain essential to the production process as integrator of these separate operations into a product for which a wide market existed; and specialization of men to tasks at the sub-product level was the hall mark of the putting-out system.

The capitalist division of labour, as developed under the putting-out system, embodied the same principle that 'successful' imperial powers have utilized to rule their colonies: divide and conquer. Exploiting differences between Hindu and Muslim in India – if not actually creating them – the British could claim to be essential to the stability of the sub-continent. And they could, sometimes with ill-concealed satisfaction, point to the millions of deaths that followed Partition as proof of their necessity to stability. But this tragedy proved only that the British had *made* themselves essential as

mediators, not that there was any inherent need for British mediation of communal differences.

Similarly, the development of an industrial system dependent on capitalist integration does not prove that the capitalist division of labour was technologically superior to integration by the producer himself. The putter-outer's peculiar contribution to production was handsomely rewarded not because of any genuine scarcity of the ability to integrate separate functions; rather the scarcity was artificially created to preserve the capitalists's role.

How could the capitalist withstand competition if his role was an artificial one? What prevented each producer from integrating his own work, and thereby coming directly into contact with a wide market? The capitalist putter-outer, who, by hypothesis, was technologically superfluous, would have been eliminated by such competition; for integrated producers would have produced pins and cloth and pottery more cheaply. Why didn't some enterprising and talented fellow organize producers to eliminate the capitalist putter-outer? The answer is that there was no profit in such a line of endeavour. If the organizer became a producer himself, he would have had to settle for a producer's wage. His co-workers might have subscribed a dinner or gold watch in his honour, but it is doubtful that their gratitude would have led them to do much more. To glean rewards from organizing, one had to become a capitalist putter-outer! The point is that no collusion was necessary between the men of talent, enterprise, and means that formed the capitalist class of putting-out days. It was in the interest of each as well as in the interest of all to maintain the system of allocating separate tasks to separate workmen. Not much wit was required to see that their prosperity, as well as their survival as mediators, depended on this system.[11]

The advantages to the mediator of standing between the producer and a wide market were apparently obvious for some time before capitalist manufacture succeeded guild manufacture. George Unwin's studies of sixteenth and seventeenth century industry suggested to him that 'the various crafts were, in fact, engaged in a constant struggle as to which of them should secure the economic advantage of standing between the rest and the market.'[12] And Unwin notes − but unfortunately does not elaborate the point − that 'by this interlacing of the interests of dealer and craftsman the way was gradually prepared for a new form of organization, embracing both classes, which naturally sought to extend its authority as widely over the manufacture as possible.'[13]

Hard evidence that 'divide and conquer' rather than efficiency was at the root of the capitalist division of labour is, naturally enough, not easy to come by. One cannot really expect the capitalist, or anybody else with an interest in preserving hierarchy and authority, to proclaim publicly that production was organized to exploit the worker. And the worker who was sufficiently acute to appreciate this could, in the relatively mobile societies in which the industrial revolution first took root, join the ranks of the

exploiters.

Nevertheless, an occasional glimmer of recognition does exist. One, although from a slightly later epoch, supports the divide-and-conquer view of specialization better than any forgery could. Henry Ashworth, Jr., managing partner of one of the Ashworth cotton enterprises, noted approvingly in his diary that a competitor did not allow any of his employees, not even his manager, to mix cotton, adding

> ... his manager Henry Hargreaves knows nothing about the mixing or costs of cotton so that he can never take his business away from him — all his Overlookers business are quite separate from each other and then no one knows what is going on but himself.[14]

This story has a recent parallel. I know a man who was for a time a sandal maker. To learn the trade, he went to work for a 'master' sandal maker. This worthy systematically taught him all there was to know about making sandals — except how to buy the leather. My friend could have learned this vital aspect of the trade on his own by the familiar and time-honoured method of trial and error — if he had had $1,000 or so to set aside for the mistakes inherent in the learning process. Lacking the capital, his boss's unwillingness to share one particular skill effectively obliged him to remain a worker as long as he remained in the trade.

One other nineteenth century comment suggests that those closer to the beginnings of industrial capitalism than ourselves were not blind to the role of division of labour in supporting a hierarchical society. *The Spectator* approved of co-operation between master and men, so long as it did not threaten capitalism. Indeed, as long as cooperation was limited to profit-sharing and the like, it might strengthen capitalism for profit sharing in no way meant an end to hierarchy. By contrast, workers' co-operatives were perceived as a distinct threat, one *The Spectator* thought it necessary to exorcise before extolling the virtues of profit sharing:

> Hitherto that principle (of cooperation) has been applied in England only by associations of workmen, but the Rochdale experiments, important and successful as they were, were on one or two points incomplete. They showed that associations of workmen could manage shops, mills, and all forms of industry with success, and they immensely improved the condition of the men, but then *they did leave a clear place for the masters*. That was a defect, for three reasons. (Emphasis added)[15]

It is of some interest to examine these reasons:

> Firstly, money in England is held in great masses in individual hands; secondly, there exists among us a vast mass of administrative or, as we call it, business ability, which is of the highest value in directing associated labour wisely, which can and does add infinitely to the value of that labour, and which is not willing to devote itself to labour in absolute or equal partnerships. It does not pay, say Mr. Brassey, to be anything but head. And lastly, cooperation among workmen is not so

consonant to the national genius as cooperation between masters and men – limited monarchy having got into our bones – and a system which harmonizes with the national genius is accepted quickly, while one which does not, even if it is superior in itself advances slowly indeed.[16]

The first – that 'money . . . is held in great masses . . . in individual hands' – is a reason for hierarchical organization only if one considers the wealth distribution inviolable. Indeed, the argument is usually put the other way around: that the superiority of hierarchical production requires great wealth inequalities! The second reason – that 'administrative . . . ability . . . can and does add infinitely to the value of . . . labour' but 'is not willing to devote itself to labour in absolute or equal partnership – is contradicted by the very successes claimed for the Rochdale experiments. The third – 'the natural genius' for 'limited monarchy' – is the last refuge of scoundrels; if one took it seriously, one could never challenge the *status-quo*.

Although the direct evidence for the divide-and-conquer view of the capitalist division of labour is not overwhelming, it is at least as impressive as the direct evidence for the efficiency view. And there is some indirect evidence too. If the specialization of workmen to tasks took place to ensure capitalist control, then where capitalist control was for other reasons beyond challenge, there is no basis, according to the divide-and-conquer hypothesis, to expect a minute specialization. And so it turns out, at least in the one case of which I have knowledge. The British coal industry offers an example of an industry in which the capitalist division of labour never took hold. Under hand-got methods, as primitive in technique as the putting-out system of manufacture, but surviving into the twentieth century, 'responsibility for the complete coal-getting task rests squarely on the shoulders of a single small, face-to-face group which experiences the entire cycle of operations within the compass of its membership.'[17] This group contracted directly with the colliery management and 'though the contract may have been in the name of the hewer, it was regarded as a joint undertaking. Leadership and "supervision" were internal to the group, which had a quality of *responsible autonomy*.'[18] Furthermore, 'each collier (was) an all-around workman, usually able to substitute for his mate . . . He had craft pride and artisan independence. These qualities obviated status difficulties and contributed to responsible autonomy.'[19] Presumably the mine owner felt no need to specialize men to tasks; the scarcity of coal seams and the institution of private property ensured that workers would not dispense with bosses.

But this is only the beginning of the story. Its most interesting chapter perhaps is the subsequent development of work organization under mechanized – longwall – conditions. As Trist and Bamforth tell the story, 'need arose (with mechanization) for a unit more of the size and differentiated complexity of a small factory department.'[20] On what model? 'At the time the longwall method developed, there were no precedents for the adaptive underground application of machine technology. In the absence of relevant experience in the mining tradition itself, it was almost inevitable that heavy culture-borrowing (of specialization of men to tasks) should have taken place.'[21]

The basic idea of the longwall system was the division of labour by shifts, each shift being responsible for a subset of the operations that move the coal from pit to ground.

The work is broken down into a standard series of component operations that follow each other in rigid succession over three shifts of seven and a half hours each, so that a total coal-getting cycle may be completed once in each twenty-four hours of the working week. The shift spread of the 40 workmen needed on an average face is: 10 each to the first ('cutting') and second ('ripping') shifts; 20 to the third ('filling') shift.[22]

Mechanized methods did not, however, yield the fruits they seemed to promise. The problem lay in the supervision of groups of specialists each responsible for only one of the operations that constitute the whole.[23] Jnd the solution lay in reconstituting work groups so that each shift was 'responsible for task continuity rather than a specific set of tasks ... with responsibility for co-ordination and control being primarily in the hands of the cycle group.'[24] The distinctive features of the new system, called the 'composite longwall system' were fourfold:

The Work Method

In accordance with the tradition of composite working which originated in the (hand got) system, the oncoming men on a shift were to take up the work of the cycle from the point at which it had been left by the previous shift group and continue with whatever tasks had next to be done. When the main task of a shift was completed the men were to redeploy to carry on with the next tasks whether they formed a part of the current cycle or commenced a new one.

The Workmen

In order for this task continuity to be practised, it was necessary for the cycle group to include men who were at least competent under supervision, if not always formally qualified, to undertake the necessary tasks as they arose. It was not essential that all members of the composite team be completely multi-skilled, but only that as a team they should have sufficient skill resources available on each shift to man the roles likely to arise.

The Work Groups

The team manning the composite longwall was to be a self-selected group. The cycle group was to accept responsibility for allocating its members to the various jobs that management specified to be filled. In order to regulate the deployment, the team was to develop and operate some system for the rotation of tasks and shifts among team members.

Method of Payment

As in (hand got) systems, there was to be a common pay-note in which all members of the team were to share equally, since all members were regarded as making an equivalent contribution to the completion of the cycle. [25]

The British coal industry is one of the few places where direct comparisons of alternative methods of organizing work have been attempted. The Tests are not absolutely conclusive, because the alternatives cannot be applied repeatedly to one and the same coal face. Nonetheless, the results are striking: the composite longwall method was found to produce 20 per cent more coal than the conventional longwall method. [26]

Equally interesting for present purposes is the effect of reorganization on management:

The effects of self-regulation by the cycle group on the management of the seam of which the composite longwall was a part ... was that the seam management structure was eventually simplified. *One overman was withdrawn;* It was found that there was no job for him. [27] (Emphasis added.)

It is not hard to imagine the difficulties reorganization would have encountered had it been in the hands of the redundant overman to decide its fate.

Essential to the willingness of the overman's superiors to allow the reintroduction into the mines of self-integrating, non-specialized, non-hierarchical work groups was the coupling of the physical scarcity of coal seams with the institution of property. [28] Had the miners been able to set up shop for themselves, management well might have found it necessary to rely, as did the capitalist putter-outer, on specialization of men to tasks as a means of keeping the worker in his 'rightful' place – and thereby the boss in his.

The coal mine is to some extent typical of the stage in the development of industrial capitalism that *followed* the putting-out system, but it is, I think, wrong to ascribe primary importance to the growth in fixed capital, to the high cost of means of production, in explaining the proletarianization of the work force. Property in machinery, like property in coal seams, was perhaps in mid-nineteenth century England as effective as specialization in insuring a role for the capitalist. Machinery was too costly for the individual workman, and the group, was for all intents and purposes, nonexistent. But before that time, machinery was not prohibitively expensive, and since then the union has become a force that might have offset the high cost of machinery – for the group if not for the individual. For some time preservation of the boss – worker hierarchy has required tacit acceptance by unions; present-day unions lack the will for change, not the strength. This is not to say that it is mere accident that unions have for the most part chosen to ignore hierarchy and its effects, and have concentrated instead on 'bread-and-butter' issues. These have been the easiest to accommodate within the framework of a growing economy and agreement to limit conflict to these issues has been instrumental in muting the conflict between capitalists and workers. But the price of accommodation has been steep; unions have become another cog in the hierarchy, not the workers' defence against it. [29] It is not, however, simply a matter of reorienting priorities within the traditional framework of union leadership. Once unions were to become interested in the relationship of men to their work, they would find themselves in conflict with the very principles of capitalist organization, not merely in conflict over the division, at the margin, of the capitalist pie. No longer could labour's spokesmen be pillars of the established order.

When the absolute scarcity of natural resources limits production to a few sites, the institution of property has itself sufficed to maintain the workers in a subordinate position. Thus it is that in an extractive industry like coal mining, specialization has proved necessary under neither a hand nor a machine technology. In manufacturing industry, where non-labour factors of production are themselves for the most part produced and, therefore, in principle accessible to groups of workers regardless of cost, specialization has continued to sustain the illusion that hierarchy is necessary for integrating the efforts of many into a marketable product.

But we get ahead of the story. At the present point in the argument, chronology suffices to refute the explanation of proletarianization of the producers by the high cost of machinery: the transformation of the independent producer to a wage labourer took place *before* machinery became expensive. It was a direct consequence of the specialization of men to component tasks that characterized the putting-out system. To be sure, capital played a role in the putting-out system; the putter-outer was after all a 'capitalist'. But machinery under the putting-out system was primitive; *fixed* capital was inconsequential. The capital provided by the putter-outer was predominantly working capital — stocks of good in process — and advances against future labour.

The role played by wage advances deserves more attention than it has received, for at least in some trades it appears to have been an important means by which the capitalist maintained his hegemony. [30] Wage advances were to the capitalist what free samples of heroin are to the pusher: a means of creating dependence. It is of little moment that one was a legal and the other a physiological dependence. Both represent an addiction from which only the exceptionally strong-willed and fortunate escape. [31] The point for present purposes is that the practice of what was virtually indentured servitude (though for shorter periods of time than were customary in the British North American and African colonies) nicely complemented the specialization of men to tasks. Wage advances legally bound the worker to his master, and specialization of his activity to a small part of the whole helped to prevent the worker from circumventing his legal obligation to work for no one else (until his debt was discharged) by restricting the outlets for his production to intermediaries, a much smaller 'market' than the market for a finished product. It was presumably much harder to dispose illegally of unwhitened pins than of whitened ones.[32]

The use of wage advances to maintain worker dependence and hierarchical control of production, however widespread under the putting-out system it may or may not have been, was no isolated historical phenomenon. It has been an important feature in other kinds of market economies where alternative means for subordinating the worker have not been available. Perhaps the most relevant example in the American experience was the development of agricultural organization in the post-1865 South. The problem of the post-bellum American planter was in many respects similar to the problem of the pre-factory British putter-outer: how to ensure for himself an essential role in the production process. The ex-slave was no longer legally tied to the land, and the land, like the means of industrial production in pre-factory days, was not sufficiently scarce or costly to maintain the dependency of workers on capitalists.

The problem was solved by coupling the crop-lien system of credit to the share-cropping system of farming. The planter-capitalist typically advanced credit in kind for food and other necessities of life, as well as for seed, fertilizer, and implements. These advances were secured by a lien on present and future crops, and the cultivator was legally under his creditor's thrall until the debt was repaid, which could be never since the creditor kept the books. Under the share-cropping system, the land-owner, not the tenant, controls the choice of crops,

> and he wants nothing brown except what he can sell. If the tenant takes time to keep a garden he does so at the neglect of his major interest, and, furthermore, he deprives the owner of the privilege of selling him additional groceries.[33]

Even the nominal independence of land-ownership was rarely of any value to the ex-slave. Debt was not a business arrangement, but subjugation. And the crop lien gave the capitalist virtually the same control over the cropping pattern as did land ownership. 'The cropper who dared to till a truck patch was quickly warned that he was lowering his credit.'[34] The result was a ruinous monoculture.

> In the greater part of the South the merchant demanded that cotton, more cotton, and almost cotton alone should be grown, because . . . the growers could neither eat it up behind his back nor slip it out for surreptitious sale.
>
> . . . Any attempt to sequester any of the cotton for sale elsewhere, even if beyond the amount due the storekeeper, was visited with quick retribution. In South Carolina, if the lien-holder even suspected such intent, he could get an order from the clerk of the court to have the sheriff confiscate the whole crop for sale . . .[35]

Generously assisted by the police power of the state, cotton enabled the capitalist to intervene between the producer and the market. Indeed, it is fair to conclude that cotton culture was to the capitalist planter what specialization was to the capitalist putter-outer: a choice dictated not by technological superiority but by his interest in interposing himself between the producer and the market.

3 THE RISE OF THE FACTORY

The minute specialization that was the hallmark of the putting-out system only wiped out one of two aspects of workers' control of production: control over the product. Control of the work process, when and how much the worker would exert himself, remained with the worker – until the coming of the factory.

Economic historians customarily ascribe the growth of the factory to the technological superiority of large-scale machinery, which required concentration of productive effort around newly harnessed sources of energy – water and steam. The first factories, according to T. S. Ashton, arose in the beginning of the eighteenth century when '*for technical reasons*, small groups of men were brought together into workshops and little water-driven mills.' [36] But the beginnings of the modern factory system are usually associated with Richard Arkwright, whose spinning mills displaced the domestic manufacture of cotton yarn. Arkwright's water frame, it is said, dictated the factory organization of spinning: 'Unlike the jenny, the frame required, for its working, power greater than that of human muscles, and hence from the beginning the process was carried on in mills or factories.' [37] Other authorities agree. Thus Paul Mantoux: ' . . . the use of machines distinguishes the factory from (the putting-out system), and gives its special character to the new system as against all preceding ones . . .' [38] And, more recently, David Landes has written

> The Industrial Revolution . . . required machines which not only replaced hand labour but compelled the concentration of production in factories – in other words machines whose appetite for energy was too large for domestic sources of power and whose mechanical superiority was sufficient to break down the resistance of the older forms of hand production. [39]

These authorities, it should be said, recognize the other advantages the factory afforded, particularly a system of discipline and supervision that was impossible under the putting-out system. 'It was', as Ashton says, 'the need for supervision of work that led Peter Stubbs to gather the scattered filemakers into his works at Warrington.' [40] Mantoux also notes the 'obvious advantages from the point of view of organization and supervision'[41] of bringing together many workers into a single workshop. According to Landes the need for discipline and supervision turned 'the thoughts of employers . . . to workshops where the men would be brought together to labour under watchful overseers.' [42] And elsewhere Landes is even more explicit. 'The essence of the factory,' he writes in an introduction to a volume of essays on the development of capitalism, 'is discipline – the opportunity it affords for the direction of and co-ordination of labour.' [43]

Nevertheless, the advantages of discipline and supervision remain, in the conventional view, secondary considerations in accounting for the success of the factory system, if not for the motivation behind it. In the same breath as Mantoux notes the organizational advantages of the factory, he concludes that 'the factory system . . . was the necessary outcome of the use of machinery.' [44] Similarly, while identifying discipline as the essence of the factory, Landes attributes its success to technological factors: 'the triumph of concentrated over dispersed manufacture was indeed made possible by the economic advantages of power-driven equipment. The factory had to beat cottage industry in the marketplace, and it was not an easy victory.' [45]

The model underlying this reasoning is easy to identify: the factory survived, therefore it must have been a less costly method of production than alternatives. And in the competitive market economy, only least-cost methods are technologically efficient, provided efficiency is defined in an economy-wide sense. Hence the factory must have been technologically superior to alternatives.

However, the very mention of supervision and discipline as motivations for the factory ought to put one on guard against a too-easy identification of cost-minimization with technological efficiency. In the competitive model, there is no scope for supervision and discipline except for that imposed by the market mechanism. [46] Any recognition of the importance of supervision and discipline as motivating forces behind the establishment of factories is tantamount to admission of important violations of the assumptions of perfect competition, and it follows that cost minimization cannot be identified with technological efficiency. Thus, technological superiority becomes neither necessary nor sufficient for the rise and success of the factory.

It will be argued presently that the agglomeration of workers into factories was a natural outgrowth of the putting-out system (a result, if you will, of its internal contradictions) whose success had little or nothing to do with the technological superiority of large-scale machinery. The key to the success of the factory, as well as its inspiration, was the substitution of capitalists' for workers' control of the production process; discipline and supervision could and did reduce costs *without* being technologically superior.

That the triumph of the factory, as well as the motivation behind it, lay in discipline and supervision, was clear to at least one contemporary observer. The leading nineteenth century apologist for the factory system, Andrew Ure, quite explicitly attributed Arkwright's success to his administrative prowess:

> The main difficulty (faced by Arkwright) did not, to my apprehension, lie so much in the invention of a proper self-acting mechanism for drawing out and twisting cotton into a continuous thread, as in . . .

training human beings to renounce their desultory habits of work, and to identify themselves with the unvarying regularity of the complex automation. *To devise and administer a successful code of factory discipline, suited to the necessities of factory diligence, was the Herculean enterprise, the noble achievement of Arkwright.* Even at the present day, when the system is perfectly organized, and its labour lightened to the utmost, it is found nearly impossible to convert persons past the age of puberty, whether drawn from rural or from handicraft occupations, into useful factory hands. After struggling for a while to conquer their listless or restive habits, they either renounce the employment spontaneously, or are dismissed by the overlookers on account of inattention.

If the factory Briareus could have been created by mechanical genius alone, it should have come into being thirty years sooner; for upwards of ninety years have now elapsed since John Wyatt, of Birmingham, not only invented the series of fluted rollers, (the spinning fingers usually ascribed to Arkwright), but obtained a patent for the invention, and erected 'a spinning engine without hands' in his native town ... Wyatt was a man of good education, in a respectable walk of life, much esteemed by his superiors, and therefore favourably placed, in a mechanical point of view, for maturing his admirable scheme. But he was of a gentle and passive spirit, little qualified to cope with the hardships of a new manufacturing enterprise. *It required, in fact, a man of a Napoleon nerve and ambition, to subdue the refractory tempers of work-people accustomed to irregular paroxysms of diligence* ... Such was Arkwright. [47] (Emphasis added.)

Wyatt's efforts, and his ultimate failure, are shrouded in mystery. Indeed, it is impossible to sort out his contribution from the contribution of his collaborator, Lewis Paul. No model of the Wyatt-Paul machine survives, but Mantoux supports Ure's judgment that Wyatt and Paul anticipated Arkwright in all technical essentials. Arkwright's machine, according to Mantoux, 'differs from that of Wyatt only in its details. These trifling differences cannot explain Arkwright's triumphal success.' [48]

Contemporary evidence suggests that the problems of organizing the workforce played a substantial part in the failure of the Wyatt-Paul enterprises. The correspondence between the principals and their officers suggest a continuing preoccupation with discipline. Edward Cave, a financial backer as well as a licensee, set up shop with hand-powered equipment in anticipation of finding a suitable water mill. Early on he wrote to Paul: 'I have not half my people come to work today, and I have no great fascination in the prospect I have to put myself in the power of such people.' [49] Discipline did not improve once the Cave factory became mechanized. When Wyatt visited the new spinning mill at Northampton in 1743 he found that 'only four frames were regularly at work, since there were seldom hands enough for five.' [50] The search for new methods of discipline continued. A month later, Cave's lieutenant wrote Wyatt:

I think they (the workers) have done as much in four days this week as they did in a week when you were here ... There were not hands enough to work all five engines but four is worked complete which did about 100 skeins a day one with another, nay some did 130. One reason for this extra advance is Mr. Harrison (the mill manager) bought 4 handkerchers one for each machine value about $\frac{1}{2}$p. each and hung them over the engine as prizes for the girls that do most ... [51]

These crude attempts to 'subdue the refractory tempers of work-people' by judicious use of the carrot apparently came to nought. One of the few indisputable facts about the Wyatt-Paul attempts is that they failed. And between Wyatt and Arkwright no one managed to bring Wyatt's invention to a successful conclusion, a remarkable failure indeed if the defects of machine spinning were primarily technological in nature.

There is additional evidence for the assertion that factory spinning did not depend for its success on a superior machine technology. Factory spinning took hold in the woollen industry as well as in cotton, and its success in the wool trade could only have been for organizational reasons. The technology of wool-spinning for many years after the factory made its appearance was the same in factory as in cottage; in both the 'spinning jenny' was the basic machine well into the nineteenth century. [52] The Hammonds suggest that factory spinning dominated by the beginning of the century:

By 1803 the transformation was practically complete. The clothiers had one by one introduced the system of 'spinning houses' on their own premises, and the weavers were filled with apprehension lest they too should be forced to work under their employer's roof. [53]

At some places water power may have been used for working the jennies, [54] but this does not appear to have been the general case. Benjamin Gott, called by Mantoux the 'first of the great Yorkshire spinners' [55] never used power in his spinning (or weaving) rooms during his quarter-century career as factory master and nevertheless appears to have made a satisfactory profit. [56] Certainly Gott never abandoned spinning and weaving to domestic workshops, although these handpowered activities could have been carried on separately from the operations to which Gott applied steam power scribbling and fulling. Indeed, the customary practice when Gott began his factory in 1793 was for scribbling and fulling to be a trade distinct from spinning and weaving. [57]

In weaving the case is even clearer than in spinning. Gott's handloom weaving sheds were not unique. Long before the powerloom became practicable, handloom weavers were brought together into workshops to weave by the same techniques that were employed in cottage industry, Clearly, the handloom shops would not have persisted if it had not been profitable for the entrepreneur, and just as clearly the source of profits could not have been in a superior technology. There is no evidence that the handloom in the capitalist's factory was any different from the one in the weaver's house.

I have found no comprehensive quantitative estimates of the relative importance of handloom factories, and it would probably require a major research effort to make even a reasoned guess.[58] A recent study of the history of cotton handloom weaving concludes that 'although (the handloom weaving shed) was never anything like the predominant form of organization in cotton weaving, it was not negligible, nor was it confined . . . to fancy goods only.'[59] The author of this study continues:

> According to the historian of Rossendale, in the period 1815–1830, when 'the trade of cotton weaving on the handloom was at its briskest, there were at the lowest computation thirty weaving shops, apart from the looms in dwelling houses, in the forst of Rossendale.' The distinguishing feature of the sheds was that they employed a number of weavers on handlooms outside their own homes and families; they were substantially larger than the small shops of four or six (looms) run by a master weaver and apprentices in some of the more specialized lines at Bolton or Paisley. Isolated cases have been found with as many as 150 or 200 handlooms, quite a few with between 50 and 100, and a considerable number with 20 or more. Such sheds were to be found in town and country throughout the weaving area.
>
> . . . For both employers and workers, the handloom shed represented a transitional stage in the organization of cotton weaving between the true domestic system and the power driven factory. It does not necessarily follow, however, that the handloom shed was a comparatively late development in cotton, or that it was a conscious imitation of the powerloom factory. With the coming of the dandyloom (an improved handloom) in the late 1820s, there was a probable increase in the number of such sheds, but there is some evidence from notices in the local newspapers for their existence in the 1780s and 1790s.[60]

Even as late as 1838, the weaver's animosity might, as in the case of Thomas Exell of Gloucestershire, be directed against the handloom shop and it's owner, not against the powerloom. 'Excell was, according to Wadsworth and Mann, "lamenting . . . the concentration of handlooms and jennies in the clothier's shop" when he wrote "They have driven us away from our houses and gardens to work as prisoners in their factories and their seminaries of vice." '[61]

The early years of the nineteenth century saw the concentration of outworkers into workshops in other trades too. Supervision appears to have provided not only the motivation for 'Peter Stubbs to gather the scattered filemakers into his works at Warrington,' but a sufficient economic rationale for maintaining a factory-like organization in place of the putting-out system. Ashton's careful study of the Stubbs enterprise[62] does not suggest any technological argument for bringing the filemakers together, at least none he considers to be compelling. Nor does Ashton suggest that the new method of organizing work was ever abandoned. On the contrary: some of the original workshops were still standing in his own day.[63]

None of this is to deny the importance of the technological changes that have taken place since the eighteenth century. But these changes were not independent causes of the factory. On the contrary, the particular forms that technological change took were shaped and determined by factory organization. It is not accidental that technological change atrophied within the putting-out system after Hargreaves's jenny but flourished within the factory. On the demand side, the capitalist provided the market for inventions and improvements, and his interest lay — for reasons of supervision and discipline — with the factory. The supply side was only slightly more complex. In principle, an inventor might obtain a patent and license the use of his inventions to putter-outers or, indeed, to independent producers. In practice, as long as production took place in scattered cottages, it was difficult if not impossible to detect and punish piracy of patent rights. It was much easier to enforce patent rights with production concentrated into factories, and this naturally channelled inventive activity into the more remunerative market. And of course many improvements were by their very nature nonpatentable, and their benefits were under capitalist economic organization capturable only by entrepreneurs.

This argument may be thought to imply a *dynamic* technological superiority for the factory system, for it may fairly be interpreted as suggesting that the factory provided a more congenial climate for technological change. A more congenial climate for innovation does not, however, imply technological superiority, dynamic or static. For the factory's superiority in this domain rested in turn on a particular set of institutional arrangements, in particular the arrangements for rewarding inventors by legal monopolies vested in patents. An invention, like knowledge generally, is a 'public good': the use of an idea by one person does not reduce the stock of knowledge in the way that consumption of a loaf of bread reduces the stock of wheat. It is well understood that public goods cannot be efficiently distributed through the market mechanism; so patents cannot be defended on efficiency grounds.

Indeed, the usual defence of patents is in terms of the incentives afforded for invention. But the argument is hardly compelling. There is no *a priori* reason why society might not reward inventors in other ways. In the eighteenth century, for example, Thomas Lombe was voted £14,000 in lieu of a renewal of his patent for silk-throwing machinery, a small amount in proportion to the £120,000 he earned during the fourteen year term of his patent, but a tidy sum nevertheless, presumably enough to coax out the secrets of all but the most diffident genius. [64] To be sure, as it was practised in Great Britain at least, the public reward of inventors was a fitful and unreliable arrangement, but this does not mean that a way could not have been found to make the system workable had the will existed. Had the patent system not played into the hands of the more powerful capitalists, by favouring those with sufficient resources to pay for licences (and incidentally contributing to the polarization of the producing classes into bosses and workers), the patent system need not have become the dominant institutional mode for rewarding inventors.

There remains one loose end in this account of the rise of the factory: why did the market mechanism, which has been supposed by its defenders from Adam Smith onwards to harness the self-interest of the producer to the public interest, fail to provide adequate supervision and discipline under the putting-out system? Discipline and supervision, it must be understood, were inadequate only from the point of view of the capitalist, not from the point of view of the worker. And though it is true that in a sufficiently abstract model of perfect competition, profits are an index of the well-being of society as a whole as well as capitalists' well-being, this identity of interests does not characterize any real capitalist economy, no more the 'competitive' capitalism of Adam Smith's day than the monopoly capitalism of our own. In the perfectly competitive model, there are no capitalists and no workers, there are only households that dispose of different bundles of resources, all of which – labour included – are traded on markets in which no one possesses any economic power. For this reason, labourers can equally well be thought to hire capital as capitalists labour, and the firm plays no significant role in the analysis. By contrast, the hallmark of the putting-out system was a specialization so minute that it denied to the worker the relatively wide (competitive!) market that existed for products, replacing the product market with a narrow market for a sub-product that, in a limited geographical area, a few putter-outers could dominate.[65] The perversion of the competitive principle, which lies at the heart of the capitalist division of labour, made discipline and supervision a class issue rather than an issue of technological efficiency; a lack of discipline and supervision could be disastrous for profits without being inefficient.

The indiscipline of the labouring classes, or more bluntly, their laziness, was widely noted by eighteenth century observers.

> It is a fact well known (wrote a mid-century commentator) ... that scarcity, to a certain degree, promoted industry, and that the manufacturer (worker) who can subsist on three days work will be idle and drunken the remainder of the week ... The poor in the manufacturing counties will never work any more time in general than is necessary just to live and support their weekly debauches ... We can fairly aver that a reduction of wages in the woollen manufacture would be a national blessing and advantage, and no real injury to the poor. By this means we might keep our trade, uphold our rents, and reform the people into the bargain.[66]

Indiscipline, in other words, meant that as wages rose, workers chose to work less. In more neutral language, laziness was simply a preference for leisure! Far from being an 'unreasonable inversion of the laws of sensible economic behaviour,'[67] a backward bending labour-supply curve is a most natural phenomenon as long as the individual worker controls the supply of labour.

At least no devotee of the conventional indifference-curve approach to leisure-goods choices would dare argue that there is anything at all peculiar about a backward bending labour-supply curve. [68] Central to indifference-curve analysis of consumption choices is the separation of substitution and income effects. A rising wage makes leisure relatively more expensive to the worker, to be sure. But against this negative 'substitution' effect must be considered the 'income' effect; besides changing the terms of trade between leisure and goods, a rising wage is like a windfall that makes the worker able to afford more leisure. As long as leisure is a 'normal' good (one for which the income effect is positive), substitution and income effects work in opposite directions. And the outcome is unpredictable; certainly no neoclassical economist worth his salt would argue that the substitution effect must be stronger than the income effect. [69]

In a competitive market, however, the shape of the labour-supply curve in the aggregate is of little moment. By definition, any individual capitalist can hire as many workers as he likes at the going wage. And the wage he pays is reflected in the market price of his product. He earns the competitive rate of profit, whether the going wage is low or high. But for the oligopsonistic putter-outers, the fact that higher wages led workers to choose more leisure was not only perverse, it was disastrous. In 1769, Arthur Young noted 'the sentiment universal' among the cotton manufacturers of Manchester 'that their best friend is high provisions.' [70]

Thus the very success of pre-factory capitalism contained within it the seeds of its own transformation. As Britain's internal commerce and its export trade expanded, wages rose and workers insisted in taking out a portion of their gains in the form of greater leisure. However sensible this response may have been from their own point of view, it was no way for an enterprising capitalist to get ahead. Nor did the capitalist meekly accept the workings of the invisible hand.

His first recourse was to the law. In the eighteenth century, Parliament twice enacted laws requiring domestic woollen workers to complete and return work within specified periods of time. In 1749 the period was fixed at twenty-one days, and in 1777 the period was reduced to eight days. [71] But more direct action proved necessary. The capitalist's salvation lay in taking immediate control of the proportions of work and leisure. Capitalists' interests required that the worker's choice become one of whether or not to work at all – the only choice he was to have within the factory system.

To a great extent, supervision and discipline meant the same thing in the factory. Under the watchful eye of the foreman, the worker was no longer free to pace himself according to his own standards. But supervision was important for another reason: under the putting-out system materials inevitably came under the control of the workman during the process of manufacture. This created a variety of ways for the workman to augment his earnings; in the woollen trade a worker might exchange poor wool for good, or conceal imperfections in spinning, or wet the wool to make it seem heavier.[72] Above all, there was the possibility of outright embezzlement. It seems likely that these possibilities multiplied as trade developed and grew, for disposing of illegally-gotten goods would appear to have been easier as the channels of trade multiplied and expanded. In any event, capitalists increasingly utilized the legislative, police, and judicial powers of the state to prevent workers from eroding their profits during the course of the eighteenth century.[73] Indeed, even the traditional maxim of English justice − that a man was innocent until proven guilty − counted for little where such a clear and present danger to profits was concerned. A Parliamentary Act of 1777 allowed search of a workman's home on mere suspicion of embezzlement. If suspicious goods were found on his premises, it was up to the worker to prove his innocence. Otherwise he was assumed to be guilty − even if no proof were forthcoming.[74]

The worker's 'dishonesty', like his 'laziness,' could not be cured by recourse to the law, however diligently Parliament might try to serve the interests of the capitalist class. The local magistrates might not be sufficiently in tune with the needs of the master manufacturers,[75] particularly one would imagine, if they were members of the landed gentry. In any event, enforcement of the law must have been cumbersome at best, especially where manufacturing was dispersed over a relatively wide geographical area. It is no wonder that, as Landes says, 'the thoughts of employers turned to workshops where the men would be brought together to labour under watchful overseers.' As late as 1824, a correspondent of the *Blackburn Mail* specifically urged the factory system as a means of combating embezzlement:

It is high time . . . that we should have a change either to powerlooms or to (hand) loom shops and factories, when at least one sixth part of the production of cotton goods is affected by (embezzlement).[76]

It is important to emphasize that the discipline and supervision afforded by the factory had nothing to do with efficiency, at least as this term is used by economists. Disciplining the work force meant a larger output in return for a greater input of labour, not more output for the same input.[77] Supervising − insofar as it meant something different from disciplining − the work force simply reduced the real wage; an end to embezzlement and like deceits changed the division of the pie in favour of capitalists. In the competitive model, innovation to improve the position of one individual or group at the expense of another may not be feasible. But the history of employer-worker relations under the putting-out system belies the competitive model. Embezzlement and other forms of deceit were exercises in 'countervailing power,' and pitifully weak ones at that.[78] The factory effectively put an end both to 'dishonesty and laziness.'

The factory system, then, was not technologically superior to the putting-out system, at least not until technological change was channelled exclusively into this mould. But was it in any event efficient? Was it not better than available alternatives not only for the capitalist, but for the factory worker as well, however severe the consequences (mere 'pecuniary diseconomies' in technical language) for those who persisted in cottage industry? After all, nobody was legally compelled to work in a factory. The worker, no less than the capitalist, 'revealed' by the very act of entering the factory a 'preference' for factory organization, or at least for the combination of factory organization and factory pay[79] – or so neoclassical logic goes.

How applicable is this logic in fact? First of all, it is a strange logic of choice that places its entire emphasis on the absence of legal compulsion. Judging from the sources from which factory labour was originally drawn, the workers had relatively little effective choice. According to Mantoux

> In the early days factory labour consisted of the most ill-assorted elements: country people driven from their villages by the growth of large estates (that is, by the enclosure movement), disbanded soldiers, paupers, the scum of every class and of every occupation.[80]

The question is not so much whether or not factory employment was better for workers than starving – let us grant that it was – but whether or not it was better than alternative forces of productive organization that would have allowed the worker a measure of control of product and process, even at the cost of a lower level of output and earnings.[81] But to grow and develop in nineteenth century Britain (or in twentieth century America) such alternatives would have had to have been profitable for the organizer of production. Since worker control of product and process ultimately leaves no place for the capitalist, it is hardly surprising that the development of capitalism, while extending the sway of the market in labour as well as goods, and extending the range of occupations, did not create a long list of employment opportunities in which workers displaced from the traditional occupations of their parents could control product and process.

Where alternatives to factory employment were available, there is evidence that workers flocked to them. Cottage weaving was one of the few, perhaps the only important, ready alternative to factory work for those lacking special skills. And despite the abysmally low level to which wages fell, a force of domestic cotton weavers numbering some 250,000 survived well into the nineteenth century. The maintenance of the weavers' numbers is, in the light of attrition caused by death and emigration, convincing evidence of persistent new entry into the field.[82] However, the bias of technological change towards improvements consistent with factory organization sooner or later took its toll of alternatives, weaving included.[83] The putting-out system, with its pitiful vestiges of worker control, virtually disappeared in Great Britain by mid-century. And weaving was about the last important holdout of cottage industry. Where this alternative was not available, the worker's freedom to refuse factory employment was the freedom to starve.

And even where the adult male had a real choice, so that the logic of 'revealed preference' is conceivably more than formally applicable,[84] his wife and children had no such prerogatives. Women and children, who by all accounts constituted the overwhelming majority of factory workers in the early days,[85] were there not because they chose to be but because their husbands and fathers told them to be. The application of revealed preference to their presence in the factory requires a rather elastic view of the concept of individual choice.

In the case of pauper children, no amount of stretching of the logic of revealed preference will do. Sold by parish authorities as 'factory apprentices' for terms of service up to ten or more years in order to save the local taxpayer the cost of food, clothing, and shelter, these poor unfortunates had no choice whatsoever, legal or otherwise. Apprenticeship itself was nothing new, nor was the binding over of pauper children to masters by parish authorities. But by the end of the eighteenth century, the institution of apprenticeship was no longer a means of limiting entry into the various crafts and trades and of ensuring the maintenance of quality standards. It had become, in accordance with the exigencies of capitalist enterprise, a system of indentured servitude.[86] As factories became prominent features of the industrial landscape, an enterprising capitalist might seize upon an advertisement like this one:

To Let, The Labour of 260 Children

With Rooms and Every Convenience for carrying on the Cotton Business. For particulars, enquire of Mr. Richard Clough, Common Street, Manchester.[87]

Mantoux goes so far as to claim that in the factory's early days, no parents would allow their own children inside, so that pauper apprentices were 'the only children employed in the factories.'[88] But despite the contemporary evidence Mantoux cites to support his claim, it may be a bit exaggerated. The Oldknow mill at Mellor appears to have relied primarily upon family groups (mothers as well as childen), and Unwin suggests that the provision of employment to fathers of these families — outside the mill in general — was a continuing concern of Samuel Oldknow. But pauper apprentices were nevertheless a significant part of the work force at Mellor, reaching a maximum of perhaps twenty-five per cent at the end of the eighteenth century.[89]

It is not directly relevant to the purposes of this paper to enter into a moral discussion of child labour generally or pauper apprenticeship in particular.[90] Given the factory, child labour was very likely a necessary evil, at least in the early days. As Ure wrote,

... it is found nearly impossible to convert persons past the age of puberty, whether drawn from rural or from handicraft occupations, into useful factory hands. After struggling for a while to conquer their listless or restive habits, they either renounce the employment spontaneously, or are dismissed by the overlookers on account of inattention.

This was not, as history has shown, to remain a permanent state of affairs: the factory did, after all, survive the abolition of child labour. Not surprisingly, recruiting the first generation of factory workers was the key problem. For this generation's progeny the factory was part of the natural order, perhaps the only natural order. Once grown to maturity, fortified by the discipline of church and school, the next generation could be recruited to the factory with probably no greater difficulty than the sons of colliers are recruited to the mines or the sons of career soldiers to the army.

The recruitment of the first generation of workers willing and able to submit to an externally determined discipline has been a continuing obstacle to the expansion of the factory system. Even mid-twentieth century America has had to face the problem, and here too the lack of alternatives has had an important role to play in aiding the market mechanism. Just after World War II, General Motors introduced machine-paced discipline to Framingham, Massachusetts, in the form of an automobile assembly plant. Over eighty-five per cent of a sample[91] of workers interviewed by a team of sociologists under the direction of Charles Walker and Robert Guest had previously worked on jobs where they themselves had determined their own work pace. When interviewed by the Walker–Guest team in 1949, half the sample cited the lack of alternatives – termination of previous jobs or lack of steady work – as the reason for joining GM. And about a quarter said that they would be willing to take a cut in pay, if they could only find another job.[92] Said one:

> I'd take almost any job to get away from there. A body can't stand it there. My health counts most. What's the use of money if you ruin your health?[93]

If the problems of discipline and supervision – not the lack of a suitable technology – were the obstacles to the agglomeration of workers, why did the factory system emerge only at the end of the eighteenth century? In fact, the factory system goes back much farther, at least to Roman times. The factory, according to Tenny Frank, was the dominant means of organizing the manufacture of at least two commodities, bricks and red-glazed pottery.[94] Interestingly for our purposes, Roman factories appear to have been manned almost exclusively by workers who had the same degree of choice as pauper children in eighteenth century England – that is to say, by slaves. By contrast, factories were exceptional in manufactures dominated by freedmen. Frank lists several – clay-lamps, metal wares, jewellery, and water pipes – in which slaves were relatively uncommon; all were organized along small-scale craft lines.[95] This dualism is not so surprising after all. Independent craftsmen producing directly for the market offer no scope for supervision, whereas slave labour is obviously difficult to mobilize without suprvision. The factory offered the ancient as well as the modern world an organization conducive to strict supervision.[96]

The surviving facts may be too scanty to prove anything, but they strongly suggest that whether work was organized along factory or craft lines was in Roman times determined, not by technological considerations, but by the relative power of the two producing classes. Freedmen and citizens had sufficient power to maintain a guild organization. Slaves had no power – and ended up in factories.

This reasoning bears on the development of capitalism in modern times. Guild organization of production and distribution eventually gave way to the putting-out system for two reasons: it was more profitable to the class that was able to interpose itself between the producer and the market, and, equally important, profits provided the nascent capitalist class with the political power to breakdown the institutional arrangements of guild organization – strict rules of apprenticeship, strict association of production with marketing, and the like – and replace them with institutional arrangements favourable to the putting-out system – the free market in labour as well as commodities, buttressed by strict rules of industrial discipline, with harsh penalties for embezzlement and other infractions. Until the political power of the small master and journeyman was broken, the putting-out system could not flourish, for the division of labour that formed the essence of the putting-out system denied both the orderly progression of apprentice to master and the union of producer and merchant in the same person.

At the same time, the putting-out system was necessarily transitional. Once a free market in labour was brought into existence, it was only a matter of time until the employer took to the factory as a means of curbing those aspects of freedom that depressed profits. Legal arrangements carefully set up to buttress the employer against the worker's 'laziness' and 'dishonesty' were, as we have seen, never enforceable to the capitalist's satisfaction.

The factory likely would have made its appearance much sooner than it in fact did if the small master and journeyman, fighting the battle of the guild against capitalism, had not been able for a time to use for their own ends the strategy of divide and conquer. Taking advantage of divisions between more powerful classes, the small master and journeyman were able to forge temporary alliances that for a time at least were successful in stalling the advent of the factory. For example, the alliance of the small cloth-making master with the large merchant not engaged in production maintained strict controls on apprenticeship well into the seventeenth century.[97]

A more striking, perhaps the most striking, example of successful alliance with more powerful interests had as outcome a Parliamentary prohibition against the loom shop. Thus runs the Weavers' Act of 1555, two hundred years before Arkwright:

> Forasmuch as the weavers of this realm have, as well at the present Parliament as at divers others times, complained that the rich and wealthy clothiers do in many ways oppress them, some by setting up and keeping in their houses divers looms, and keeping and maintaining them by journeymen and persons unskilful, to the decay of a great number of artificers who were brought up in the said art of weaving ... it is therefore, for remedy of the premises and for the averting of a great number of inconveniences which may grow if in time it be not foreseen, ordained and enacted by authority of this present Parliament, that no

person using the mystery of cloth-making, and dwelling out of a city, borough, market town, or incorporate town, shall keep, or return, or have in his or their houses or possession more than one woollen loom at a time . . . [98]

The main purpose of this Act may have been, as Unwin suggests, 'to keep control of the industry in the hands of the town employers (who were exempted from its coverage) by checking the growth of a class of country capitalists.'[99] It was precisely by riding the coattails of more powerful interests that the small master and journeyman were able to hold their own as long as they did.

Indeed, the important thing about the 1555 Act is not the precise alignment of the forces for and against, but its very existence at such an early date. Where there was so much smoke there must have been some fire, and some powerful motivation to the agglomeration of workers – long before steam or even water power could possibly have been the stimulus. Witch hunts apart, important legislative bodies are not in the habit of enacting laws against imaginary evils. To be the occasion of parliamentary repression, the loom shop must have been a real economic threat to the independent weavers even in the sixteenth century. By the same token, there must have been a class that stood to profit from the expansion of factory organization. The difference between the sixteenth and later centuries was in the relative power of this class and the classes that opposed the development of capitalist enterprise.

Industrial capitalism did not gain power suddenly: rather it was a fitful and gradual process, as a history like Unwin's makes clear. [100] But by the end of the eighteenth century the process was pretty well complete. The outright repeal of statutes limiting apprenticeship or otherwise regulating capitalists only reflected the new realities. By this time the process of innovation towards the form of work organization most congenial to the interests of the capitalist class was in full sway. The steam mill didn't give us the capitalist; the capitalist gave us the steam mill.

4 VARIATIONS ON A THEME

The resort of economically and politically powerful classes to innovation in order to change the distribution of income in their favour (rather than to increase its size) was not unique to the industrial revolution. Marc Bloch's 'Advent and Triumph of the Water Mill' tells a fascinating story of a similar phenomenon in feudal times. [101] The dominance of water-powered flour mills may reasonably be thought to be a consequence of their technological superiority over handmills. But Bloch's article suggests another explanation: water mills enabled the feudal lord to extract dues that were unenforceable under a handmilling technology.

What is the evidence for the assertion that the water mill was inspired by distributional rather than technological considerations? First grinding at the lord's mill was obligatory, and the milling tolls varied inversely with the status of the owner of the grain. Justice Fitzherbert's *Boke of*

Surveying (1538) noted the systematic variations:

> There be many divers grants made by the lord: some men to be ground
> to the twentieth part (a toll in kind of 1/20 of the quantity ground) and
> some to the twenty-fourth part; tentants-at-will to the sixteenth part;
> and bondsmen to the twelfth part. [102]

In extreme cases, the toll on grain grown on the lord's manor was as high
as one-third, [103] which suggests that the obligation to grind at the lord's mill
(the milling 'soke') was in the extreme merely a device for ensuring that the
peasant not evade what was actually a payment for the use of the lord's
land, by secretly harvesting and sequestering grain due the lord. The close
relationship in the minds of contemporaries between the milling soke and
land rent is indicated by an extensive controversy over the application of
the milling soke to bought grain. [104] Despite the obvious possibilities for
evasion of dues on home-grown grain that an exemption for purchased
grain would have provided, Justice Fitzherbert came down firmly for
limiting the soke:

> To the corn mills, to the most part of them, belongeth Socone (soke) —
> that is to say, the custom of the tenants is to grind their corn at the
> lord's mill; and that is, me-seemeth, all such corn as groweth upon the
> lord's ground, and that he (the tenant) spendeth in his house. But if he
> buy his corn in the market or other place, he is then at liberty to grind
> where he may be best served. [105]

Whether the obligation to grind grain at the lord's mill (coupled with
confiscatory tolls) was a more enforceable version of a land rent, or
whether it was an additional device for enriching the landlord at the
expense of the tenant may not be terribly important for present purposes.
Both hypotheses are consistent with the proposition that distributional
rather than technological considerations dominated the choice of milling
technique. In arguing for this proposition Bloch finds it signifcant that 'All
the (water) mills whose history we can more or less follow were in fact
seignorial in origin.' [106]

> ... where — as in Frisia — the community was exceptional in managing
> to avoid being stifled by seignorial authority, the peasants only took
> advantage of their liberty to remain obstinately faithful to their own
> individual mills. They were not prepared to come to a friendly
> agreement with one another and adapt technical progress to their own
> requirements. [107]

Presumably the lord, as he gained power, would have been content to
allow peasants to continue with their handmills if he could have extracted
milling dues independently of milling technique. Thus, at certain places
and times, the lords 'did not so much claim to suppress (handmills) as to
make the use of them subject to the payment of a due.' [108] But enforcement
must have posed the same problems it later did for the putting-out master.
It must have been extremely difficult to prevent the peasant from
'embezzling' the lord's 'rightful' portion of grain if the milling operation
took place within the peasant's own house. Bloch mentions the 'lawsuits

which grimly pursued their endless and fruitless course, leaving the tenants always the losers' [109] – but at great expense of time, effort, and money to the lord as well. Moreover,

> In the countryside, seignorial authority, harassing though it was, was very poorly served. It was therefore often incapable of acting with that continuity which alone would have made it possible to reduce the peasants, past masters in the art of passive resistance, to complete submission. [110]

Just as later the master manufacturer's 'thoughts turned to workshops where the men could be brought together to labour under the eyes of watchful overseers,' so must the feudal lord's thoughts have turned to a centralized water mill where grain would be ground under the watchful eyes of his bailiffs. Essential therefore to the triumph of the water mill was not only a monopoly of the sources of water power, but an absolute prohibition against the use of handmills – the establishment of the soke.

> A very great piece of luck enables us to see the monks of Jumierges, in an agreement dated 1207, breaking up any handmills that might still exist on the lands of Viville. The reason is no doubt that this little fief, carved out of a monastic estate for the benefit of some high-ranking *sergent* of the abbot, had in fact escaped for a long period the payment of seignorial dues. The scenes that took place in this corner of the Norman countryside under Philip Augustus must have had many precedents in the days of the last Carolingians or the first Capetians. But they escape the meshes of the historian's net. [111]

At about the same time the milling soke was being explicitly incorporated into English milling rights. ' "The men shall not be allowed to possess any handmills" – such was the clause inserted by the canons of Embsay in Yorkshire between 1120 and 1151, in a charter in which a noble lady made over to them a certain water mill.' [112]

The struggle between the lord and peasant was hardly an equal one, and the history of grain-milling reflects this asymmetry: the handmill gradually disappeared from the scene. But when the peasant temporarily gained the upper hand, one of the first casualties was the lord's monopoly on grain-milling – and maybe the lord and the water mill for good measure. After recounting a half century of intermittent struggle between the people of St. Albans and the abbot who was their lord, Bloch nears the end of what he calls, without exaggeration a 'veritable milling epic:' [113]

> ... when in 1381 the great insurrection of the common people broke out in England and Wat Tyler and John Ball emerged as leaders, the people of St. Albans were infected by the same fever and attacked the abbey ... The deed of liberation which they extorted from the monks recognized their freedom to maintain 'hand-mills' in every home. The insurrection however proved to be like a blaze of straw that soon burns itself out. When it had collapsed all over England, the charter of St. Albans and all the other extorted privileges were annulled by royal statute. But was this the end of a struggle that had lasted over a century? Far from it.

The (monastic) chronicler, as he draws to the close of his story, has to admit that for malting at any rate the detestable hand-mills have come into action again and have been again forbidden. [114]

What lessons do we draw from Bloch's account of the conflict between alternative milling techniques? Most important, it was not technological superiority, but the nature of feudal power and the requisites of enforcing that power that determined the replacement of handmills by water mills. It was not the handmill that gave us feudalism, but the feudal lord that gave us the water mill.

A model of feudalism that assumes a given distribution of power between master and man would naturally suggest that milling techniques should have been chosen on the basis of technological efficiency. But such a model implicitly ignores the dynamic conflict between classes and the need of the controlling class to choose technologies that facilitate the exercise of its power. A static analysis of the choice between handmill and water mill, or of feudalism generally, is as far off the mark as an analysis of the choice between domestic and factory production, or of capitalism generally, based on the neoclassical model of perfect competition. The key roles played by supervision and discipline – or, more generally, the exercise of power – in the determination of technology require models that are grounded in the challenge-response mechanism of class conflict, models at once dynamic and dialectic.

The collectivization of Soviet agriculture makes clear that efficiency is not necessarily the determinant of technology under socialism any more than under feudalism or capitalism. Stalin's arguments, to be sure, stressed the technological superiority of collective farming:

> The way out (of the difficulties of the twenties) is to turn the small scattered peasant farms into large united farms based on the common cultivation of the soil, to introduce collective cultivation of the soil on the basis of new and higher technique. The way out is to unite the small and dwarf peasant farms gradually and surely, not by pressure but by example and persuasion, into large farms based on common co-operative cultivation of the soil, with the use of agricultural machines and tractors and scientific methods of intensive agriculture. [115]

A different rationale emerges from the account of even the most sympathetic of outside observers – for example, Maurice Dobb. [116] The difficulty from which a way out was most urgently needed was not low agricultural output, but the mobilization of enough surplus grain to permit the Government both to maintain the level of real wage rates in industry and at the same time to launch an ambitious programme of capital accumulation, which would require both exports to pay for imported machinery and expansion of employment in capital-goods producing industries. Under the New Economic Policy of the twenties, the Soviet Government's ability to impose on the peasants its own conception of the size of the agricultural surplus was limited to its control over the terms on which grain would be exchanged for industrial products.

Inadvertently, the Revolution had exacerbated the problem of mobilizing the agricultural surplus. In sharp contrast with the methods followed in reorganizing large-scale industry, the Revolution broke up large landholdings and maintained the principle of private property in agriculture.[117] Until the collectivization drive at the end of the 1920s, grain production was overwhelmingly in the hands of *kulaks, sredniaks,* and *bedniaks* – rich, middle, and poor peasants. So when the dislocations of civil war were surmounted and production restored to pre-war levels, peasant producers controlled the allocation of grain between on-farm consumption and market sales. And just as the British workman of the eighteenth century wanted to take a significant portion of any increase in real income in the form of leisure, so the Russian peasant of the twentieth chose to eat better as he became the master of the grain formerly due the landlord. However desirable this was for the peasant, the results were disastrous for the rest of the economy. Grain production 'was (in 1925-26) nearly nine-tenths of 1913; but the marketed surplus was less than one-half of the pre-war amount.'[118]

Of course, the Soviet Government could and did levy taxes upon the peasant, but there remained the age-old problem of enforcement. Moreover the civil war had made the peasant-worker alliance politically essential, which, as Lenin told the Tenth Party Congress in 1921, posed certain constraints on agricultural policy:

> The interests of these classes do not coincide: the small farmer does not desire what the worker is striving for. Nevertheless, only by coming to an agreement with the peasants can we save the socialist revolution. We must either satisfy the middle peasant economically and restore the free market, or else we shall be unable to maintain the power of the working class.[119]

As long as the market remained the principal means of mobilizing an agricultural surplus out of the countryside, the Government could do little more than manipulate the terms of trade. The debate that ensued between the proponents of high prices for agricultural goods (to coax out the surplus) and those who favoured low prices (to minimize the costs in terms of industrial goods of mobilizing the surplus) was, alas, largely beside the point. Against the argument for high prices was first of all the possibility that *no* price policy would have coaxed out enough grain both to maintain the urban real wage and to launch an ambitious programme of capital accumulation. The supply curve for grain under small-holder agriculture could, like the supply curve of labour under the putting-out system, have both forward-sloping and backward-bending ranges; there may simply have been no terms of trade at which the peasant would have freely parted with enough grain to allow the Government both to pay for imports and to feed a work force swelled by the addition of workers building machines and factories, dams and highways – without sharply reducing the real wages of all workers. But even if sufficiently high relative prices would have coaxed out adequate supplies of grain, the cost in terms of industrial consumer goods, domestic or imported, would probably have made capital accumulation all but impossible – save by a reduction in the real wage. Low agricultural prices were no solution, however. For, beyond a certain point at least, lower prices would simply encourage peasants to eat more and sell less.

Faced with this dilemma, the Soviet authorities could have sacrificed either capital accumulation or the real wage. But in the twenties, at least, the Revolution was not sufficiently secure to permit a conscious policy of reducing real wages, whatever the convictions of the leaders. [120] As a result, capital accumulation suffered. Thus it was that

> the apparent gap in urban consumption which (the) shortage of marketed grain supplies occasioned was met by reducing the export of grain, which even in the peak year of the post-war period did not exceed a third of its pre-war quantity. [121]

And thus it was that 'in the middle and late '20s, unemployment (skilled and unskilled) was large and was tending to increase.' [122]

The decision, towards the end of the decade, to double or triple the rate of capital accumulation over a period of five years – the goal of the 'minimal' and 'optimal' variants of the First Five Year Plan [123] – required either a policy aimed at reducing the industrial wage rate (though not the wage *bill*) or a policy designed to reduce total consumption in the countryside. [124] To reduce industrial wages would have undermined the support of the most revolutionary class – the proletariat. Besides such a policy would surely have made it more difficult to recruit new entrants to the industrial labour force once the initial backlog of unemployment had been overcome. [125] This left no choice but to break the peasants' control over the disposition of agricultural production. It is hard not to agree with Dobb's conclusion: 'Collective farming was (an) expedient for solving the difficulty of supplying aggricultural produce to an expanding (industrial) population.' [126] With collectivization, the Government at last determined not only the terms of trade, but the *quantities* of agricultural and industrial products flowing between the countryside and the city.

The economic problem posed by peasant ownership of land was, in short, not one of insufficient production, and not necessarily one of a surplus insufficient for feeding the nonagricultural population. It was rather that land ownership gave the peasants too strong a voice in determining the rate of capital accumulation. 'New and higher technique' was no more the basis of collective farming than it was, centuries earlier, of the water mill. Had technological superiority rather than control of the surplus really been the basis for collectivization, the Soviet Government would have had no more reason to renege on Stalin's promise to rely on 'example and persuasion' to bring the peasants aboard [127] than the feudal lord had to outlaw the handmill in order to ensure the success of the water mill.

A due regard for the role of economic power and the institutional constraints on the use of power are as important to understanding socialist economic development as to understanding the development of earlier economic systems. Under socialism (at least in its Soviet strain), no less than under feudalism and capitalism, the primary determinant of basic choices with respect to the organization of production has not been technology – exogenous and inexorable – but the exercise of power–endogenous and resistible.

NOTES

1 F. Engels, 'On Authority,' first published in *Almenacco Republicano*, 1894; English translation in Marx and Engels, *Basic Writings in Politics and Philosophy*, L. Feuer (ed.), Doubleday and Co., Garden City, New York, 1959, p, 483. Emphasis added.

2 The attribution of the division of labour to efficiency antedates Adam Smith by at least two millenia. Plato, indeed, argued for the political institutions of the Republic on the basis of an analogy with the virtue of specialization in the economic sphere. Smith's specific arguments were anticipated by Henry Martyn three quarters of a century before the publication of the *Wealth of Nations*. See *Considerations Upon the East-India Trade* (London, 1701).

3 For a concise and elegant discussion of the relationship between technological efficiency and least-cost methods of production, see Tjalling Koopmans, *Three Essays on the State of Economic Science*, McGraw-Hill, New York, 1957, essay 1, especially pp. 66-126.

4 At least in the constant-returns-to-scale version of the competitive economy. Any other version implies the existence of a factor of production (like 'entrepreneurial effort') that is not traded on the market, and with respect to which the model is therefore non-competitive.

5 'We may, therefore, assume either that the landowner will hire labourers for a wage . . . or that the labourers will hire the land for rent.' Knut Wicksell, *Lectures on Political Economy* (translated by E. Classen), Routledge & Kegan Paul, London, 1934, Volume I, p. 109.

'Remember that in a perfectly competitive market it really doesn't matter who hires whom; so have labour hire "capital" ' . . . Paul Samuelson, 'Wage and Interest: A Modern Dissection of Marxian Economic Models,' *American Economic Review*, December, 1957.

6 A. Smith, *The Wealth of Nations* (Cannan edition) Random House, New York, 1937, p. 7.

7 Smith, *op. cit.*, pp. 734-35.

8 Smith, *op. cit.*, pp. 4–5.

9 T. S. Ashton, 'The Records of a Pin Manufactory – 1814-21', *Economica*, November, 1925, pp. 281–292.

10 For another example, cotton handloom weaving, though described by J. L. and Barbara Hammond in a volume entitled *The Skilled Labourer* (Longmans Green, London, 1919), was apparently a skill quickly learned (p. 70). A British manufactuer testified before a parliamentary committee that 'a lad of fourteen may acquire a sufficient knowledge of it in six weeks.' Duncan Bythell's *The Handloom Weavers*, (Cambridge University Press, Cambridge, England, 1969), which is my immediate source for the manufacturer's testimony, is quite explicit: 'Cotton handloom weaving, from its earliest days, was an unskilled, casual occupation which provided a domestic by-trade for thousands of women and children . . .' (p. 270)

The apparent ease with which, according to the Hammonds, women replaced male woollen weavers gone off to fight Napoleon suggests that woollen weaving too was not such a difficult skill to acquire (*op. cit.*, pp. 60–162). Indeed the competition of women in some branches of the woollen trade was such that in at least one place the men felt obliged to bind themselves collectively 'not to allow any women to learn the trade' (*ibid.*, p. 162), an action that would hardly have been necessary if the requisite strength or skill had been beyond the power of women to acquire. The role of war-induced labour shortages in breaking down artificial sex barriers, and the subsequent difficulties in re-establishing these barriers is reminiscent of American experience in World War II.

11 This is not to say that the putter-outer, or 'master manufacturer' never contributed anything of technological importance to the production process. But where the capitalist did contribute a useful technological innovation, he could effectively appropriate to himself the gains (of what in economic terms is a 'public good') by preventing others, particularly his workers, from learning and imitating his trade secrets. What better way to achieve secrecy than to insist that each worker know only a part of the whole? The patent system was notoriously ineffective, and the benefactions of a grateful nation all too haphazard to rely upon, especially for the marginal improvements that are the most all but a handful of innovators could possibly achieve.

12 George Unwin, *Industrial Organization in the Sixteenth and Seventeenth Centuries,* first published by the Clarendon Press, Oxford, England, 1904 and republished by Cass, London, 1957, p. 96.

13 *Ibid.*, p. 96.

14 Quoted in Rhodes Boyson, *The Ashworth Cotton Enterprise,* Oxford University Press, Oxford, England, 1970, p. 52.

15 *The Spectator,* London, May 26, 1866, p. 569.

16 *Ibid,* p. 569.

17 E. L. Trist and K. W. Bamforth, 'Some Social and Psychological Consequences of the Longwall Method of Coal-Getting,' *Human Relations,* Vol. IV, NO. 1, 1951, p. 6.

18 *Ibid.*, p. 6.

19 Trist and Bamforth, *op. cit.*, p. 6.

20 *Ibid.*, p. 9.

21 *Ibid.*, p. 23-24.

22 *Ibid.*, p. 11.

23 As we shall see, supervision was a problem endemic to the specialization of men to tasks under the putting-out system. The factory system was a solution to this problem, one, it will be argued, that reflected capitalists' interests rather than a supposed technological superiority.

24 Harvard Business School Case Study, 'British Coal Industries (C)', prepared by Gene W. Dalton under the direction of Paul R. Lawrence and based on E. L. Trist and H. Murray, 'Work Organization at the Coal Face,' No. 506, Tavistock Institute,London, England.

25 Harvard Business School Case Study, 'British Coal Industries (B),' prepared by Gene W. Dalton under the direction of Paul R. Lawrence, and based on E. L. Trist and H. Murray, 'Work Organization at the Coal Face,' Doc. No. 506, Tavistock Institute, London, England.

26 'British Coal Industries (C),' *op. cit.*

27 *Ibid.*

28 Nationalization did not change the concept of property; it merely transformed title of the mines to the state.

29 Paul Jacobs' is a voice crying out in the wilderness:

If unions are going to survive and grow in the coming period, they have to break with their old patterns. First of all, they have to break with their pattern of not thinking about *work,* the nature of work, their relationship to work, and what they can do about work. What do we do about work now? Well, we say we're going to fix the wages, we're going to try to establish what we think ought to be minimal working conditions, we're going to slow down the line, we're going to argue about the speed of the line. But do we ever say: Hey, the whole concept of production of an automobile on a line stinks; the whole thing is wrong; what we ought to be doing is figuring out new ways of looking at the problem of work? No, these are questions from which every union withdraws.

I heard the vice-president of Kaiser explain their new agreement with the Steelworkers Union, and he was asked what the union would have to say about the nature of work processes in the plant. 'Nothing', he said. 'My goodness, the Steelworkers Union wouldn't ever dream of venturing into this area . . .'
(Center for the Study of Democratic Institutions, *Labor Looks at Labor*, Fund for the Republic, Santa Barbara, California, 1963, pp. 14–15).

30 See T. S. Ashton, *An Eighteenth Century Industrialist*, Manchester University Press, Manchester, 1939, chapters 2–3, for an account of the importance of wage advances in the metal trades. Advances to weavers were common in the putting-out enterprise run by Samuel Oldknow. However, the amounts were relatively small, of the order of a week's wages. (G. Unwin and others, *Samuel Oldknow and the Arkwrights*, Manchester University Press, Manchester, 1924, p. 49). If, in fact, wage advances were an important instrument of capitalist control only in the metal trades, it would be interesting to know why. George Unwin gives one instance of a debt-employment nexus in the cloth industry as early as the reign of Henry VIII. (*Industrial Organization in the Sixteenth and Seventeenth Centuries*, p. 52).

31 It is of equally little moment that the worker's dependence was 'freely' entered into, any more than the pusher's enticement of the unwary is any less destructive because one has the right to refuse the come-on.

32 Though presumably not impossible. Embezzlement was a continuing problem under the putting-out system, and it will be argued presently that the chief advantage of the factory system in its early days was the ability to provide the supervision necessary to cure this and other ills.

33 Fred Shannon, *The Farmer's Last Frontier*, Holt, Rinehart and Winston, New York, 1945, p. 88.

34 *Ibid.*, p. 92.

35 *Ibid.*

36 T. S. Ashton, *The Industrial Revolution 1760–1830*, Oxford University Press, London, 1948, p. 33 (emphasis added).

37 *Ibid.*, p. 72.

38 P. Mantoux, *The Industrial Revolution in the Eighteenth Century*, Harper and Row, New York, 1962, p. 39. (First English edition published in 1928).

39 D. S. Landes, *The Unbound Prometheus*, Cambridge University Press, Cambridge, England, 1969, p. 81.

40 *The Industrial Revolution, op. cit.*, p. 109. See also Ashton, *An Eighteenth Century Industrialist*, p. 26.

41 *The Industrial Revolution in the Eighteenth Century, op. cit.*, p. 246.

42 Landes, *op. cit.*, p. 60.

43 D. S. Landes (editor), *The Rise of Capitalism*, Macmillan, New York, 1966, p. 14.

44 Mantoux, *op. cit.*, p. 246.

45 *Ibid.*, p. 14. C.F. Herbert Heaton, *The Yorkshire Woollen and Worsted Industries*, Oxford University Press, Oxford, 1920: 'the major part of the economic advantage of the factory springs from the use of machinery capable of performing work quickly, and the use of power which can make the machinery go at high speed.' p. 352.

46 Ronald Coase appears to be unique in recognizing that the very existence of capitalist

enterprise is incompatible with the reliance of perfect competition on the market mechanism for co-ordinating economic activity. Coase, however, sees the capitalist firm as the means not for subordinating workers but for saving the costs of the market transactions:

> . . . a firm will tend to expand until the costs of organizing an extra transaction within the firm become equal to the costs on the open market or the costs of organizing in another firm.

See 'The Nature of the Firm,' *Economica* vol. IV, 1937, pp. 386–405, reprinted in Stigler and Boulding (eds.), *Readings in Price Theory,* Irwin, Chicago, Illinois, 1952, pp. 331–351. The quotation is from p. 341 of Boulding and Stigler.

47 A. Ure, *The Philosophy of Manufacturers,* Charles Knight, London, 1835, pp. 15–16. Military analogies abound in contemporary observations of the early factory. Boswell described Mathew Boulton, Watt's partner in the manufacture of steam engines, as 'an iron captain in the midst of his troops' after a visit to the works in 1776. (Quoted in Mantoux, *op. cit.,* p. 376).

48 Mantoux, *op cit.,* p. 223. Wadsworth and Mann differ. See Alfred P. Wadsworth and Julia DeLacy Mann, *The Cotton Trade and Industrial Lancashire,* Manchester University Press, Manchester England, 1931, pp. 482–3.

49 Quoted in Julia DeLacy Mann, 'The Transition to Machine-Spinning' in Wadsworth and Mann, *op. cit.,* p. 433.

50 *Ibid.,* p. 436.

51 *Ibid.,* p. 437.

52 'Up to the close of the period (1820), and probably until after 1830, when Crompton's mule had been made "self-acting," it made no headway in the woollen industry.' W. B. Crump, *The Leeds Woollen Industry 1780–1820,* Thoresby Society, Leeds England, 1931, p. 25.

53 J. L. Hammond and Barbara Hammond, *op. cit.,* p. 146.

54 *Ibid.,* p. 148.

55 Mantoux, *op cit.,* p. 264.

56 Crump, *op. cit.,* esp. pp. 24–5, 34.

57 *Ibid.,* p. 24.

58 Albert P. Usher, *An Introduction to the Industrial History of England,* Houghton Mifflin, Boston, 1920, reports some statistics for 1840, but does not give his source: 'In the Coventry ribbon district, there were 545 handlooms in factories, 1264 handlooms employed by capitalists outside the factories, and 121 looms in the hands of independent masters. At Norwich 656 handlooms were in factories out of a total of 3398 for the district as a whole.' (p. 353).

59 D. Bythell, *op. cit.,* p. 33.

60 *Ibid.* pp. 33–34.

61 Wadsworth and Mann, *op. cit.,* p. 393.

62 *An Eighteenth Century Industrialist.*

63 *Ibid.,* p. 26.

64 Mantoux, *op. cit.,* pp. 195–196. In the case of Lombe and his brother, genius, apart from organizing talent, consisted in pirating an Italian invention.

65 On the power of bosses over workers see, among others, Landes, *op. cit.,* p. 56; E. P. Thompson, *The Making of the English Working Class,* Random House, New York, 1963, chapter 9, especially the quotations on pp. 280, 297. Adam Smith was quite explicit: 'Masters are always and everywhere in a sort of tacit, but constant and uniform combination, not to raise the wages of labour above their actual rate. To violate this combination is everywhere a most unpopular action, and a sort of reproach to a master among his neighbours and equals. We seldom, indeed hear of this combination, because it is

the usual, and one may say, the natural state of things which nobody hears of.' *The Wealth of Nations, op. cit.,* Book 1, Chapter 8, pp. 66–7.

66 J. Smith, *Memoirs of Wool* (1747); quoted in E. P. Thompson, *op. cit.,* p. 277.

67 The characterization is Landes's, *Unbound Prometheus,* p. 59.

68 Contrary to Landes's implication, 'a fairly rigid conception of what (is) felt to be a decent standard of living' (*ibid.,* p. 59) is not required for a backward bending supply curve of a good or service that (like time) affords utility to the seller.

69 It may be slightly ironic that an important necessary condition for the indifference-curve model to be applicable to one of the most fundamental problems of economic choice is inconsistent with capitalism. For the indifference-curve model to be applicable to goods-leisure choices, control of the hours of work must rest with the worker. But this is inconsistent with capitalist control of the work process, and hence with capitalism itself.

70 A. Young, *Northern Tour;* quoted in Wadsworth and Mann, *op. cit.,* p. 389.

71 Heaton, *op. cit.,* p. 422. These laws had historic precedents. Unwin reports a municipal order dating from 1570 in Bury St. Edmunds requiring spinsters to work up six pounds of wool per week. Employers were to give notice to the constable in the event any one failed to obey the order (*op. cit.,* p. 94).

72 Heaton, *ibid.,* p. 418.

73 See Heaton, *ibid.,* pp. 418–437 for an account of the woollen industry, Wadsworth and Mann, *op. cit.,* pp. 395–400 for the cotton industry.

74 Heaton, *op. cit.,* p. 422.

75 Heaton, *ibid.,* p. 428.

76 Quoted in Bythell, *op. cit.,* p. 72.

77 In technical terms, the shift from workers' control of goods-leisure choices to capitalists' control meant a shift *along* a given production function not a shift in the function itself.

78 Any comment on the alleged immorality of these defences is probably superfluous. This was after all an era in which unions were illegal 'combinations,' proscribed under common law of conspiracy (and later, by statute).

79 Factory wages for handloom weaving were higher than wages earned for the same work performed in the worker's cottage – presumably the reward both for longer hours and for submitting to the factory supervision and discipline. See Bythell, *op. cit.,* p. 134.

80 Mantoux, *op. cit,* p. 375.

81 'Better' is used here in a broader sense than it is conventionally used by economists when comparing different bundles of commodities even when they bother to count leisure as one of the goods. Integrity – personal and cultural – can hardly be represented on an indifference curve. For a discussion of the effects of economic change on cultural integrity, see Karl Polanyi, 'Class Interest and Social Change' originally published in *The Great Transformation,* Rinehard, New York, 1944; reprinted in *Primitive, Archaic and Modern Economies,* edited by George Dalton, Doubleday, Garden City, New York, 1968, pp. 38–58.

82 On the size of the labour force in domestic cotton weaving, see Landes, *op. cit.,* pp. 86–7; Bythell, op. cit., pp. 54-57. On wages, see Bythell, *ibid.,* chapter 6 and appendices; Sydney J. Chapman, *Lancashire Cotton Industry,* Manchester University Press, Manchester, England, 1904, pp. 43–4.

83 The amazing thing is that the cottage weavers held out as long as they did, testimony as Landes says, 'to the obstinacy and tenacity of men who were unwilling to trade their independence for the better-paid discipline of the factory.' (*Unbound Prometheus,* p. 86).

The reluctance of cottage weavers to submit to factory discipline was widely commented upon by contemporaries. As late as 1836, a noted critic of the factory, John Fielden, wrote 'they will neither go into (the factories) nor suffer their children to go.' (Quoted in Bythell, *op. cit.*, p. 252). Another critic testified to a Select Committee of Parliament that a cottage weaver would not seek factory employment because 'he would be subject to a discipline that a handloom weaver can never submit to.' (Select Committee on Handloom Weavers' Petitions, 1834; quoted in E. P. Thompson, *op. cit.*, p. 307.)

Whether the cottage weavers' inadaptability to the factory was a matter of taste or of the lack of psychological attitudes essential to factory discipline is a question of present as well as historical significance. (Ure, for what his opinion is worth, clearly sides with the view that the cottage *could* not adapt as opposed to the view that he *would* not.) For the argument that the role of schools is precisely to inculcate attitudes conducive to labour discipline see Herbert Gintis, 'Education, Technology, and the Characteristics, of Worker Productivity,' *American Economic Review*, May, 1971.

84 For men, factory employment could be quite attractive. Agglomeration of workers did not by this one fell swoop solve all problems of discipline. In spinning mills, for example, adult males formed a corps of non-commissioned officers; women and children were the soldiers of the line. And factory employment was relatively attractive for these 'labour aristocrats.' To quote Ure,

> The political economist may naturally ask how . . . the wages of the fine spinners can be maintained at their present high pitch. To this question one of the best informed manufacturers made me this reply: 'We find a moderate saving in the wages to be of little consequence in comparison of contentment, and we therefore keep them as high as we can possibly afford, in order to be entitled to the best quality of work. A spinner reckons the charge of a pair of mules in our factory a fortune for life, he will therefore do his utmost to retain his situation, and to uphold the high character of our yarn.'
>
> Ure, *op. cit.*, p. 366.

85 For example, in the Oldknow spinning mill at Mellor, only ten per cent of the workers were male heads of families, even excluding child apprentices. G. Unwin and others, *Samuel Oldknow and the Arkwrights*, Manchester University Press, Manchester, England, 1924, p. 167.

86 See Ashton, *An Eighteenth Century Industrialist*, p. 28 who cites as his authority O. J. Dunlop, *English Apprenticeship and Child Labour*, p. 196. See also Bythell, *op. cit.*, p. 52; Wadsworth and Mann, *op cit.*, pp. 407–8.

87 *Wheelers Manchester Chronicle*, August 7, 1784. Quoted in Wadsworth and Mann, *op. cit.*, p. 408. If inclined to business on a more modest scale, one might be tempted by a package offer of a factory of sixteen looms and the labour of twelve apprentices. *Manchester Mercury*, December 1, 1789. Quoted in Bythell, *op. cit.*, p. 52.

88 Mantoux, *op. cit.*, p. 411.

89 G. Unwin and others, *Samuel Oldknow and the Arkwrights*, pp. 166–175.

90 The evils speak for themselves, and it will suffice perhaps to note that a man like Unwin reveals more than anything else the poverty of his own imagination when, in bending over backwards to be fair and objective, he defends the system (*ibid.*, pp. 170–5) on the grounds that it was superior to the alternative of the workhouse.

91 The sample was just over one-fifth of all the production workers.

92 Charles R. Walker and Robert H. Gust, *The Man on the Assembly Line*, Harvard University Press, Cambridge, Mass., 1952, chapter 6. A follow-up survey of worker attitudes would be fascinating: To what extent did those who initially resisted and resented the dehumanizing aspects of assembly-line work come to accept them — in return for relatively high pay and job security? What was the process by which workers' values and tastes changed in response to their employment at GM? To what extent did they eventually seek more congenial work?

93 *Ibid.,* p. 88. Sometimes, it would appear, the problem of recruiting a suitable labour force is resolved in ways that inhibit rather than foster the work attitudes necessary for expansion of industrial capitalism. The abundance of unemployed and underemployed workers in India, for example, appears to have permitted foreign and Indian enterpreneurs to graft an alien factory system into indigenous society without developing the discipline characteristic of factory labour. Indian workers are much freer than their Western counterparts to come and go as they please, for a contingent of substitute workers stands ready to fill in as needed. See A. K. Rice, *Productivity and Organization: The Amhedabad Experiment,* Tavistock, London, 1958, pp. 79, 118 for incidental support of this hypothesis.

94 Tenney Frank, *An Economic History of Rome,* Second Revised Edition, Johns Hopkins University Press, Baltimore, 1927, chapter 14.

95 *Ibid.,* chapter 14.

96 Freedmen, it should be noted, did apparently work for wages, though not in factories. The existence of a proletariat seems beyond dispute. *Ibid.,* pp. 269–270 and chapter 17.

97 Unwin, *Industrial Organization in the Sixteenth and Seventeenth Centuries,* p. 199.

98 3 & 4 Philip and Mary, c.II. Quoted in Mantoux, *op. cit.,* pp. 34–5.

99 Unwin, *Industrial Orgnization in the Sixteenth and Seventeenth Centuries,* p. 93.

100 *Ibid.*

101 Reprinted in Marc Bloch, *Land and Work in Medieval Europe,* (translated by J. E. Anderson), Harper & Row, New York, 1969, pp. 136–168.

102 Quoted in Richard Bennett and John Elton, *History of Corn Milling,* vol. III, Simpkin, Marshall and Company, London, 1900, p. 155.

103 *Ibid.,* pp. 221, 253.

104 *Ibid.,* chapter 9.

105 Quoted in Bennett and Elton, *op. cit.,* p. 242. By the time of Henry VIII, feudal institutions had begun to decay and it is hard to decide between the hypothesis that the learned justice's remarks reflects this decay and the hypothesis that the milling soke was bound up with land rent.

106 Bloch, *op. cit.,* p. 151.

107 *Ibid.,* p. 151.

108 Bloch, *op. cit.,* p. 156.

109 Bloch, *op. cit.,* p. 157.

110 *Ibid.,* p. 155.

111 *Ibid.,* p. 154.

112 Bloch, *op cit.,* p. 157. Bennett and Elton denote a whole chapter to the institution of soke. *Op; cit.,* chapter 8.

113 Bloch, *op. cit.,* p. 157.

114 *Ibid.,* p. 158.

115 Report to the Fifteenth Congress of the Communist Party of the Soviet Union, December 1927. Quoted in Maurice Dobb, *Soviet Economic Development Since 1917,* Fifth Edition, Routledge and Kegan Paul, London, 1960, p. 222.

116 *Ibid.,* especially chapter 9.

117 According to official Soviet figures, less than two percent of total grain production was accounted for by state and collective farms in 1926–27, *ibid.,* p. 217.

118 *Ibid.,* p. 214.

119 Quoted in Dobb, *ibid.,* p. 130.

120 Abram Bergson quotes a study based on Soviet statistics to the effect that real wages rose by eleven per cent between 1913 and 1928. *The Structure of Soviet Wages,* Harvard University Press, Cambridge, 1944, p. 203.

121 Dobb, *op. cit.,* p. 214.

122 *Ibid.*, p. 189.

123 *Ibid.*, p. 236.

124 It was not necessary to reduce the *average* standard of living, as the Plan's provision for increased total consumption makes clear. That part of the labour force that was unemployed or underemployed in the twenties would receive employment and wages as a result of the expansion envisioned in the Plan, and the improvement in their standard of living could more than make up for the deterioration of the standard of living imposed on everybody else, both in terms of distributive justice and statistical averages.

125 Whatever reductions in real wages accompanied the First Five Year Plan were probably, as Dobb says, the unforseen result of the resistance of peasants to collectivization and the consequent reduction in agricultural output. *Ibid.*, p. 237.

126 Dobb, *op cit.*, p. 225.

127 Compare Dobb, *Ibid.*, pp. 228–229.

ANDRÉ GORZ

The Tyranny of the Factory: Today and Tomorrow*

The tyranny of the factory is as old as industrial capitalism itself. The aim of production techniques and the work organization they dictate has always been a double one: Labour must be made as productive as possible for the capitalist, and thus maximum output must be forced from the worker through the organization and the objective requirements of the means of production. The production process must be organized so that the worker experiences the coercion to maximum output as an unalterable requirement of the machine or an imperative inherent in matter itself. Inexorable and incontestable, this imperative seems to be a result of the apparently neutral laws of a complex machine, beyond volition and dispute. The worker must submit to the quantity and the nature of his daily work as the only possible way to serve a machine. And he must see the machine as the only possible one: the only possible solution to the technical problems of production.

One may argue that all machinery is invented by non-workers serving the interests of capital, who thus predetermine the nature and quantity of work. One may add that the output imposed by the plant's inherent constraints *could have been* or *could be* attained and surpassed without constraint *if* workers could participate in conceiving and organizing production and in defining its aims and determining how they are implemented. Today these points are becoming clear, but they miss the essential issue: they could not even be stated this way until capitalist industry encountered them as *external limits* of its aims and external negations of its logic, that is, as so strong a resistance by the workers that production goals could no longer be reached by the usual means – the compulsion to work.

In fact the fundamental reason for this compulsion is not the greater efficiency of work which is imposed (forced labour) rather than voluntary. The root of forced labour and its necessity from capital's viewpoint, lies instead in the *social division* of labour. Capital's aims are foreign to the worker and *must* remain so: workers must be led to work to the limits of

* This article originally appeared in *Les Temps Modernes*, (September-October 1972). Translated by Bart Grahl.

their strength for a result in which they have, and can have, no share: the accumulation of capital. To say that they work better and more efficiently and give their all to work without compulsion, when their products and the unfolding of the work process seem to be their own affair – this only amounts to saying that the optimization of the work process is incompatible with capitalism. Manufacturers already knew this.

In fact, if workers had a say in the goals and arrangement of the work process, the accumulation of capital would cease to be the dominant goal of production. It would be subordinated to or balanced by other aims such as the pleasure, interest, and usefulness of work, the use-value of the products, the increase of free time and so on. In other words, the accumulation of capital can be maximized only if it is imposed on workers as an alien demand to which all others must be subordinated. For capitalism to develop and perpetuate itself, the demand of capital – to increase – must be embodied in the person of the capitalist as a *separate* demand. As a functionary of capital, he must retain absolute despotic power over the work-place. The oppressive organization of work is designed to affirm this power: like the oppressive industrial architecture, the ugliness, the filth, the noise, the stench, and the discomfort of the workshops, it reveals the undivided domination of capital.

On the level of production, the history of industrial capitalism's birth can be read as the history of capital's constitution as a separate power, and thus of the proprietors as *exclusive* owners of the means of production. These could function *as capital*, purely according to its demands exclusive of all others, only if the workers had first been dispossessed and *separated* from their machines. This separation occurred even before the transcendence of artisan technology: the weaving machines in the earliest manufacturing establishments were indistinguishable from artisan looms. Their concentration in capitalist manufacture – not technically motivated – allowed the owners to take possession of and control over all that was produced by all available labour, and to enforce work on these machines at a pace and for a number of hours that no independent weaver would have imposed on himself.

Capitalist technology and the capitalist division of labour were thus developed not because of their productive efficiency *in itself* but because of their efficiency in the context of alienated and forced labour: work subjugated to an alien goal. Capitalist techniques were not meant to maximize the production and productivity *in general* of all workers *whatsoever*. Instead they were to maximize the productivity *for capital* of workers who had no reason to give of themselves since an enemy will had dictated the aims of their production. To make them bow to this will it was not enough that they should lose the ownership of the means of production. In so far as possible, they also had to lose control over their functioning. They had to lose what their professional and practical knowledge and skills had given them so far: the power to run the machines without the assistance of a hierarchial corps of engineers, technicians, maintenance experts, foremen and so on. *Technically,* the factory could dispense with such functionaries[1] but their *political* function is to perpetuate the workers' dependence, subordination and separation from the means and process of production. By making control a separate function, the factory hierarchy is instrumental in denying the workers any possible control over the conditions and methods of machine production. Only in this way can the means and process of production be set up as an alien, autonomous power that exacts the workers' submission.

As a whole, the history of capitalist technology can be read as the history of the dequalification of the direct producers. The dequalification process is certainly not linear: at the beginning of each technical revolution it seems partially inverted. But the general tendency immediately reasserts itself: the new qualifications demanded by new techniques are redecomposed. The most qualified production workers' professional skills are carved up into sub-specializations shorn of autonomy. The power of control which they carried – and thus power over the production process – is transferred to non-workers as a separate function. The effects of automation are entirely consistent with this process. Accompanying mechanization, which dequalifies and fragments production tasks, automation dequalifies and fragments control itself. After mechanization has dispossessed workers of all power of control and transferred it to separate agents, automation transfers the function of control to machines, which now control their former supervisors.

But a partial inversion of the dequalification process has tended to appear during the last few years. Manufacturers in certain sectors are discovering that the oppressive organization of work deprives the firm of the valuable inventiveness and 'creativity' of the workers by provoking resistance, indolence and diffuse hostility. Defects, errors, sabotage and accidents are increasing; absenteeism and turnover are growing alarmingly high; and taking on staff is becoming difficult.[2] The owners, having done everything to deny workers any possibility of initiative or control in their jobs, are now discovering something that the workers have always known: if workers stop giving of themselves and stick rigorously to what is prescribed, the factory jams.[3] The rigorous predetermination of tasks turns against its authors. Productivity drops.

Has 'rationalization' been pushed too far? Or has the same old oppression become insufferable to changed workers? In fact, both hypotheses are true. 'Failures' have assumed such proportions that half the equipment lies idle in General Motors' most modern factory, where the intensity and monotony of work surpasses anything previously imposed on assembly-line workers.[4] But this fact in itself cannot explain the jamming of the industrial system. Capital encounters a fundamental contradiction stemming from the fact that, step by step with the *dequalification* of work, there is an increased social qualification of *workers* and a social *disqualification* (or devaluation) of all work as a productive force.

Contrary to popular theory, the social qualification of workers does not accrue from their increased useful or useless (school) knowledge. At school they learn less than in the past. *Teaching* is not and has never been the aim of School. People are not taught by education; they are taught by being placed in 'pedagogical situations' that lead them to *teach themselves* according to the practical-theoretical demands of their *praxis*. As Ivan Illich has ably shown, there are many learning methods more fruitful and efficient than schooling. If people are schooled, it is because under the pretext and on the occasion of teaching (thus deflected from its apparent purpose), the system is anxious to *socialize* them in a certain way. They must be educated to venerate the Knowledge of Others and the monumental learned culture to the detriment of uncodified living culture; they must be educated into submission, discipline and respect for hierarchy. And this is precisely what no longer works: there is a link between the education crisis of (school instruction) and the crisis of despotism in the factory. School instruction becomes unacceptable because there is a new culture (or subculture) on the edge of the learned culture and codified knowledge. It is made of bric-à-brac but it is alive, developing against society and the socialization attempted by the schools. The 'work culture' also becomes unacceptable, since it long ago turned into its opposite in deculturing the worker to adapt him to the barbarity of the factory, to the hierarchical, fragmented division of militarized labour.

More fundamentally, through *this* school, *School* becomes unacceptable because beyond *this* work, *work* is disqualified from now on. Although it is still necessary to the reproduction of capitalist social relations, it is *virtually* no longer needed for the individual production of subsistence in the imperalist metropolis. Not that work has become superfluous: in the final analysis it remains the source of all wealth; and after the communist revolution we will work more, not less. But necessary work and superfluous work, useful production and waste production, creation and destruction of wealth, use-valve and uselessness – indeed, counter-usefulness ('disutilities') – are inextricably commingled in mature capitalist society. Privation and penance are no longer the conditions for (postponed) enjoyment. Victory over scarcity and the domination of nature no longer require mortification in and outside work: 'Repression is losing its rationality.'[5] We could live better while producing less if we worked, consumed and lived in another way. All work in the framework of the capitalist system, is discredited and meaninglessness and devalued, just as a marginal surplus of goods dumped on a saturated market devalues the totality of its goods and returns them to a marginal price. All forced, alienated, mortifying work imposed for the sake of capital becomes an unacceptable, arbitrary vexation when accumulation can continue only at the price of destruction, sumptuous over-consumption and waste.

In this context the attempts of the corporations' psycho-sociologists to reconcile workers with their work by abolishing the despotism of the factory appears to be a new manipulation rather than a solution to the basic contradictions. The psycho-sociologists attempt to explain disaffection and resistance towards work by the mere lack of intrinsic interest in fragmented, repetitive, militarized jobs. Frederick Herzberg writes that 'indolence, indifference, and irresponsibility are the correct attitudes toward absurd work'. Recompose and enrich jobs, he adds; give the worker conrol over his pace and (within limits) over his hours; end his separation from the means of production and from his product by entrusting him with an intelligent job that includes possibilities for voluntary co-operation, initiative and responsibility. His job will regain a 'meaning' and an 'interest' for him; his output will increase; the proportion of errors, rejects, absenteeism and quitting will decrease.

Is this true? Where job enlargement or enrichment has been tried experimentally the results have almost always been convincing.[6] Does this prove that *workers* can be reconciled with *work;* that its absurdity and their exploitation can be effectively concealed; that their domination by and separation from the means of production are no longer necessary to capital's power; that it is becoming possible to abolish factory despotism and introduce 'industrial democracy' in the interests of capital itself? In short, can techniques of production and techniques of domination, which have not been distinguished until now, really be separated, and the workers' revolt against forced work be co-opted?

In this abstract form these questions do not mean very much. So far, it is impossible to generalize the conditions for the success of experiments in job enlargement and enrichment. Each one – there have been only a few dozen in the world – required long preparation. Each required a rigorous selection of participants, first on the basis of volunteers and then by co-optation. In short, the formula has succeeded in so far as it has been limited to groups of workers with a 'positive attitude' towards work. No combative, unsubmissive, politicized working class has ever been won over by the amelioration – however genuine – of work conditions and climate made possible by job recomposition (which always includes the elimination of petty bosses and superintendents). At Fiat, for example, the workers' struggle against the capitalist work organization has produced *autonomous* workers' demands and organizational forms (assembly line and shop committees revocable by the base, self-limitation of work pace, and so on). In such situations owners have not only made no 'democratic' concessions but have done everything possible to smash workers' autonomy and resistance, and to prohibit organs of direct democracy in the factory (assemblies, committees, councils) and re-establish the power of trade-union regimentation based on indirect representation.[7]

Thus, as with any reform, the meaning of new non-despotic forms of work organization depends on the relation of the forces presiding over their introduction. Introduced cold at the owner's initiative, to defuse or prevent atomized and diffuse worker resistance (absenteeism, indolence, quitting, bad work), they can be profitable to capital and consolidate its hegemony, at least for a time. On the other hand if new forms of work organization are demanded or imposed in the heat of organized workers' action, the owner fights them as a workers' power that cannot be reconciled with his own authority. Only when the workers' autonomous power has been smashed and the owner's power re-established will he be able to consider granting changes that he refused when the initiative was not his own. Thus the ambiguity of 'democratization' of the work process is that of all reform. When instituted from above, it is a reformist co-optation by capital of workers' resistance; when imposed from beneath in a test of strength, it opens a breach in capital's system of domination. But that test of strength can be won only if it goes beyond the limits of the factory.

Thus there is no point in coming out for or against job enlargement *in itself*. To the extent that it smashes the myth of the objective technical necessity of a certain type of work organization and frees workers from stupefaction, isolation and the oppression of petty bosses, it gives the working class weapons for sharpening the contradictions of capitalism and aggravating its problems. Still, the working class must learn to use these weapons by immediately linking the struggle against factory despotism and idiotic jobs with the struggle against every form of domination and exploitation, and with the struggle against the 'rationality' of capitalist production.

The psycho-sociologists' gamble depends on the assumption that 'work well done' requires intelligence, responsibility and 'creativity' and has its own inner meaning regardless of its final result. Is it really possible to find meaning and take interest in assembling televisions when the programmes are idiotic; or in making fragmentation bombs, throw-away fabrics or individual cars built for obsolescence and rapid wear and destined to sit in traffic jams? What meaning does work have when its dominant aim (the accumulation of capital) is meaningless? Challenging the capitalist organization of work implies challenging the system as a whole. Reformist subjugation and co-optation of workers' resistance to factory despotism can be prevented only if this challenge is made explicit and autonomous.

NOTES

1 As opposed to job *enlargement* – which consists of recomposing a certain number of fragmentary jobs (in assembly, for example) into a complex and less monotonous job – job *enrichment* consists precisely of giving back to the production worker the responsibility for regulation, preparation, maintenance and supervision of which he has been deprived. Job enrichment thus eliminates the 'control staff' and 'NCOs of production'. There are several examples in Yves Delamotte, *Recherches en vue d'une organisation plus humaine du travail* (Paris: Ministère du Travail 1972).

2 See the article by Dominique Pignon and Jean Querzola in this book.

3 A virtuoso demonstration of this came from the Fiat workers in Turin in summer 1969.

4 On this subject see Emma Rothschild, *Paradise Lost* (New York; Random House 1973).

5 Herbert Marcuse, *Counterrevolution and Revolt* (New York: Beacon 1972), pp. 22–3.

6 For an analysis of two American examples of job enrichment see Pignon's and Querzola's article in this book.

7 Toward the end of 1971 the Italian owners (Confindustria) unleashed a general

counteroffensive to free factories of workers' power at the base (assemblies, shop committees, factory councils), to re-establish the authority of the trade-union apparatus and, in this way, to submit claims to juridical rules and compulsory procedure.

'The question is to see if the increase of power obtained by the unions can find its rational function in a system which permits syntheses and an equilibrium, and restores the rules of the game,' said Lombardi, president of Confindustria, on 9 March 1972. (See Pino Ferraris, 'La Confindustria e la costruzione del nuovo ordine sociale', *Fabbrica e Stato,* 3, via della Scala 9, Roma.)

This preoccupation of the owners was shared by the union confederations (if not by the federations). At the beginning of July 1972 the executives of the three confederations decided that 'factory councils' – an outgrowth of shop committees, elected and subject to recall by the workers as whole – should be replaced by union councils in which all political tendencies of the federal bureaucracies would be represented. In this way the factory councils ceased to be the councils *of workers* in order to become the parliaments of parties represented in the unions. The fusion of the metal workers' federations in a unified organization depending on the factory councils' autonomous unity, was put off till domesday.

DOMINIQUE PIGNON AND JEAN QUERZOLA

Dictatorship and Democracy in Production*

'The consumption of labour-power is at one and the same time the production of commodities and of surplus value. The consumption of labour-power is completed, as in the case of every other commodity, outside the limits of the market or of the sphere of circulation.

Accompanied by Mr Moneybags and by the possessor of labour-power, we therefore take leave for a time of this noisy sphere, where everything takes place on the surface and in view of all men, and follow them both into the hidden abode of production, on whose threshold there stares us in the face: *No admittance except on business.*

(Karl Marx, *Capital*, I, ch. 6) [1]

'How long can our political democracy stand the 70,000,000 who live the majority of their waking hours in an atmosphere that is totalitarian?' [2] The question is posed by Robert J. Doyle, personnel manager of Donnelly Mirrors of Holland, Michigan, a small firm which supplies car mirrors to the big car manufacturers in Detroit. In an interview he said 'I was talking recently with somebody who has just come back from Yugoslavia ... some interesting things are going on there. I'm not for a moment suggesting that we must accept communism, but the idea of electing managers is a very interesting one, and it seems to me that it is compatible with our social system.'

The style is becoming familiar. It is the new language of capitalism – the end of work on the line, the arrival of job-enrichment, participation in target-setting, retraining and a career structure for all workers etc. All Doyle is doing is giving these tendencies a more radical ideological form. His form of discourse is possible, and is listened to, because in the last few years on the western stage there has been a change of scene. 'Everyday life' has emerged into the light of day. The concrete conditions of labour (not merely in industry), which until the last few years had been almost entirely excluded from the arena of class struggle, are now beginning to occupy the centre of the stage. Many things that used to be accepted have suddenly become socially intolerable.

It could be said that behind the scenes the reality of relations between labour and capital at the point of production does not change. This unchanging reality is still as expressed in the labour code: 'The employee who refuses to carry out an order given by his employer is thereby guilty of

---

* This article is a revised and extended version of one that appeared, under the same title, in *Les Temps Modernes* (September-October 1972). Translated by Geoffrey Nowell Smith.

a serious offence such as to justify his dismissal without notice or compensation.' Despotism is masquerading as democracy. Nobody is fooled. All that has changed is the forms of subordination of labour to capital.

Fair enough. But this question of the change of forms and the transformation of the mode of capitalist domination is also the political question of the forms of change. For this transformation of the system can equally well mean its consolidation or the possibility of its overthrow.

1 SYMPTOMS AND FIRST MEASURES

Absenteeism, labour turnover, botched work and even active sabotage have become the running sores of the American automotive industry. *Fortune*, the monthly magazine of the managerial élite, describes in gory detail all these manifestations of working-class resistance to methods of organization and dominance that have not changed since the beginning of Taylorism. *Fortune* offers its own explanation of this increasing resistance, particularly notable among younger workers, as follows: 'The new workers have had more years in school . . .; blue-collar workers between twenty-five and forty-four years old have completed twelve years of school, compared with ten years for those from forty-five to sixty-four. It doesn't sound much of a difference, but it means an increase of 20%.' [3] (Note, in passing, this managerial mania for quantification. Does staying on at school from 16 to 18 instead of leaving at 16 really mean a 20 per cent increase in schooling? Do each of the last two years really have the same value as each of the first ten? Is there really such a linear progression?)

Whatever the value of this explanation, the fact is that in the eyes of American bosses the resistance and insubordination of young workers represents an urgent problem. The resulting disorder affects the rate of profit and the 'competitivity' of American industry. 'The result of all this churning labour movement is, inevitably, wasted manpower, less efficiency, higher costs, a need for more inspections and repairs, more warranty claims – and grievous damage to company reputations as angry customers rage over flaws. . . .' [4] Such, according to *Fortune*, are the effects of 'blue-collar blues'.

The symptoms are these:

a) *Absenteeism* (despite the fact that hourly paid workers have their wages docked for every absence) has gone up massively over the last ten years. It has grown particularly in traditional branches of industry where there is assembly line work – the car industry, light engineering, electronics etc. At General Motors, Ford and Chrysler absenteeism has doubled in the past ten years, reaching a peak in the last two, and now averages between 5 and 10 per cent. Five per cent of hourly paid workers are regularly absent without cause (i.e. for reasons other than illness, holidays etc.) at General Motors. On Fridays and Mondays the figure goes up to 10 per cent. This increase in absenteeism, general throughout industry, also extends into the service and white-collar sectors. The same tendency can be observed in typing pools, in drawing offices and in big bureaucracies.

b) *Turnover*, that is to say the voluntary movement of workers who change job in order to find better working conditions, is another nightmare for American capitalists. In 1969 Ford lost 25 per cent of its labour force. These were mostly younger workers, which suggests that the rate can be expected to increase further with the entry of a new age-group into production. Some workers, a manager remarked in amazement, leave their job in the middle of the day, without even bothering to collect their wages.

At the world's biggest private capitalist employer, American Telegraph & Telephone (AT&T), the personnel managers face a nightmare task just trying to recruit people. They have had to carry out more than 2 million interviews a year in order to take on 250,000 new employees.

c) *Falling productivity* is a further index of workers' resistance to exploitation.[5] This resistance, manifested in go-slow techniques, hidden sabotage and an increasing number of defective and rejected products, represents a particular threat to the employers. For in the present phase of concentration of capital, redistribution of production units and international competition, any fall in productivity can be a fatal weakness for a capitalist enterprise.

In the face of resistance and revolt, the Taylorist and post-Taylorist school can respond only by repression, intimidation and physical violence. This terrorist regime is still the order of the day in big mass-production plants. The car industry is famous for its private security forces – the supervisors at Ford and General Motors, the members of the scab foremen's union at Simca and Citroën, the 'flying squad' at Renault.

But repressive methods are powerless against widespread and ever-present resistance. Strictly organizational and repressive measures to increase productivity, such as the authoritarian imposition of speed-up or productivity bonus schemes etc., find their effectiveness limited by shop-floor power, and lead only to strikes, go-slows and a considerable increase in production faults. No supervision can stop a worker missing a piece and enforcement itself places a formidable burden on the productive apparatus.

A repressive intensification of Taylorism does not provide an acceptable response, in the eyes of 'capital', to working-class rejection of degrading, tedious and exhausting forms of industrial work. Some remedy had to be found, and American capitalists were the first to pursue it.

An initial policy was worked out in the United States in the late forties, at the instigation of a former steelworker and trade-unionist, J. N. Scanlon.[6] This policy works on basically the same principles as what in France has come to be called 'participation'. It starts from the observation that workers don't 'go all out' or 'give their best' in their work because they are struggling against the boss. It follows that attempts should be made to eliminate this (class) struggle by means of a process of economic and ideological integration.

From an economic point of view what we find here is the good old theory of material incentives, already practised by Taylor, but in a new form. From an ideological point of view, however, the 'Scanlon plan' is part of the movement integrating social science into the theory of industrial organization that has been operative in the United States since the New Deal.[7] The main aim of the new policies is not pressure on wages or resistance to bargaining claims. They were instituted with the collaboration of corporatist but quite combative trades unions, and the strategy involved from the outset the establishment of labour agreements. The aim is an increase in the overall productivity of an enterprise, among junior management and white-collar workers as well as among the industrial workforce proper, and the means adopted are those of integration.

The first firm to apply the new scheme was the Lapointe Machine Tool Company, with 350 workers. The scheme required the active participation of the unions, who, while continuing in their role as defenders of the workers' economic interests, received equal representation on a newly created body, the Productivity Commission.

The principles of the 'Scanlon plan', as applied at Lapointe, can be summarized as follows:

1 The total wage-fund for the productive labour-force is set at an average value that depends on the firm's market position and corresponds to a given average productivity. Productivity in any month is compared with average productivity and the total wage-fund for workers and other staff is calculated by means of a coefficient based on the productivity increase achieved.

2 The wage-fund for management is tied to increases in turnover.

3 Productivity bonuses are distributed evenly to all workers in a particular category, irrespective of the personal productivity of each single worker.

4 Individual initiative aimed at improving the organization of labour is mediated through production committees, which take up and discuss suggestions made by the workers. The process of discussion (in two years 513 suggestions were taken up, of which 380 were accepted, 28 were carried out, 32 are in the pipeline and 65 were rejected) involves collaboration between people at widely different levels of the hierarchy.

The results of the experiment were encouraging. The firm acquired a very competitive position on the market, the workforce was brought together and stabilized and the workers obtained a productivity bonus of 18 per cent.

But it is clear enough what the limits of such participation are. The economic class struggle is merely pushed back a little and in any case the possibility of pursuing this sort of integrationist policy is very dependent on the firm's position relative to its competitors, the state of the labour market in the area and the general economic situation. But we should not dismiss this kind of policy too lightly as just yet another of traditional paternalism's reach-me-downs. The whole contemporary modernist trend in organizational methods derives from these experiments and preserves their essential foundation, which is the idea that the repressive organization of production systematized by Taylor is a hindrance to the development of productivity under present-day economic and cultural conditions in the industrialized western nations. The modernists explain the relative failure of job-enrichment programmes in the sixties and the accumulated difficulties encountered in dealing with young workers as being due to an inadequate recognition of the real contradictions. Let's face it, they say, the interests of bosses and workers *are* opposed. But the thing to do is not to cover up this opposition, in the way that 'industrial relations' policies tend to do, but to institutionalize it. In this way worker initiative can be liberated but at the same time kept under control.

At this point we may turn to two case histories that seem to us exemplary in a number of ways: the story of Donnelly Mirrors Corporation, which employs a few hundred workers; and that of AT&T, which is one of the biggest firms in the world.

2 THE MASS LINE

Donnelly Mirrors is a small family business. Its president, John F. Donnelly, who took over from his father in 1932, and is now in his sixties is fairly representative of a certain paternalist and Christian-inspired tradition. For example one of his favourite authors is G. K. Chesterton, a Catholic convert, who was extremely popular not only as a novelist but also as a moralist throughout the interwar period. Donnelly's company has a dominant position on the market. Eighty per cent of American motorcars are equipped with Donnelly rear-view mirrors. Over the last few years expansion has been very rapid. Turnover rose from $3.6 million in 1965 to $15 million in 1971. Profits are increasing at an average rate of 22 per cent a year. The main plant, at Holland, Michigan, employs about 300 workers.[8]

The mirrors are made of glass, which is backed with silver and set in a plastic mount. The production process consists of the following stages:

a) *Plating* Sheets of glass about 2ft (60cm) square are silvered and painted on a machine with five work positions: setting up the glass, electrolysis, painting, drying and removal of the mirror. It is line work in particularly poor conditions. The air is foul because of the electrolytic baths and the painting. The work rhythm is very fast and the handling of the glass is dangerous.

b) *Cutting* There are various cutting machines, each with five workers. The sheets of mirror glass are moved into place and cut to size. The equipment looks very old and here again the rhythm is fast.

c) *Polishing* Each mirror now goes to a polishing machine, which employs a single worker. There are five machines in all. The work is extremely unpleasant because of the noise produced. It is also dangerous because it generates a dust of powdered glass and polishing materials that coats the lungs and can lead to silicosis. Work is therefore done with a mask.

d) *Making the mounts* The mounts are pressure-moulded out of plastic. Machines are of a standard type for this sort of operation. Each one employs three workers and again the rhythm is high.

e) *Finishing* The final stage is the fitting of the mirrors to the mounts, which is done on automatic machines, each with three workers.

As far as the form of the technical process of production is concerned, there is therefore no difference between Donnelly Mirrors and many small European firms. The factory is old, working conditions are appalling and no attempt has been made to make them more bearable. Visiting the workshops one sees no signs of differences in organization. The division of labour appears to be the standard one. The only thing to be noted is that the workers operate in teams, each team being assigned to a particular operation or a series of operations on one machine.

But this apparent similarity in fact conceals real differences. A reform of the work organization has been in progress for some years. The avowed purpose of the instigators of the reform was to put the firm in a strong competitive position by reducing costs to the minimum. To attain this end, they reckoned to rely essentially on the initiative of the workers themselves, on the grounds that nobody else knew as much about production and that they should therefore be allowed to express their point of view on how the production process was organized.

A special machinery was set up for this purpose. From time to time meetings are held of work committees, consisting of representatives of all the work teams, the foreman and a manager and, where necessary, technicians and engineers. The meetings discuss possible modifications aimed at increasing productivity. Suggestions are put forward by shop-floor workers and engineers alike. Although each team is under the direct supervision of a foreman, the expression of opinions on how work is to be carried out is not mediated through him, as it would be in more traditional organizations.

This modification of labour relations is put forward as a natural development of the 'Scanlon plan', which has been in operation at Donnelly for the past fifteen years. But, Donnelly maintains, 'the committee structure created by Scanlon was not sufficiently wide-ranging to involve everybody in the company's affairs or to apply to all problems ... so a broader committee structure had to be set up so as to give everybody a chance to learn and to contribute and so as to co-ordinate the resulting suggestions.'[9]

The new structure is based on the idea of the work team. It is organized as a hierarchy of functional committees. Certain members of each team, known as 'link-pins', are also part of an 'executive work team'. The link-pins have a dual function. On the one hand this is conventionally hierarchical and co-ordinating, but they also have an informational function that operates in all directions, since organization has to be made transparent from whichever point of view it is looked at. [10]

The informational system is highly developed. Information is one of the primary functions of the link-pins. They are assisted in this task by a company newspaper (the *Donnelly Mirror* – management-edited), in which you get all the usual guff you would expect from this kind of publication, but also precise details about the methods used by different work teams to reduce production costs. Meanwhile occasional broadsheeets (*Donnelly Flash*) provide frequent doses of summary information of a technical, organizational or commercial kind – arrival of a new machine, formation of a specialized work group, market successes and so on. This information helps to transmit to the workers a sense of the pressure of the market. At the same time the informative content is interspersed with exhortations to initiative. Take this example from a *Donnelly Flash* of 1971: ' IDEAS WANTED. The Research and Development department of the Automotive Optics division is designing a periscopic mirror for the Buick Riviera and aims to land a substantial contract ... It is launching a large brainstorming movement to get the best ideas for the best periscope possible.'

The new organization has a pay and wages structure that is also derived from Scanlon. A global involvement plan takes into account the total wages fund, turnover and so on, and collective productivity bonuses are assigned to each area of production. The wage negotiating procedure links the basic wage directly to economies realized in production costs.

This is how the procedure worked in 1970.

The basic wage is reassessed annually on 1 May, which is the beginning of the fiscal year in American business. On 22 January the council of work-team delegates asks for an increase of 11 per cent. In response management present accounts to show that in order to increase both the basic wage *and profits* by 11 per cent, production costs will have to be cut to the tune of $374,000, calculations being based on the 1970/1 fiscal year. This proposal is aired division by division. Automotive Optical, which is by far the biggest, has to cut its costs by $292,000. The question is put on the agenda for the team meetings. Working groups are formed and 'brainstorming' sessions take place. Every idea is analysed. Bob Doyle told us: 'The engineers resisted the idea of developing closer links with production workers ... but after a pretty good experience in the last few years ... the situation is improving, and they are much more open to the fact that blue-collars may have ideas. It's a beginning, only a beginning.'

'Cost reduction committees' centralize information at divisional level and each team presents its own 'cost reduction commitment' plan. The first plating team commits itself to reducing production costs by $15,000, which is further divided as follows:

quality improvements	$4,900
maintenance economies	400
economies on control operations	4,800

increased productivity   4,900
                                                    total: $15,000

All the teams of workers engaged in direct production in the Automotive Optical division then finally commit themselves to an aggregate cost reduction of $174,000, of which only $39,000 are in the sphere of increased productivity proper.

This is important. Faced with a demand for a pay increase, the management could have responded by making counter-demands based on productivity alone. It would have tried in the usual way to lessen the impact of the increase in labour costs by means of an increase in direct productivity. It could have done this either overtly, by insisting on a productivity deal as a condition during negotiation, or covertly, by conceding the pay increase with no short-term strings attached, and then at a later date taking advantage of a cooling-off in militancy once agreement had been reached, stepping up work rhythms stealthily and bit by bit — a normal tactic, for example, among French employers.

By going about things in a different way, the Donnelly management succeeded in conjuring up an additional $135,000 of potential economies. And it is the producers themselves who commit themselves to achieving it. This is the crucial point. For even if management had been able to establish the *technical possibility* of such economies, to impose their achievement against the will of the direct producers would have been politically impossible.[11] The sheer cost of the apparatus of technical and repressive control that would have had to be set up would have made most of the potential technical economies more or less unprofitable.

The directly productive work teams are not the only ones to send in cost-reduction projects. Technical innovations that depend on the engineering team are taken into account as well, leading to $295,000 of economies, net of amortization and reinvestment costs. Similarly with the sales department: $40,000 of 'economies' were to be derived from increasing the already negotiated and agreed price of products sold to Chrysler. Thus it is the entire foreseeable surplus that, in theory at least, is brought into play in the 'division of spoils between labour and capital'.

In the Automotive Optical division alone the projected cost reduction has now reached $557,000. Management then grants *on the spot* the increase demanded, in exchange for the commitment of the personnel to reaching the target.

As the year goes on the position of the different teams in relation to their targets is regularly marked up on a board. Since these targets are higher than was strictly necessary for the increase demanded and granted in basic pay, achievement of the new targets also means massive collective bonuses. The quicker the target is reached or even exceeded, the larger the bonus, because it is calculated on the basis of the fiscal year. Over the last few years, targets have always been surpassed.

We must re-emphasize the point. In this system, unlike the traditional one, pressure is not brought to bear directly on productivity in the narrow sense. For the direct producer, reaching a target is not just a question of keeping up a set rhythm. Liberating the worker's initiative, while at the same time keeping it firmly under control, is Bob Doyle's real ambition. We quoted him at the beginning of this article. Here he is again: 'Most firms under-utilize the mental potential of their labour force . . . In a firm with 500 employees, 50 do the thinking work and the other 450 just do the sweating work. . . . You've got to get all 500 working with their heads. . . . Everyone's got to play a part in managing the business. . . . This is a real revolution in managerial thinking.' He also tells this exemplary little tale: when a new machine had to be bought for cutting the mirrors, the engineers met the workers on the old cutter to study the specification book in the light of their practical experience; the engineer sent over to California to negotiate the purchase will go with a shop-floor worker by his side.

To liberate mass initiative, the masses must be given a voice. But how? Supervisors, for example, make poor spokesmen for the work teams. In their relations with their superiors in the hierarchy they have a tendency to cover over facts that are unfavourable to themselves and to represent the workers below them as responsible for all the problems. Furthermore they are in a precarious position, looked on by the engineers as jumped-up nobodies (most of them at Donnelly's have been promoted from the shop floor) and by the workers as agents of the bosses. The supervisors either feel threatened by shop-floor initiative or try to claim credit for it themselves. One result is that mass initiative is stifled. It was after a careful analysis of this delicate problem of the 'gaffers' that management decided to set up a work-team council where criticism by the workers of managerial decisions not only would be permitted but actively encouraged. Another block on technological and organizational innovation was that rationalizing the labour process leads to an increase in productivity that is not always matched by a corresponding increase in output. This in turn leads to fewer jobs and to workers being laid off. Workers know this. So an agreement was reached that any innovation that meant the loss of a job would not be carried out unless the worker in question was guaranteed another job at the same wages for at least six months.

In a similar vein, in order to prevent individual competition over productivity proposals hindering the development of collective initiatives, individual rewards are not offered. All bonuses go to the team as a whole.

The results of this reorganization were very much as expected. Productivity showed a significant increase. Absenteeism without cause dropped from 4 per cent to 1 per cent. Labour turnover was halved. The quality of work went up. The number of faulty items dropped from 25 per cent in 1967 to a mere 5 per cent in 1971. This then meant a reduction in the number of quality-control personnel. Products returned to the factory went down from 3 per cent to 0.2 per cent.

We can see here the emergence, alongside traditional factory organization with its highly differentiated hierarchical levels, of an organization of a partly democratic type. Thus members of the work-team council are elected by the workers – but their powers are strictly limited. The council, for example, fixes work speeds – but within limits already determined by management, and so on.

We are not claiming that these forms of organization and their corresponding ideologies are entirely new in the history of capitalism, but we shall try to interpret them, within their present context, as some of the signs among others pointing to a 'revolution' in forms of production that are at the same time forms of domination of capital over labour.

It should also be noted that the new organizational forms do not entirely replace the old forms. They are added to and combined with what was there before. At Donnelly's, for example, management has used quite traditional methods – paternalism, repression, setting up a house union – to prevent the trade unions from acquiring a foothold with the company. Alongside the 'workers' councils' the old hierarchy still exists. It is being deprived of its overtly despotic character, inherited from the factory system of early capitalism, while its controlling and dominating function persists, taking advantage of the competence and ideological integration of the labour force. This change in the forms of domination is visible in the elimination of a number of intermediary hierarchical categories. The supervisors with least technical competence, those whose role, when it comes down to it, is merely repressive, are the first to be threatened by the new organization. They know this, and keep up a sullen resistance to the reforms.

3 A RATIONAL DEMOCRACY

The present organization of Donnelly Mirrors is put forward as the (admittedly provisional) result of a rigorously scientific process of organizational reform. Innovations are worked out in the light of a 'theory' and their direct and indirect effects are checked with the aid of a series of statistical indicators devised by the Michigan Survey Research Center. The theory being applied is that of Rensis Likert, director of the Ann Arbor Institute of Social Research, to which the Survey Research Center belongs.

Likert's name is generally linked with those of Herzberg, McGregor, Argyris and other theorists of modern management. Their theories are certainly close (though in what space?) but by no means equivalent. Herzberg, for example, relies on a purely individualist conception of motivation.He makes explicit reference to Jung, Adler, Rogers and so on, and his theory of 'job-enrichment' is based on the concept of the individual's need for 'self-actualization' in his work. [12] Robert Ford, personnel manager at AT&T, belongs to the same school. His account of the organizational policies carried out at AT&T, aspects of which we shall discuss later, is given in a book called *Motivation Through the Work Itself* (New York 1969), which is dedicated to Herzberg ('to Frederick Herzberg, humanist and psychologist . . .').

None of this psychological humanism is to be found in Likert. There is no explicit theory of Man. His research is concerned with organizations and command systems, in an attempt to establish 'experimentally' the characteristics of the most efficient methods. Likert belongs to a current of American social psychology dominated by Kurt Lewin. The methodological and conceptual dependence on Lewin's theories of Likert's ideas on efficient organization is cemented by an institutional link: the Institute of Social Research, which Likert has directed since its creation in 1948, is the result of a fusion between the Michigan Survey Centre and the Research Centre for Group Dynamics, which had been directed by Lewin until his death that same year.

Former students and collaborators of Lewin, such as French, Lipitt and Zander, took part in the experimental studies that led to the organizational schemes applied at Donnelly. Likert is quite open about this inheritance and presents his theory of management systems as deriving from research started by Lewin thirty years ago on forms of command. [13]

Modern management shows a tendency to give an increasingly systematic place to 'human factors'. But this tendency does not reflect any basic change in its rationale, which remains the traditional compromise between the demands of technology and the principles of humanism. [14] On the contrary it marks an extension of technical rationality to the management of human resources. Likert, for example, insists that the human capital of an organization should be included among the assets on its balance sheet and should be managed as scientifically as any other form of capital. [15]

As Marcuse writes in *One Dimensional Man*, 'The dominant forms of social control are technological in a new sense.' [16] And, at the beginning of *The Human Organization*, Likert explains how the art of management becomes a technology:

> Now, research on leadership, management, and organization, undertaken by social scientists, provides a more stable body of knowledge than has been available in the past. The art of management can be based on verifiable information derived from rigorous, quantitative research. Independent investigators can repeat the research and test the validity of the findings. Not only is the body of knowledge more stable and accurate, but it is likely to grow continuously as the results of additional research on management are accumulated. Quantitative research anywhere in the world can add to this body of knowledge. Its rate of growth can be accelerated by increasing the expenditure for social science research focused on organization. [17]

So, no real break with Taylor. The objective remains the same – to transform into a science the art of organization and command. The difference is simply that in Taylor's day this objective could not really be attained because the social sciences were not so highly developed. [18]

We might add that during the war Likert was head of the 'Morale Division' of Strategic Air Command. It was there that he put into practice the results of interdisciplinary organizational research, and it was there that he and his colleagues formed the project for the Institute of Social Research.[19]

4 THE POWER OF THE MARKET

The American Telephone & Telegraph Company is the biggest firm in the world in terms of number of people employed (860,000 in Canada and the United States). It includes telephone companies, research organizations (Bell Laboratories), electrical engineering firms in the Western Union Group and so on. We shall here be considering only the organizational changes that have taken place in the telephone service.

These services consist on the one hand of installation and repair and on the other hand of administration and accounting. The work of the installation engineers is relatively independent. They work their way round towns and country districts in accordance with the requests that come in for installation and repair work. Their work is closer to that of an artisan than to that of a factory worker.

The women clerical workers, for their part, carry out the massive task of sorting and preparing invoices for computerization. Their work is formally very similar to line work in a factory, with pools of typists, punch-card operators and so on. What we find here is a type of work that has developed in its present form as a result of the massive introduction of computers in business management. As is well known, this has led to a heightening of the division of labour and a simplification of tasks for certain groups of employees, a phenomenon often referred to as 'white-collar proletarianization'.

Ostensibly the main reason behind the reorganization was the high proportion of workers leaving their jobs within six months of entering the company. This turnover was experienced in two ways, from the point of view of recruitment and from that of loss of personnel. During the years of full employment from 1962 to 1967 the number of people leaving their jobs went up from 5 per cent to over 7 per cent. The recruiting policy at first introduced to counter this tendency was aimed at selectivity and at eliminating in advance people who were thought likely to leave soon. In 1970 the company carried out $2\frac{1}{2}$ million interviews of personnel in order to take on only one-tenth of that number of new employees. The sheer cost of this policy, which had no appreciable positive result, led the top management of the telephone group to look for less narrowly organizational solutions. As one manager said in 1968: 'We have to change our way of thinking about the behaviour of young people today. . . . We have to rethink our work, our control methods, our whole style of management.'

The conclusion reached was along these lines: money is not enough to satisfy human needs; job-content is an essential component of the satisfaction or distaste a worker feels when carrying out his work; we cannot make labour acceptable just by tinkering with things external to the work itself. The planners therefore concentrated on work itself and set out to modify work organization proper in certain selected sectors. This pilot reorganization, judged to be a success by the heads of the company, is now being steadily extended to other sectors of the group's operations. [20]

Let us take the example of the punch-card operators and checkers. The job of the employee is to mark on a punched card the customer's statement of account; the account number (ten digits) is written in pencil in the middle of the card to be punched; in New York alone 200,000 cards of this type are handled every day. Before the reforms the job was organized in the following way: the women employees were divided into two groups of card-punchers and checkers, with about ten to fifteen women in each; a supervisor divided the work out each day among the workers.

After some discussions that will be described later, a modification was decided on. Instead of being divided up at random between the operators, the account cards were grouped according to their place of origin. Each employee was thus given a particular geographical sector to deal with, which also meant a particular group of customers, for whom she now became personally responsible. After trials, the checker working opposite each card-puncher was eliminated, early results having shown that the percentage of errors had shrunk from 4 per cent to less than 1 per cent.

A modification of the forms of constraint had in fact had the effect of an increase in productivity. The constraint no longer appears as the product of a hierarchical authority that imposes work rhythms from above, but as determined by the market, and thus acquires a new semblance of objectivity.

An AT&T manager explained the situation as follows:

There are 2,000 cards to be punched and there are 20 of you, which means 100 cards each. What is the stimulus that will get the job done faster? There isn't one, because when you've done 100 cards all that means is you've got to do another 100. There's no incentive to good work. So we figured that instead of splitting the work up into 20 operations spread around a large pool, why not give each operator the customers of a particular exchange to look after? Before there was no way of identifying the card-puncher who had made a mistake. Now we cut out the checker and a disputed card is always returned to the same original operator. This provides a stimulus to the operator not to make mistakes.

The reorganization therefore does not modify the technical content of the work. Instead it modifies its social form. There is a certain degree of reinsertion of the job into the process of commodity exchange. The employees are no longer confronted with the boss as the person they are responsible to but rather with their customers and with the market.

This labour reorganization can be formally analysed as a 'democratization' that leaves the domination of capital over labour to be exercised through the mediation of the capitalist commodity market. This tendency to open a firm up to the market and to consider each department as a firm on its own subject to criteria of profitability is quite generalized throughout contemporary capitalism.

Another example of the same type of reorganization within the administrative sector is offered by the Centralized Mail Remittance Department. The subscriber's bill is sent out on a punched card and the subscriber pays by sending the card back to the Center along with a cheque. The staff at the Center deal with 7,500 envelopes a day. Before the service was restructured, the job was broken down into 9 separate operations, divided among 20 employees:

a supervisor sets and divides up the day's work

the envelopes are put in special containers

they are put in a vibrating machine, which separates the cards and the cheques

the sum on the cheques is compared to the sum invoiced on the cards

a group of subscriber accounts is checked by comparing the total sum received with the total of invoices for the group

certain individual payments are passed on to another department

a machine is used to make up the day's accounts

the accounts are checked

the overall total is sent, along with the cards, to the computer centre.

What we see here is a division of office labour analogous to the division found on an industrial production line. The job to be done is in each case very simple – comparing the sum on a cheque with that on a bill for example. But the extreme fragmentation of tasks brings with it control functions that split up the labour process still further. The traditional structure of this form of labour organization combines a sequential decomposition of tasks with a military-style discipline over the employees. The fact that the women have been reduced to carrying out the most menial work renders both necessary and at the same time easier a control by capital on what they are doing.

The reorganization consists quite simply of cutting down the division of the labour process. What we now have is a recomposition of tasks, 'job-enlargement'. Each employee carries out all stages of the labour process. But the bills are not handed out at random to each employee. Each one always deals with the same subscribers at the same exchange. Any mistake detected by a customer is immediately attributed to the employee responsible. Again recomposition is combined with a degree of reinsertion into the market.

Furthermore the reorganization cuts out a number of control functions. A group of 20 workers was reduced to 16 after a rearrangement of work positions, for the same total volume of work. Productivity thus went up by 20 per cent. Meanwhile the number of errors went down from 10 per cent to 2 per cent between November 1969 and May 1971, although it had been consistently above 10 per cent for the last 10 years. At the same time turnover was noticeably reduced.

Working conditions are objectively better, and this improvement can be seen in the abolition of the authority of the supervisors. Employees are now free to move round the department, and indeed they have to do so in order to carry out their work. Furthermore on a number of questions they no longer have to pass through the intermediary of an hierarchical superior in order to contact staff in other departments. The assembly-line chain is broken, and the same work position recombines a number of tasks, with a consequent extension of the 'responsibility' of the individual worker.

The corollary of this capitalist democratization is the introduction of competition within a group of employees in the same department. Previously it had been effectively impossible for an hierarchical superior individually to control the quality of each employee's work. Responsibility got diluted round the whole of the department. A promotion policy based on results (measured in terms of customer satisfaction) is a further way of reinforcing the domination of capital.

In the installation and maintenance sector, the control both of the quality of work and of labour productivity is made difficult because of the geographical dispersion and the autonomy of the jobs being done. As far as its technical form is concerned, the work of fitting, repairing and maintaining telephones is similar to artisanal labour. Here too the fundamental principle of reorganization was to make direct use of market constraints. Instead of being sent out at random to cope with jobs as they come in, repair teams are assigned to a particular neighbourhood or geographical area. An immediate consequence of this change is an increase in the pressure exercised by customers on the quality of work. A team constantly on the move round New York City is in virtually no danger of encountering the same customer twice. A badly done job does not mean that the same team will come back but that a new one will be brought in. Under the new system, anything that goes wrong is immediately blamed on the team responsible, and they have to go back and make good the mistake. The constraint exercised on the team is of the same type as that experienced by the artisan or small tradesman exposed to the pressures of competition. Control by a bureaucracy is replaced by control by the consumer. The team works in a more flexible and decentralized manner than before, which lightens the burden of administration and so leads to a gain in productivity. The quality of work is higher because the engineer can no longer shelter behind 'the company' but is directly responsible to the customer. In exchange, the team can enjoy a relative freedom in its conditions of work.

One aspect of this form of labour organization is its recognition of the competence of the worker or employee in the sphere of his or her own work. In a technocratic organization, the domination of capital over the direct producer takes the form of an absolute and despotic control over all aspects of working life. The categorization of every work position by the 'Organization and Methods' (o & m) specialists can, however, lead to all sorts of problems. The division between conception and execution swells the red tape, and distortions appear in the way reality is perceived. It is evident that it is the workers themselves who know most about their own work. But this experience and direct knowledge is repressed in the militaristic Taylorist and post-Taylorist organization of labour, where individual initiative is totally crushed. To activate this source of mass initiative, in the interests of capital, while retaining complete control of the production process, this in a nutshell is the aim of the reorganization we have been studying.[21]

5 THE TWO FORMS OF THE AUTHORITY OF CAPITAL

In all areas where work has become very fragmented, reorganizations of this type are beginning to be introduced. Texas Instruments, Polaroid, Corning Glass, IBM – many such firms, each of them with tens of thousands of employees, are working intensively on reorganization programmes. It might appear as if such reorganization is concentrated in 'spearhead' companies, with advanced technologies, and that it is connected with the privileged strategic character of their production. But this is not the main issue, and in fact the same organizational current is sweeping through areas as traditionalist as the motor industry. The Chrysler Corporation has been working since January 1971 on a vast 'job-enrichment program' for its Detroit production lines. Ford, somewhat more cautious, is introducing job-enrichment at selected assembly plants, inspired by the methods in use at Donnelly Mirrors. (Ford has sent some of its experts to study and training sessions at Donnelly.) General Motors is moving in the same direction.

In Europe, too, increasing numbers of experiments with reorganization are being made. To quote only some of the better known: Volvo in Sweden, ICI in Britain, Philips in Holland, Olivetti in Italy.[22]

In the two examples of reorganization that we have analysed, the transformations concerned the content of labour and the forms of authority. At the level of the forms of authority, the reorganization of Donnelly Mirrors demonstrates clearly that, in the last resort, power always belongs to capital. But the powers of the intermediate hierarchy, say at foreman level, have been diminished. Reorganization tends to cut out the repressive function of supervisory staff and to leave only their technical function. The workers have the right to a voice, and the domination of capitalist over worker is assured by ideological apparatuses outside the workplace.

The reorganization at AT&T was possible only because a measure of initiative was allowed to the person on the job, a measure of trust. This trust is quite relative and the freedom granted to the employee in carrying out his or her work is strictly circumscribed by the needs of the market. It is customer demand that imposes the rhythm of work. Thus hierarchical control can be reduced. But this does not in any way mean that hierarchy is suppressed, and it continues to control the degree of integration and submission to the system.

It can be seen very clearly from the two examples cited that the reorganization of labour in a 'democratic' perspective, consciously opposed to the despotic tradition systematized by Taylor, has as its essential complement an extension of the power of the market over the worker. This poses a challenge to the fundamental conceptual opposition set up by Marx between the two social forms of the division of labour.

In the chapter in *Capital*, I, on 'Division of Labour and Manufacture', Marx writes: 'In spite of the numerous analogies and links connecting them, division of labour in the interior of a society and that in the interior of a workshop differ not only in degree but also in kind' (*Capital* I, ch. 14, sec. 3, p. 354). This opposition provides the basis for the Marxist characterization of bourgeois society in terms of 'anarchy in the social division of labour and despotism in that of the workshop' (*ibid.*, p. 356). On this question Marx refers in a footnote (p. 357) to his own earlier remarks in *The Poverty of Philosophy:* 'It can also be established as a general rule that the less authority controls the division of labour in the interior of a society, the more the division of labour is developed in the interior of the workshop, and the more it is subjected to the authority of a single person. Thus authority in the workshop and in society, in relation to the division of labour, are in an inverse ratio to each other.'

But the absence of authority in bourgeois society – 'anarchy of production' – is also the presence of another authority, 'an *a posteriori*, nature-imposed necessity, controlling the lawless caprice of the producers, and perceptible in the barometric fluctuation of market prices', the authority of competition.[23]

We are therefore in the presence of two forms of social authority, 'the *undisputed authority* of the capitalist over men that are but parts of the mechanism that belongs to him', and the *authority of competition* imposed on the capitalist through the coercive laws of the market. In capitalist production these two forms of authority are combined. The question of bourgeois democracy in production becomes the question of the delimitation or combination of these two forms of the authority of capital, the abstract and general authority of capital as a whole exercised through market forces, and the particular authority of a single capital exercised locally in the form of legal relations.

To this question Marx gave a simple answer. What characterizes the division of labour in manufacture is the fact that the detail labourer does not produce a commodity.[24] Not being his own commodity-producer, he is subjected to the authority of a capitalist. 'On the basis of capitalist production, the mass of direct producers is confronted by the social character of their production in the form of strictly regulating authority and a social regulation of the labour process organized as complete hierarchy.'[25]

Whether or not to be a commodity is undoubtedly an important question for a product, but it is not in a position to choose the answer. Certainly the product of certain activities is hard to individuate in commodity society. But capitalism's capacity to develop commodity forms has no bounds.[26] It is well known that within firms exchanges (whether or not of material goods) between one department and another tend to acquire notional commodity value, because of the demands of an economic rationality that cannot comprehend technical relations except when they are disguised in commodity form, and that this art of disguise is practised today in business schools under the name of analytic compatibility. The increasing scale of economic units clearly encourages the development of these fictitious internal markets that communicate, under the control of a central authority, with the real market on the outside. [27]

Parallel with this, states and financial groups extend the first form of authority (the administrative form) to the division of labour in society and even – and this is just a beginning – to the international division of labour.

The two forms of the authority of capital are combined today in a more complex manner than before. The frontier that still separates the world of labour (where the despotism of capital persists) from civil society is tending to disappear. In May 1968 a slogan on a factory wall read 'Here freedom stops'. Maybe the wall will crumble away. But on the side where the writing was there was no freedom yet, and the crumbling of the wall would seem perhaps to announce the extension to society at large of a new, and very democratic, factory regime.

6 THE DESPOTIC ORGANIZATION OF PRODUCTIVITY

What is it that determines the specifically capitalist character of the organization of production under capitalism? To answer this question in historical materialist terms, we should perhaps rephrase it, and ask: how is it that capitalist relations of production, seen as relations of formal subordination, determine the concrete forms of the capitalist organization of immediate production? [28]

Every complex productive process has to be organized. But under capitalism, where the consumption of labour-power is at the same time production of commodities and of surplus-value, the organizational function becomes a function of capital and so acquires a special character. A denial of the specifically capitalist character of the organizational forms of the productive process is typical of bourgeois ideologies in this domain. Bourgeois economy, Marx remarks, identifies the function of directing and superintending (in so far as it derives purely from the nature of the co-operative labour process) with the exercise of this function in a form that is specifically capitalist and consequently antagonistic to the process itself.

Thus for the captains of capitalist industry, the organization of labour corresponds at the same time to an economic necessity (obtaining maximum productivity) and to a political one (keeping the direct producers in a subordinate position relative to capital).

Now these necessities contradict one another, and in the last analysis capitalist forms of organization aim to resolve this contradiction.

Necessary productivity, from the standpoint of capital, is a purely economic form of productivity. It brings into relation labour, means of production and products by means of a price system. This form of productivity depends, at an ideal level, on the one hand on the efficiency of the material production process[29] (a concept that directly relates the product to the quantity of labour and of means of production consumed in the course of the labour process) and on the other hand on the pricing system of the various kinds of labour, means of production and finished products in question.

The organization of labour, however scientific, is clearly powerless to reduce the price of means of production or to raise the price of the product. So there remains the price of labour. To reduce this, at least relatively, is a question of method, and it was this grandiose idea that animated Taylor until his dying breath.

This means that the organization of labour can be used by capital as a means of raising productivity in two ways: by means of an increase in the efficiency of the production process, and by means of a relative reduction in the price of labour.

The efficiency of the production process in relation to a given quantity of labour depends simultaneously on production proper and on the means consumed.

Marx devoted a chapter of *Capital* (III, ch. 5) entitled 'Economy in the Employment of Constant Capital' to the question of economies in the consumption of means of production. Here he analyses the different methods used by capitalists to attain their ends. The use of particular methods determines certain concrete forms of capitalist organization of the labour process.

a) In a branch of production where fixed capital is relatively important, the capitalists always try to use the means of production for as long as possible each day. This led in the nineteenth century to a lengthening of the working day and nowadays to a 3 x 8 shift system, wherever technical conditions permit. 'A prolongation of the working day does not entail any fresh expenditures in this, the most expensive portion of constant capital. . . . [It] therefore increases the profit, even if overtime is paid, or even if, up to a certain point, it is better paid than the normal hours of labour. The ever-mounting need to increase fixed capital in modern industry was therefore one of the main reasons prompting profit-mad capitalists to lengthen the working day' (*Capital*, III, ch. 5, p. 77).

b) Again in cases where fixed capital is relatively important, the capitalists will further try to increase the intensity of labour when the productivity of a given set of means of production depends on it. This applies every time production speeds are held down by shop-floor resistance rather than by technical characteristics of the means of production.

It should be clearly noted that the capitalist is not at this point trying to reduce the price of labour. As Marx observes, he is ready to pay over the odds either for overtime or for higher work-intensity or for night-shift work. But this is merely a measure of the importance of fixed capital costs, and usually what happens is that any revolt over speed-up or extra hours is turned simply into a question of how much the capitalist is prepared to pay in extra wages.

c) In cases where the effective consumption of material means in the process of production is not purely determined by the level of technology but also depends to a large extent on the direct producers on the shop floor, the capitalists try to impose economy measures.

The capitalists' fanatical insistence on economy in means of production is therefore quite understandable. That nothing is lost or wasted and the means of production are consumed only in the manner required by production itself, depends partly on the skill and intelligence of the labourers and partly on the discipline enforced by the capitalist for the combined labour. This discipline will become superfluous under a social system in which the labourers work for their own account, as it has already become practically superfluous in piece-work [*ibid.*, p. 83].

The importance of this objective in determining the form taken by capitalist organization of labour is often underestimated. It is in fact harder to grasp than intensification or speed-up, for example, by people who do not have direct knowledge of technological processes. The interested parties, who generally do have such knowledge, know where the game is being played. The operative who has been forbidden to adjust his own machine, when the person doing the adjusting has to ask him, the operative, how to adjust it, is not in the habit of naively attributing this aspect of the division of labour to the simple necessities of technology. The organization of labour that allows the boss to control this aspect of the production process also allows him to achieve another objective at the same time – the reduction of status qualification. The operative who is adjudged incompetent to adjust his own machine is paid (or not paid) accordingly.

d) In a general way capitalism tries to economize over conditions of work that do not actually form part of the technical production process. 'Such economy extends to ... crowding dangerous machinery into close quarters without using safety devices, to neglecting safety rules in production processes pernicious to health, or, as in mining, bound up with danger. Not to mention the absence of all provisions to render the production process human, agreeable, or at least bearable. From a capitalist point of view this would be quite a useless and senseless waste' (*ibid.*, p. 86). And yet, Marx continues, 'more than any other mode of production, it [capitalism] squanders human lives, or living labour, and not only blood and flesh, but also nerve and brain' (*ibid.*, p. 88).

f) For a given overall quantity of living labour and a given system of material and intellectual means, production can be increased only by transforming the labour process, generally in conjunction with a change in the level of qualification demanded of the labour force. The forms of rationalization of the labour process that enable the people who have control of production to attain their goal of immediate efficiency constitute the hard nub of capitalist organization of labour. Here the forms of the division of labour are presented as completely determined by an imperative of direct efficiency, independent of any social system. And yet this is precisely the stage on which the social game is played, in the assignment of each direct producer to a given place in the labour process. It is here too that the very content of labour acquires fixed form, as do the relations established at the level of direct production among the workers themselves, and between them and the management.

g) The forms of organization that enable the quality of production to be raised are in all respects similar to those anlaysed above in the achievement of economies on means of production. First the task of preparing and maintaining the means of labour are withdrawn from the worker. Now he is deprived too of the control of the quality of his production and this function is exercised not through him but in opposition to him.

These six specific aims that the controllers of capitalist production set themselves are just so many aspects of a general aim of 'efficiency'. They are not always of equal importance in determining the forms of organization. Leaving on one side the questions of the lengthening of the working day and of economies in general working conditions, we should like to focus on the following observations: the two basic conditions under which, from the point of view of capitalist control of production, the organization of labour contributes to increasing the efficiency of the production process are: (i) if it means that the wage-earners are made to work harder (even though they may be paid for this more than proportionally, particularly where there is a lot of fixed capital tied up in means of production); and (ii) if it succeeds in imposing on the labour process a form that results in higher productive efficiency in the strict sense and tighter control on consumption of means of production and on the quality of the product.

A reduction, at least a relative reduction, in the price of labour is important to 'capital' to the extent that wages represent a major factor in production costs. To achieve this reduction, capitalists have two basic methods at their disposal: intensification of labour and disqualification of the labourer.

In theory the only means of constraint available to the capitalist to enable him to impose his will on the 'free' labourer are economic, and normally intensification of labour is introduced with the aid of a suitable system of wage adjustments. We have already seen how this works when the capitalist is in a position to pay 'above the odds' for labour because of the importance of the fixed capital element in his business. But in the present case it is a question of reducing the price of labour, where it is essential to pay supplementary wages that are less than proportional to the increase in labour performed. Taylor himself gives an example of how this can be done. In 1884 the workers at Midvale Steel Co. were on piece-work at a rate of 50c per piece. Average daily production was 5 pieces. After an analysis of the work and an assessment of the minimum time necessary for each of the basic operations, Taylor came to the conclusion that it was possible to produce 10 pieces a day. So instead of 50c he set the rate at 35c per piece if the workers produced ten or more pieces a day, and 25c if they produced less. [30]

Dequalification as a means of reducing labour costs is obviously based on the existence of different prices for sections of the labour force with different skills and qualifications. These prices are imposed on the capitalist producers in the same way as any other price system.

We should emphasize here that we are talking about a purely economic aspect of wage differences, and not about their ideological function in preserving the hierarchy. At this level capitalist labour organization aims to allow the controllers of production to achieve two main objectives simultaneously – increased efficiency in the productive process and a relative reduction in the price of labour. The former objective is not in itself unique to the capitalist mode of production. What is specifically capitalist, however, is the forms of organization of the productive process that are used to achieve it.

In all modes of production, even the most primitive, we will find people looking for ways to make their labour more efficient. But when the direct producers are in a position to organize their own labour freely and to dispose of its results, pressure for higher efficiency can be balanced against the cost to the producers themselves. They may decide to opt for a slower rhythm of work, for less division of tasks, for more free time and so on, rather than for an increase in production.

Capitalism does not allow such options. Competition turns the search for efficiency into a matter of economic life or death. And this search for efficiency in the context of capitalist social relations leads of necessity to specific forms of organization.

7 REAL SUBORDINATION

Will capitalism be in a position to hold back the movement of revolt that is developing today, in the most highly industrialized countries of the West, against the conditions of labour and the labouring condition itself? Do the new forms of organization of production and a transformation of the concrete conditions of labour offer it the possibility of so doing? Should we see in these new forms of organization a crafty move on the part of a capitalist class that, in the present historical conditions, reckons that it is able to renounce obsolete forms of domination, to 'recuperate' revolt against these forms, to extend bourgeois democracy to work relations and thus consolidate its authority? Or should we say on the contrary that techniques of domination and techniques of production, hitherto confused within the context of a capitalistic technology sheltering behind the ideological alibi of scientific neutrality, [31] are now revealed as distinct, and that for the revolutionary movement this distinction opens a breach that it can exploit to assault the dominion of capital in all its forms? Are these two interpretations contradictory? Can the Leninist problematic of democratic revolution (bourgeois or proletarian according to the hegemonic capacity of the classes in the struggle) be transposed to meet the new situation? Or must we look elsewhere for the beginnings of a political answer to these questions?

It seems to us that the development of a political response demands a reformulation of the questions, for today more than ever before the future is being decided fundamentally elsewhere than in the sphere of production as such. The objectively real but undoubtedly very localized modifications that can be seen to be taking place in the productive organizations of industrialized western countries are merely effects in the 'sphere of production' of a wider transformation of the mechanisms of social power. This transformation is characterized by the emergence, alongside the 'old manifest forms of coercion', of new and rationally based forms of subordination and control. When they are interpreted in this wider context these modifications can be seen to be vehicles of a radical change in the forms of capitalist authority over production, and thereby in the forms and contents at stake in the class struggle.

We are still at the stage of beginning to explore, theoretically and practically, with old concepts and old methods, the political space that has thus been opened out.[32] Let us start by saying that in the 'sphere of production' the issue at stake is being displaced from formal subordination to real subordination.

These concepts date back to Marx. In capitalist production the elements of the labour process belong to the capitalist. Means and objects through which production is carried out are his property, as is the labour-power expended in the process and, of course, the resulting product. The whole process unrolls 'under his authority'. The direct producers engaged in the process are subordinated to him. In the early days capital began by subordinating the direct producers in a merely formal way, that is to say without modifying the labour process itself. The old-fashioned artisan, for example, continued to work as before, the only difference being that the product of his labour no longer belonged to him, but became the property of the man who advanced to him his means of production and his wages — the capitalist.

In some manuscript notes on the question of subordination, Marx wrote: The general characteristic of formal subordination is the direct subjection of the labour process to capital, whatever the technological methods employed. But on this basis there arises a quite specific technological mode of production, which transforms the nature and the real conditions of the labour process. This is the capitalist mode of production. It is only when this appears that the real subordination of labour to capital takes place ... Science and technology are applied to immediate production ... On the one hand, constituted by now in its specificity, the capitalist mode of production creates a new type of material production; and, on the other hand, this material transformation constitutes the basis of the development of the capitalist system.[33]

At a second stage, then, the labour process is itself transformed. The traditional unity of the craft is destroyed, the direct producer finds himself subordinated to capital not only by means of market relations but also (or should one say, above all?) by means of the new technical relations of production that are being set up. Here the subordination becomes real.

From the point of view of the direct producers, this transition from formal to real subordination, from artisanal labour to modern industry, passing through the various stages of manufacture, is the history of their progressive dispossession. [34] **How is the autonomy of the direct producers in the labour process reduced? How is the authority of capital made absolute? The answer is: by the division and organization of labour in strictly hierarchized forms,** [35] **with extreme fragmentation of tasks, generalized productivity-related wage rates and a constantly multiplying control system. At least this is the answer given by the theorists of factory despotism – Taylor, Bedaux, Rowan and their ilk.**

But how does it come about that over nearly a century the real subordination of labour to capital has survived uncontested, to the point of being barely affected by even the most radical revolutions? [36] Why is it only now beginning to be exposed? And to what is it exposed? How, and to what extent, do the forms of real subordination depend on the production techniques in use?

If on this last question we understand by production technique a concrete system of material and intellectual means of production, then the answer is not in doubt. The structure of the labour process is almost always completely determined by the system of means of production; and in large-scale capitalist production the specific characteristics of this structure – hierarchy and fragmentation of labour – will present themselves as endowed with the same quality of technical objectivity as the material process itself.

In capitalist practice the system of means and the corresponding organization and division of labour are conceived, in all essential respects, not as successive but as simultaneous. Certainly problems of the organization of the labour process have to be coped with on a day-to-day basis by the controllers of production, in the context of a system of material means that cannot be radically modified overnight. But this system of means was itself conceived and erected in function of an organization of the labour process whose fundamental forms were determined in advance. This fusion of technical and organizational know-how in a single conception of the material means of production is crystallized in the concept and practice of 'engineering' as a social as well as a material science. [37] In large-scale industry the organization of the labour process, in the context of an already existing material system, is the function of a department called 'Methods', or 'Organization and Methods' (O&M). It is at this level that detailed modifications of the means of production are worked out and knowledge is accumulated that will come into its own later, when new systems are installed.

The problem here lies in the fact that the dual determination of the organization of the productive process, technological and social, can be grasped only by means of the analysis of concrete production conditions. But these conditions always appear as if already given and predetermined, in their essential features, outside the sphere of immediate production. The technological imperative that dictates the organization of production operates in economic and cultural conditions that are historically determined according to a logic and on the basis of a 'state of science and technology' that are themselves the product of a very long history.

Over the last twenty years American specialists in organizational theory have been developing a systematic critique of the so-called technological imperative in the organization of production. Echoes of old polemics come up in this quotation from Louis Davis, Professor of Industrial Engineering at Berkeley, writing in 1960:

> [Harvey] Swados (1959) indicates that industry cannot satisfy both the needs of attaining high productivity and the aspirations of human beings employed in the production system. He raises the question of whether our society can afford the consequences of lower productivity which may result from putting people before production. The job design studies challenge this assertion because of its essential assumption that production technology is inviolate and its present organization and translation into jobs is the only one possible. Wide latitude appears to be available in organizing production technology, given adequate decision rules. The needs are for determining the decision rules and needed inclusive criteria for determining organizational effectiveness. [38]

Davis had argued for some time that specialization had been taken too far and that an increase in productivity could be obtained by a move in the opposite direction. But he saw an obstacle to this in the idea 'implicitly accepted by managers and engineeers, sociologists and psychologists alike' that 'the content of any job within an organization was determined by the needs of the production process, so that the organizational structure could not be changed except to the detriment of its economic efficiency'. [39]

What this critique brings out, indirectly, is the 'ideological' function of technology. Where the division of labour is basically seen as corresponding to an objective necessity, the authority of capital is confused with the authority of technical know-how. We are not claiming that it is perceived as corresponding *only* to that necessity. Under ordinary conditions the controllers of production are not in a position to dissimulate totally to the direct producers the real function of the division of labour, that of organizing their subordination and exploitation in the production process. But they are in a position to dissimulate it to a large extent, at least to the extent that the division does have an objective basis in a technology and in an allocation of technical skills seen as already given. The capitalist division of labour is thus better sheltered from the effects of the class struggle than is the wages system, and serves the function for capital of a second line of defence.

What has to be done is to question this technological imperative in political terms,[40] and to analyse how labour is divided and organized and how the effects of domination are spread across all forms of divided and hierarchized labour, not only through hierarchies of specialization and skill, but also through the economic hierarchy of firms and branches of industry and the hierarchy of the international division of labour.

This questioning belongs within a wider movement of contestation of capitalist science and technology. The ideological unity of this movement is still in doubt. For example, it is not yet clear how to connect the growing struggle against labour conditions with the contestation that is being directed in the first instance against the forms of consumption, the destruction of natural resources or the use of science for military ends.

But there is no doubt that questions of technology are today becoming political at every point in the chain. Lenin once said that the political is the concentrated essence of the economic. It will not take us long to recognize **that the technological is the concentrated essence of the political.**

The basic problem raised by Taylor is still present for capitalism today: how to impose 'real subordination' on the direct producers. Taylor was the first to raise this problem *in a scientific manner*. If the particular solutions that he reached – the system that goes under the name Taylorism – was determined by the technical, economic and cultural conditions of the age he lived in, nevertheless, in the eyes of its ideologues, his objectives and his methods are as eternal as capitalism itself.

'The age that we live in is no longer Taylor's,' say our friends, the modernizers. 'The economic and cultural standards of the workers have risen greatly. The claims of democracy are harder and harder to withhold from the sphere of production. The workers no longer accept that freedom ends when they enter the factory gates. These tendencies cannot be checked. New devices are needed. If formal democracy has permitted us, the capitalist class, to maintain political domination over the masses for long periods of history, why should not the subordination of the direct producers in the production process be achieved in similar ways? Not only is this a possibility, but all the evidence goes to show that the control of this impending new democratic revolution will be a crucial political question. It is up to us now to seize the initiative in this field.

In this light, the despotic or democratic form taken by the subordination of labour to capital in the production process is not to be seen as directly determined by the relations of production in the strict sense, nor by technology, any more than the political forms of class domination are completely defined by the class structure of a society.

Thus, too, the opposition between parliamentary political democracy outside and despotism inside the factory is no longer to be seen as a fundamental characteristic of capitalism. More exactly, it no longer corresponds to the economic and ideological imperatives of the centre, and for this reason a democratic revolution in production is perfectly easy to imagine without the central structures being profoundly affected, and above all without any change in relations with the periphery.

If one pushes to the extreme the analogy with political democracy, the conclusion one reaches is roughly this: the despotic forms of subordination of labour to capital in the production process have come to represent obstacles to the free economic and technological development of capitalism. These forms of organization are capitalist only to the extent that they are the historical result of the development of capitalist production. But they have been determined by the relations of production only through the concrete conditions of this historical development. Capitalism began to develop at the centre, and is continuing to develop at the periphery, in economic and ideological conditions that are characteristic of earlier modes of production.[41]

These conditions have been transformed, at the centre, by the development of capitalism itself on a world scale.

At the centre the necessary prior conditions for a change in the forms of subordination have gradually been fulfilled, and the dominant class is aware of the need for such a change. But (if our analogy holds) this is the case only at the centre, since, with rare exceptions, it is only in the imperialist metropoles that formal political democracy has itself taken root.

The need for change makes itself manifest in the eyes of the capitalist class as a result both of the erosion of their authority over the production process and of the seizing up of the mechanisms of reproduction of the ideology on which their authority is founded. In brief, the division of labour and the forms of authority that constitute present-day capitalist organization of production now appear obsolete in terms of the logic of capitalist rationality itself.

NOTES

1 The (standard) Progress Publishers/Lawrence & Wishart, (1961) edn, pp. 175–76. All subsequent page and chapter references to the three volumes of *Capital* are to this edition.

2 Quotations from an article by Doyle in *Management Accounting* (USA) (September 1970), reproduced as an appendix to this text, pp. 94-6 of this volume, and from a private interview with him, recorded at Holland, Michigan.

3 Judson Gooding, 'Blue-Collar Blues on the Assembly Line', *Fortune* (July 1970).

4 *ibid.*

5 High work rhythms can actually go hand in hand with low productivity. Technical breakdowns on the line and a large increase, once a certain threshold is passed, in the proportion of missed or faulty pieces are notorious plagues of the O&M or 'methods' men. Such factors lead to a loss of efficiency that more than compensates for the nominal or expected increase in production.

6 Cf. *The Scanlon Plan*, ed. F. Lesieur (Cambridge, Mass: MIT Press 1968).

7 The 'human relations movement' was developed, with the support of the Roosevelt administration, as a reaction against the traditional theory of management as practised by Taylor, Fayol and others. It can be considered to have begun with the report on Western

Electric by Roethlisberger and Dickson, demonstrating 'the importance of human factors in industry' (cf. Elton Mayo, *Human Problems of an Industrial Civilization* [1933]. The Harvard Business School was founded at about the same time. (The movement was introduced and popularized in France by Georges Friedman, from 1945 onwards.)

8 The firm also has other lesser factories in the United States and in Ireland. Our inquiry was based exclusively on the Holland plant.

9 See the letter from Donnelly to his employees, reproduced in an appendix to this essay, pp. 96-7.

10 Power is up above. It wants to be informed, to have all possible light cast on what is below. It wants to see. It also wants to cast a blinding light so that it itself can't be seen from below.

These metaphors are a way of raising quite concrete questions for analysis, for example that of the function of social science in the power structure, or that of mechanisms of ideological repression of revolt and the neutralization of each single revolt through objectification, statistical generalization, obstruction and so on. These questions, which are of crucial importance for any problematic of 'democracy', are not really gone into in this essay. Here we may observe simply, on the question of the 'democratization' of Donnelly's, a lessening of the opacity of organization from the point of view of those at the bottom.

11 If the direct producers are in a position to discover points where economies can be made, they are usually equally capable of keeping them hushed up. When the work in question is relatively simple and is always carried out in identical conditions the methods people still have a way of calculating the rates at which the job is to be carried out. In practice these rates are really applicable only after a long period of trial and error, which supposes continuous mass production over a longish period. These conditions (and in general the conditions most favourable to the application of strict Taylorism) are apparently all present at Donnelly's. This makes the experiment in 'democratization' there particularly interesting.

12 'The factors that lead to positive job attitudes do so because they satisfy the individual's needs for self-actualization in his work' (*Motivation to Work*, [1959], p. 114). How far is this from the problematic of alienated and unalienated labour?

13 Cf. Deutsch and Krauss, *Theories in Social Psychology* (New York/London: Basic Books 1965), p. 49.

> [These researches] have been useful in explaining some of the differences in behaviour under autocratic and democratic leadership (Lafitt and White, 1943), a difference that was a focus both for Lewin's scientific interests in the study of leadership and group processes and also for his concern about the effects of autocratic governments. [These researches have also allowed us] to explain why workers are usually happier and more productive when they can participate in the decisions which affect their work.... [this work] has helped to stimulate changes in style of leadership in industrial, educational and military groups.

But we are not analysing this work here: our purpose in presenting Likert and Lewin in this way is merely to preface what is in fact a note of general application in regard to the rationality of modern management.

Let us add, for anyone who is interested in the conceptual genealogy of modern management, that Lewin's experimentalist orientation is that of the psychology of form (Lewin was, moreover, a member of the Berlin gestaltist group – here too conceptual kinships can be traced in the institutions and biographies). The gestaltist influence is to be found, for example, in the attention that Donnelly's pays to every aspect that is likely to modify the way in which work and the work environment are perceived – hence the importance of an information system.

14 The very idea of a 'humanization of technology', of a 'more human organization of industrial work', implies the separation of the technical and human elements. Humanism claims that the social organization of industry must change, because it impedes 'a free development of the human personality', because it is contrary to the eternal principles of 1789 and so on. The humanist tradition can play a revolutionary role here. The theorists of management say, more soberly, that it must change because it no longer works.

15 See ch. 9 ('Human asset accounting') of R. Likert, *The Human Organization,* (New York: McGraw Hill 1967), notably p. 146, where Likert talks of 'the necessity of including estimates of the current value of the human organization . . . in all financial reports of a firm'.

16 *One Dimensional Man* (London: Sphere 1968), p. 24. Marcuse continues:

> To be sure, the technical structure and efficacy of the productive and destructive apparatus has been a major instrumentality for subjecting the population to the established division of labour throughout the modern period. Moreover, such integration has always been accompanied by more obvious forms of compulsion: loss of livelihood, the administration of justice, the police, the armed forces. It still is. But in the contemporary period, the technological controls appear to be the very embodiment of Reason for the benefit of all social groups and interests – to such an extent that all contradiction seems irrational and all counteraction impossible [p. 25].

17 Likert, *op. cit.*, pp. 1–2.

18 'The social sciences and their ability to measure human and organizational variables are making possible the extension of this fundamental idea from the organization of the work itself to the problem of building the most productive and satisfying form of human organization for conducting any enterprise' (*New Patterns of Management* [New York: McGraw Hill 1961], p. 3. See appendix 3, below.

19 *ibid.*

20 The person mainly responsible for the 'Job-enrichment Program' at AT&T is none other than Robert N. Ford, mentioned above as a member of the Herzberg school.

21 The liberation of the workers' initiative is institutionalized at AT&T by discussion 'workshops' that bring together workers, supervisors and departmental heads. These workshops include criticism (or 'green light') sessions at which everyone, whatever his or her level in the hierarchy, freely discusses the labour process in the department.

22 For a detailed analysis of some of these experiments see Yves Delamotte, 'Recherches en vue d'une organisation plus humaine du travail industriel', *La Documentation française* (1972).

23 'The division of labour within the society brings into contact independent commodity-producers, who acknowledge no other authority but that of competition' (*Capital,* I, p. 356).

24 'But what is it that forms the bond between the independent labours of the cattle-breeder, the tanner and the shoemaker? It is the fact that their respective products are commodities. What, on the other hand, characterises division of labour in manufactures? The fact that the detail labourer produces no commodities. It is only the common product of all the detail labourers that becomes a commodity' (*ibid.*, pp. 354–5).

25 *ibid.*, III, ch. 51, p. 881. The paragraph continues:

> This authority reaches its bearers, however, only as the personification of the conditions of labour in contrast to labour, and not as political or theocratic rulers as under earlier modes of production. Among the bearers of this authority, the capitalists themselves, who confront one another only as commodity owners, there reigns complete anarchy within which the social inter-relations of production assert themselves only as an overwhelming natural law in relation to individual free will.

26 See the footnote on umbrellas on p. 355 of *Capital*, I.

27 For example the productive unit that is no longer capable of holding its own against 'outside' competition will be shut down or its work will be contracted out, in the same way as one might change one's supplier.

28 We are dealing here with capitalist relations of production as defined in the second and third parts of *Capital*, I, before the introduction of the concepts of relative surplus-value and division of labour in part 4.

29 It is not a question merely of the materiality of the product. Most non-material services are the result of largely material processes. Still less is it a question of the intellectual and manual aspects of labour, the predominance of one or the other being a characteristic of the functions of an already divided process.

30 Example quoted by Leclère in *Les Méthodes d'organisation et d'engineering*.

31 See André Gorz's essay 'Technology technicians and class struggle' in this book.

32 Since 1968 the *Cahiers du Mai* have done more than any other militant group in France to follow up this 'theoretical and practical exploration'. See the 'Dossier sur la division entre travail manuel et travail intellectual', *Cahiers du Mai*, XXXVIII (November 1972).

33 From Marx's economic MSS of 1861–5. Sections of these MSS were published in Moscow in the *Arkhiv Marksa i Engelsa*, II (vii) (1933), and republished in French in the Pléiade Edition of Marx's works, ed. Maximilien Rubel. This quotation is on p. 379 of vol. II of the French edition. 'Formal and real subordination' translates Marx's proposed category in the MSS of 'Formelle und reale Subsumption der Arbeit unter das Kapital'.

34 Marx observes that during the manufacturing period 'capital is constantly compelled to wrestle with the insubordination of the workmen' and throughout the whole period 'there runs the complaint of want of discipline' (*Capital*, I, ch. 14, p. 367). It is with industrialism proper that capital *really* subordinates the direct producers by means of a completely objective and impersonal productive organism (*ibid.*, ch. 15, sec. 1). Insubordination becomes 'irrational', and therefore individual, and no longer constitutes a political category.

35 On the origin and function of hierarchical organization in capitalist production see the remarkable study by Stephen Marglin, 'What do bosses do?' (A French translation of this essay appeared in the French edition of this present volume; it is excluded from this English edition for copyright reasons, and has not yet appeared in English.) Marglin observes that the hierarchical organization of production did not begin with capitalism and he analyses what distinguishes capitalist hierarchy from precapitalist forms.

However Marx notes that in capitalist society 'there is no politically and socially fixed relationship of supremacy and subordination ... To the extent that there is subordination, it derives from the specific content of the sale [of labour power] and not from a subordination prior to the sale.' (From the MSS notes on subordination, p. 370. See n. 33, above.)

Capitalism has, in fact, destroyed the bonds of personal dependence and has deprived economic authority of any religious or political character. (See n. 25, above.)

The term 'hierarchy' is of ecclesiastical origin and derives from Greek *hieros* (sacred) and *arché* (command). The root word *arché* means origin, principle, beginning, and subsequently power, command, authority. 'Anarchy' is the absence of *arché*. Similarly the words 'authority', 'author' and so on are cognate with the Sanskrit *ojas*, indicating the power of the gods. Benveniste notes (*Vocabulaire des institutions indo-européennes*): 'Obscure and powerful values dwell in this "auctoritas", this gift reserved to few to bring something into being and, literally, to produce existence.'

36 The privileged role of large-scale industry in the theory of scientific socialism is well known. An example can be found in Lenin's *The Immediate Tasks of the Soviet Government*, written in 1918. (Page references are to the three-volume edition of *Selected*

Works, II, already referred to. The number in square brackets that follows give the page from the *Collected Works*, based on the 4th Russian edn, vol. XXVII. Italics Lenin's.)

'In every socialist revolution, after the proletariat has solved the problem of capturing power . . . there necessarily comes to the forefront the fundamental task of creating a social system superior to capitalism, namely, raising the productivity of labour, and in this connection (and for this purpose) securing better organization of labour' (p. 662 [257]).

'The victory of socialism is inconceivable without the victory of proletarian conscious discipline over spontaneous petty-bourgeois anarchy' (p. 663 [258]).

'Large-scale machine industry – which is precisely the material source, the productive source, the foundation of socialism – calls for absolute and strict *unity of will,* which directs the joint labours of hundreds, thousands and tens of thousands of people. The technical, economic and historical necessity of this is obvious, and all those who have thought about socialism have always regarded it as one of the conditions of socialism. But how can strict unity of will be ensured? By thousands subordinating their will to the will of one' (pp. 672–3 [268–9]).

'*Unquestioning subordination* to a single will is absolutely necessary for the success of processes organized on the pattern of large-scale machine industry . . . Today the revolution demands – precisely in the interests of its development and consolidation, precisely in the interests of socialism – that the people *unquestioningly obey the single will* of the leaders of labour' (p. 673 [269]).

These quotations call for an observation and a question. a) They are taken from a polemical text produced, as is emphasized in the notes for the first draft, 'in an extremely critical and even desperate situation with regard to ensuring the subsistence of the greater part of the population'. As always, Lenin insists strongly on what he considers to be the principal danger of the moment. The persistence of anarchy in production could only lead inevitably to the collapse of soviet power and the triumph of counter-revolution. b) How are the statements quoted above to be reconciled with the Leninist theory of mass initiative, the withering away of the State etc? We cannot go into the question here, but would like to draw attention to another quotation from the same text: 'We must learn to combine the "public meeting" democracy of the working people – turbulent, surging, overflowing its banks like a spring flood – with *iron* discipline while at work, with *unquestioning obedience* to the will of a single person, the Soviet leader, while at work. We do not yet know how to do this. We shall learn' (p. 675 [271]).

37 In French *la pratique de l'engineering*. In order to render this quaint piece of franglais we have taken certain liberties with the text.

38 Louis E. Davis and Richard Werling, 'Job Design Factors', in *Occupational Psychology*, XXXIV: 2 (1960), pp. 109–32.

39 Louis E. Davis, 'Job Design and Productivity: a New Approach', *Personnel*, XXX (1957), p. 418.

40 The political questioning of western technology is opened up (from several angles simultaneously) in *One Dimensional Man*. See, on the new technological world of labour ('the containment of social change'), pp. 34–52; on the technological forms of social control ('total administration'), pp. 91–102; on the complicity of technological rationality and political power ('from negative to positive thinking'), pp. 120–38; on the necessity of a new technology ('the catastrophe of liberation'), pp. 178–93.

41 Just as today it can develop in the ideological and institutional conditions of socialism.

Appendix 1

'New Methods of Management'
by Robert J. Doyle*

THE PROBLEM:

1. Most companies presently underutilize the mental and human capabilities of the bulk of their work force which, if employed, could contribute much to the success of the enterprise.

2. Most employees feel that they do not receive an equitable share of the benefits of the enterprise.

3. Most employees neither trust nor respect their industrial leaders. They feel that labour has been viciously exploited in the past and only the presence of a strong union and the threat of strike is keeping things on an even keel. Similarly most managers neither trust nor respect people they employ to do the work.

The Scanlon plan has been called a labour-management co-operative plan, a labour costs savings plan and a group incentive plan. But it is **actually a Better Management Plan, it is a better way to manage a firm.** Its application is not too complex. Perhaps it is so simple, we do not trust it.

The plan goes like this: in a firm employing 500 people, usually 10 per cent or 50 of the 500 do the thinking work and 450 do the sweating work. In a Scanlon Plan the effort is made to reduce the sweating work and get the 500 doing thinking work . . . 'Work smarter, not harder.'

Talk to *everyone;* tell him what the problems are, that management genuinely wants *everyone* on board and helping to balance the system.

Let everyone question what management is doing until they can begin to trust their sincerity. This is easier to say than to do. Managers are not used to having their plans and decisions questioned but if progress is to be made they must let these discussions happen. At this point, if management gives any brush off answers, or tries to bluff their way through a question, they will blow the whole deal. If a difficult question is raised, it should not be answered until the correct answer is found and then it should be told straight. If management handles this step well, they are in for a terrific education. They will find an understanding of the operation of the business among the 450 that they never thought existed.

Assuming that everyone is with you, get to work. Drag out your list of problems and get everyone interested help solve them. Develop a structure to handle new ideas and suggestions as they come up.

Traditionally, the structure is a two-level committee. The Production Committee is made up of the first-level supervision and representatives elected by the employees. This committee receives suggestions and engages in first-level production problem solving.

* Extracts taken from 'A New Look at the Scanlon Plan', *Management Accounting*, Sept. 1970.

Suggestions should be processed as quickly as possible. They should be put into effect or returned to the suggestor with reasons for not being accepted. Here is where the 450 find out how serious you are about their participation. If the janitor's suggestion is treated with as much respect and dispatch as one from the president, the reaction will be, 'By George, they really mean it.' If not, you simply do not have a Scanlon Plan.

Beyond the Production Committee, there is a Screening Committee made up of other elected representatives or delegates from the Production Committees and top management. This committee looks at overall company progress and problems. It resolves suggestions that are too big or too involved to handled at the lower level.

These committees are working groups that solve problems and make plans. They are formal embodiments of the principle of participation.

At this point, many managers will say, 'That's a pretty good theory, Charlie, but let's be practical. The average guy and gal in the shop has no interest beyond getting a paycheck for the least amount of time and effort.' And for this manager, there is no retort except, 'How can you be sure of this, if you have never tried another approach?'

George Bernard Shaw said, 'The exercise of power is delightful and absolute power is absolutely delightful.' This is probably true, but how long can we allow 10 per cent of our economic community to enjoy this delight at the expense of the 90 per cent? How long can our political democracy stand the 70,000,000 who live the majority of their waking hours in an atmosphere that is totalitarian?

IF YOU APPLY THESE PRINCIPLES:

1. You have everyone (the 500) aware of the nature, status, problems and plans of the enterprise in which they are employed.

2. You have changed practically everyone's attitude toward the management of the firm. Formerly everyone thought that there were two, or perhaps three, classes of employment . . . doers and thinkers, (if you had three classes, the third was 'superthinkers'). Now you have one class – managers, because everyone is committed to and actively involved in managing the enterprise to higher goals and greater accomplishments.

3. Employees at every level are learning new skills. Top-level managers are learning how to involve more personnel in the solution of problems. Lower-level managers are learning how to participate more fully in the total work of the enterprise.

4. You are beginning to see results that you never thought possible. People who formerly were apathetic toward the company are now engaging in constructive problem solving with supervisors and department heads. And to everyone's benefit problems are being solved. Most Scanlon Plans have suggestion records that far exceed the suggestion box and individual award system. Costs are holding the line or going down and production per unit of investment is going up.

5. Everyone associated with the enterprise is being rewarded for his new

initiative. Employees of the firm from president to janitor are earning a cash bonus monthly. Because company earnings are increasing, it is possible to pay higher dividends, increase capital investment, expand facilities, increase services (such as R & D, engineering, training), and expand market activities (such as advertising).

6. In addition to increased economic rewards, everyone is enjoying the whole affair more. Dick Arthur the Executive Vice-President of Donnelly Mirrors, Inc. expressed it this way: 'We are in business to make a profit. There are two ways to do this. The first and more traditional makes profit at the expense of human dignity and personal satisfaction. The second, which we have learned through our Scanlon Plan experience, does so in a way that enhances human dignity and increases personal satisfaction.'

BUT THERE ARE OBSTACLES:

The greatest pitfall facing a company wishing to install the Scanlon Plan is to underestimate the process of changing the attitudes and habits of managers who are used to traditional management ... The modern manager who is not looking into what this science can offer him in managing his business is playing a very dangerous game with the future of his company.

Competition has never been kind to the mossback manager or to the company that has developed hardening of the managerial arteries, but it would seem that in 1970 with profit margins slimmer than in 1928, with younger, better educated, more mobile employees, with more complex technology and distribution, it could be even more unkind.

Change can be delayed for a while, but not resisted forever.

Appendix 2

Letter to Employees, January 1969,
by John F. Donnelly *

What is a work team? How does the work team idea fit with the Scanlon Plan and the Grid and the ICLS survey? Whose team am I in?

A work team is simply a boss and the people who work directly with him. It can be a foreman and his operators, or an executive president and his division managers. It could also be a special task team set up to solve a problem or guide a new product from development to sale and first production.

The difference between the notion of a work team and the old boss-subordinate relationship is the idea of a team. This puts to one side the old assumption that the boss knows all and should give the orders and see that they are carried out. On the contrary, it says everyone on the work

* From *The Donnelly Mirror*, Jan. 1969

team has some special knowledge about the work done by his team. So when plans need to be made or problems need solving, he should have an opportunity to speak his piece.

So what's new about this? Joe Scanlon said this thirty years ago. True, he did, but the structure of committees that Scanlon set up was not quite ambitious enough to involve all the people in the company, nor to cover all its problems. He had basically the right idea – that everyone has something important to say. At the time when he said this he sounded like a revolutionary. To most people he still does. So he had to move cautiously. The committees that he recommended were about all any company would accept at that time.

Where his ideas have been tried out, people have found that a wider structure of committees, or as we now call them, 'teams', should be set up so that everyone gets a chance to learn and contribute and that all the resulting ideas can be co-ordinated.

This does not mean the Scanlon committees are useless or should be discontinued. Rather we should be looking to strengthen and supplement them.

Another new feature regarding work teams is the training program called work team development. A part of the Managerial Grid, which helps the teams to work more smoothly and effectively.

A third novelty is the idea of 'overlapping teams'. The head of each team is also a member of his boss' team. He links the two teams and provides communications upward and downward.

The team concept has a fourth advantage. A person dealing with his boss as a member of a team finds it more comfortable to talk about problems, especially controversial ones, than he would on a one to one basis. He gains support from his teammates. Beyond this is the fact that one person's idea sparks ideas in others, so that the solution arrived at comes closer to being a total solution.

So the work team development program is a 'next step' in the Scanlon Plan. . . .
Sincerely,
Signed: John F. Donnelly

Appendix 3

'On Modern Management'
*by Rensis Likert**

[On the basis of the management practices of those who hold the best records of performance in American business and government, and with the aid of the social sciences, it is now possible to formulate a general

* Extracts taken from *New Patterns of Management* (New York): McGraw Hill 1961).

theory of efficient organization.]

Important forces and resources are accelerating this new development. Others are delaying it. One of the accelerating forces likely to grow in importance in the United States is the competition from the industrially developed countries throughout the world. We are already experiencing this competition and are apt to feel its effects even more acutely in the next decade. Other highly developed countries are using modern industrial technology with skills approaching ours and in some instances equal to ours. With lower labour and salary costs and other lower fixed costs, they can compete with us in world markets on very favourable terms. One way of holding a satisfactory share of the market, domestically and abroad, will be to increase the productivity of our enterprises.

[This increased productivity can be obtained by developing new forms of social organization.]

People are less willing to accept pressure and close supervision than was the case a decade or two ago. . . . The trend in our schools, in our homes and in our communities, is toward giving the individual greater freedom and initiative. There are fewer direct, unexplained orders in schools and homes, and youngsters are participating increasingly in decisions which affect them.

These fundamental changes in American society create expectations among the employees as to how they should be treated. Expectations profoundly affect employee attitudes, since attitudes depend upon the extent to which experiences meet our expectations. If experiences falls short of expectations, unfavourable attitudes occur. When our experience is better than our expectations, we tend to have favourable attitudes. This means, of course, that if expectations in America are changing in a particular direction, experience must change in the same direction and at the same or at a greater rate. Otherwise, the attitudinal response of people to their experience will be unfavourable.

[The educational level of the labour force is increasing considerably, and as people acquire more education their expectations rise as to the amount of responsibility, authority and income they will receive.]

Coupled with the cultural trend in American homes, schools, and communities is an increasing concern about mental health and an emphasis on the growth of individuals into healthy, emotionally mature adults. These developments are also creating pressures in business and government which may well lead to important changes in the management system. Argyris has a volume devoted to the dilemma which management faces in endeavouring to adhere to accepted management principles and at the same time to fulfil the personality needs of the emotionally mature people which our homes and schools are trying hard to produce. . . .

Several decades ago Taylor (1911) pointed to the fact that human variability in performance could be used to discover better ways of doing work. The social sciences and their capacity to measure human and organizational variables are making possible the extension of this fundamental idea from the organization of the work itself to the problem of building the most productive and satisfying form of human organization for conducting any enterprise.

(Managers who achieve the best performances today — greater productivity, higher profits — differ from those achieving poorer performance in their assumptions about ways of managing people.)

The full significance of the contribution of the high-producing managers to the creation of a better management system is not recognized even by the managers themselves. Each has made his changes gradually over time, often by intuition and, as a consequence, tends not to be entirely aware of the magnitude of the changes he, himself, has introduced. Nor is he fully aware that his improvements and insights and those of other successful managers as well, are beginning to form a general pattern.

Social sciences research is providing systematic evidence that such a pattern is emerging. It is also providing a body of organized data from which a valid statement of this better management system can be made.

Part Two
THE STRUGGLE AGAINST THE CAPITALIST DIVISION OF LABOUR

MARCO MACCIÓ
Party, Technicians, and Working Class in the Chinese Revolution*

1 CONSTRUCTION OF SOCIALISM AND BOURGEOIS DIVISION OF LABOUR

In the transitional stage from capitalism to communism the triumph of the proletariat or, on the contrary, the resurgence of a bourgeoisie, depends on the domination by one or other of these classes of the technical organization of production and of technico-scientific development. At first the bourgeoisie ensures its ownership of technology and intellectual labour through the bourgeois division of labour and prevents the working class and the broad masses from taking them into their hands. This is achieved by limiting the number of technical colleges and universities, but principally by reducing manual labour to a simple physical work-operation, by preventing co-operation between manual and intellectual labour; and by denying the workers the possibility of utilizing the practical experience acquired in production to take technology and science into their own hands and to ensure the full growth of the productive forces. On the one hand the proletarian revolution must therefore overcome the obstacles imposed by the bourgeoisie on the technico-scientific education of the masses of working people (all socialist revolutions have immediately greatly expanded the educational sector); but on the other hand it must also overcome the bourgeois division of labour that represses the creative energies of the working class and prevents the whole people from actively participating in the development of the productive forces, by taking science and technology into their own hands.

The bourgeoisie enforces its division of labour because this is one of the two basic sources of its privileges (the other one being private ownership of the means of production). The minority who possess technical skill can demand certain privileges without which they will refuse to work efficiently, the consequences of this attitude having repercussions on the

*This account of the Chinese cultural revolution was originally published in Italian in *Giovane Critica*, XXI. The French version translated here has also appeared in *Les Temps modernes* (August-September 1970). Translated by John McGreal.

whole production of social wealth. Even if it is deprived of the ownership of the means of production the bourgeoisie can hold on to its privileges by maintaining its division of labour, that is, by remaining in control of technology. Bourgeois division of labour and bourgeois privileges are therefore interconnected. Only if technology is in the hands of the whole people is it possible to achieve equality and to put production at the service of the masses.

Consequently, after seizing power the working class cannot limit itself to expropriating the bourgeoisie and abolishing the anarchy of bourgeois production by socialist planning; it must also establish proletarian relations of production. It must take control of the technical organization of production and of technico-scientific development.

After the seizure of power the proletariat cannot abolish the bourgeois division of labour by a simple act of will. In fact this division of labour has *really* given the bourgeoisie competence in technical work and the workers competence only in performing manual labour. Nevertheless the working class, with its broad mass of skilled workers, would be able to begin immediately the long process aiming to establish proletarian relations of production, which would clearly immediately provoke a bitter class conflict with bourgeois technicians. But if, as in the Soviet Union and in China, the working class is very much in a minority and there are very few skilled workers, the process of transforming the relations of production must be postponed. The communist leadership must then make use of bourgeois technicians to develop the socialist economy. It is therefore understandable that the socialist societies have at the beginning maintained a fundamental element of capitalist society: the bourgeois division of labour. However one fact must be explained: why, in all the socialist countries with the exception of China, has the classic communist programme not been taken up with a view to going beyond the bourgeois division of labour once an advanced stage of industrialization has been reached? Why, in certain cases, has this division of labour even been strengthened?

The fundamental problem in the construction of socialism is to develop the socialist economy by making use of bourgeois technicians, while at the same time progressively increasing working-class control over the technical organization of production. It is a matter of a difficult and complex programme, but one that must be carried out consciously and resolutely. The proletariat must seize every opportunity to push forward its policy of transformation of the relations of production; and in times of retreat it must be capable of limiting the damage in order to safeguard its ultimate objectives.

During the period of construction of socialism the organized vanguard of the proletariat, the Communist Party, must pay the greatest attention to:

1) the relations it establishes with bourgeois technical workers, as well as with the new technical workers trained in socialist schools; in fact the attitude of the latter with respect to their work and to the working class

will delay or advance the start of the process of going beyond the bourgeois division of labour;

2) the relations it establishes with the working class; in fact the total adherence of the working class to the new socialist society is essential to launching the process of transformation towards proletarian relations of production.

2 SOCIALIST TRANSFORMATION OF THE ECONOMY AND BOURGEOIS DIVISION OF LABOUR

After seizing power the proletariat is faced with an economy that is still capitalist and must be socialized without precipitating a crisis. After the liberation in China (1949) two lines developed in the Communist Party. On the right Liu Shao-chi advocated conceding full guarantees of development to capitalism, provided that the bourgeoisie concerned itself with the development of production. But it was the left line that prevailed.

The Party socialized the large capitalist enterprises (coal, steel, railways) and placed in the most important managerial posts *reliable communist personnel who were able to exercise direct control over the enterprises.* These were cadres trained within the revolutionary bases. Without them the Party would have had to call in representatives from the People's Army, who would have exercised only *indirect control.* It would then have encountered enormous difficulties in running the large socialized enterprises.

To this control exercised by reliable communist cadres was added a policy tending to put higher-ranking technical and administrative bourgeois personnel in an *economic position that gradually accustomed them to a lessening of their privileges* and former powers.

However the Party did not have at its disposal an unlimited reserve of communist cadres immediately able to replace the bourgeois administrative and technical experts, particularly in the small and medium-sized enterprises. Now this productive sector was important because it supplied the towns and, above all, the peasants, with whom the Party had to be able to maintain a solid alliance. For a transitional period the Party therefore preferred to entrust the management of small and medium-sized industries to capitalists. But it was necessary to rid the national bourgeoisie of any illusion about capitalism becoming stronger in the future. The Party therefore concentrated all its efforts on the socialization of trade. On the one hand it was a question of cutting the capitalists' economic links with the peasants by setting up peasant marketing co-operatives in the countryside and state trading departments in the towns; on the other hand the market relations between the capitalist enterprises themselves had to be cut by the creation of trading departments with the task of distributing raw materials or semi-manufactured products before they were processed according to precise instructions.

The Party had anticipated that the bourgeoisie would react against the measures socializing trade and it *acted so that capitalist profit would not be too low.* Some of the bourgeoisie nevertheless ceased to care for productivity, (i.e. the cost of the products): they expected the State to continue to pay them a fixed percentage in addition to the cost price.

In general the Chinese economy developed fairly well during this period, in spite of worsening wastage, fraud and corruption because the bourgeois managers could not be completely deprived of their decision-making power and were not adequately controlled. So the Party fell back on a second method of control: control exercised by the base, by the workers who *reported the numerous deficiencies that stemmed from the lack of interest and the corruption of the bourgeois managers:* very strong pressure was thus put on the latter's conduct.

3 PRIVILEGES AND CONTROLS

After the seizure of power the proletariat is confronted by a profound contradiction: *just at the time when it is striking at the economic power of the bourgeoisie by restricting its privileges, the proletariat has to secure from the same bourgeoisie its co-operation in organizing production, administration and the development of technology.* But if the capitalists, transformed into salaried staff, and the other bourgeois managerial staff are deprived of their privileges, their work efficiency deteriorates to the extent of injuring the country's economy. *Moreover even if privileges are maintained as a reward for efficient work, the proletariat must be in a position to exercise control so as to prevent continued wastage and corruption.* The proletariat must therefore have a sufficient number of reliable communist cadres to take some of the basic decisions away from the bourgeois personnel to exercise control over the bourgeois technicians' degree of efficiency and to expose corruption. But this control is not enough; its success also depends on the control exercised by the base, by the workers.

4 TRAINING OF SOCIALIST OR BOURGEOIS TECHNICIANS?

In the first period the relations of production are characterized by the maintenance of the bourgeois division of labour, the privileges conceded to the bourgeois technicians and the control of their work efficiency exercised by the Party and the masses. At the beginning of the second period of planned industrialization, proletarian policy is presented with a favourable opportunity: *to train technicians with socialist consciousness.* In fact industrial expansion makes evident a great shortage of technicians and this must be overcome as quickly as possible by a policy of training thousands of technicians in socialist schools.

After the liberation in China the basic principles of the new type of schools (15 per cent of the total) were introduced into the traditional type of schools run by bourgeois teachers. These principles referred to the 'necessity for the working people to take science, technology and culture into their own hands', and to the necessity of 'creating intellectuals of a new type who belong to the working class'.

Students were therefore selected from among those sons of workers and peasants who had a revolutionary consciousness by virtue of having taken part in three great mass movements: anti-corruption, anti-misappropriation and agrarian reform. The students showed their class-consciousness by helping one another in their studies, by displaying neither submissiveness before the abstract power of the teachers nor contempt for the labour of workers and peasants. ('If students attend courses in the factories, they work with the workers instead of being satisfied with looking on and taking notes.') But the running of the schools remained in the hands of bourgeois intellectuals; the students therefore rebelled against incompetent teachers ('they cannot solve practical problems'), against the speciousness of examination questions and against the domination of teachers responsible for the courses.

From 1953, the date of the first Five-Year Plan, the right-wing tendency in the CCP grew progressively stronger in education. The demands of rapid industrialization, which required the training of numerous technicians as quickly as possible, favoured the right-wing of the CCP, which proposed a radical transformation of education. This transformation was to follow the same path as the Soviet system in the thirties: polytechnic education had been abandoned; the importance given to competition between students, to marks and to exams had been restored; the teacher's supremacy over the students had been reinstated; finally the idea that the factory partly replaces certain school functions had been abandoned.

In the end this political line prevailed: from 1953 to 1954 a new educational system was progressively organized. Its characteristics can be summarized as follows:

a) admission to colleges on the basis of strict selection to avoid 'inadmissible wastage' and to avoid having 'backward students' at differing levels of education who were therefore difficult to teach; the apparent impartiality of the entrance examination therefore meant objectively that the colleges were closed to children of workers and peasants, while students attending urban middle schools, chiefly the children of the bourgeoisie, were favoured;

b) the principles of selection determined the syllabus, which included a great many subjects that were often too abstract and therefore particularly difficult to assimilate;

c) the student was thus induced to concentrate unduly on his studies, seeking only to obtain 'good marks' and to pass exams; he was satisfied with ideas learned by heart, retired into his books and withdrew from politics; he aspired to a career, to prestige (to be better than the others) and finally to economic privileges; the personalities formed in this way were individualistic, selfish and élitist; the students considered their intellectual work to be a reward for their superiority and looked down on the manual labour of the industrial worker and the peasant.

These methods of education produce fairly serious consequences: instead of contributing towards the training of technicians of working-class origin, trained in contact with the workers so as to encourage positive attitudes with respect to manual labour, absence of privileges and co-operation with the workers, the right-wing policy organizes a selection system favouring the bourgeoisie and a system of ideological education that retransmits to these students the values of the bourgeoisie.

Instead of isolating the old bourgeois cadres in a rising tide of young technicians of working-class origin, the right-wing education policy gives rise to a flood of bourgeois technicians, and thus deepens the contradiction between proletariat and bourgeoisie.

5 PLANNED ECONOMY AND BOURGEOIS DIVISION OF LABOUR

If, concurrently with planned industrialization, there is no training of skilled technicians who adhere to socialism, and if the workers do not progressively take technology and management into their own hands, a profound contradiction immediately arises at the very centre of the socialist economy: in fact planning, which cannot function effectively within the framework of the bourgeois division of labour, leaves technology in the possession of a minority of specialists.

In a system of planned economy the relations of exchange between the enterprises do not depend on the market but on the operation of the plan. This means that the management of the enterprises do not have to concern themselves with purchasing, sales, selling prices or wages. It is the planners who provide the funds necessary for wages and future investments, and who decide on the suppliers and clients of the enterprises. Managers have to concern themselves with one thing only: the production in a specified time of a given quantity of goods, fixed by the central plan. If all enterprises carry out the specified plan correctly, the economy as a whole will advance without difficulties: all enterprises will be stocked in time and will supply the client enterprises. The mark of success in a socialist enterprise is not profit but success in meeting production targets as specified in the central plan; this is the criterion on the basis of which the ability of enterprise managers is assessed.

But if the economic process is to develop without difficulty it is not enough for each enterprise to carry out the plan: it is also necessary *to ensure the quality, durability and variety of products.* These important factors of economic development do not always lend themselves to control by a central planning organization or by bodies to which local control has been delegated; in fact it is impossible to establish quantitative indices for quality and variety of products.

Only the client and commercial enterprises can control the quality of products, as well as their durability and variety. So if planning is to work well enterprises must co-operate actively among themselves and client enterprises must be able to exercise controls over the output of the supplying enterprises and to specify requirements for them. In other words, planning requires a degree of decentralization and local autonomy.

Yet this co-operation and autonomy can work, only if the working class collectively gains control of the technical organization of production and technical development. If, on the other hand, management and technology remain in the hands of a minority of specialists, the latter, a privileged group, tend not to be concerned about the quality of the output of their own enterprises or about that of their suppliers. In fact these aspects of production cannot be effectively controlled either by the central planning bodies or by the local supervisory bodies. The technicians are concerned only with the quantitative aspect of production, precisely because it is easier to control. They even use the qualitative aspects of production as a kind of safety net: they tend to lower quality in order to meet the quantitative production targets more easily.

In the period when the plan is being prepared it is in the manager's interest to give the lowest possible estimate of the productive capacity of the plant. In this way he can obtain lower quantitative production quotas from the planning centre. It is also in his interest to keep the amount by which output exceeds the planned target for the year as low as possible, so as not to incur an excessive increase in the target the following year. If the target is expressed quantitatively in tons, for example, it is in the enterprise's interest to make the unit product heavier so as to be able to produce a smaller number of them. In which case raw materials are used in excessive quantities. If the target is expressed in square metres then priority is given to the most lightweight models, and this has damaging consequences for the range of production. It is in the manager's interest to neglect the quality of the product, because this requires more careful and therefore slower work and consequently prevents him from attaining the quantitative quotas; the introduction of technological innovations is also considered to be disadvantageous because they always constitute a risk, and in all cases bring about a drop in production for a short while.

Centralized planning within the framework of the bourgeois division of labour is therefore responsible for mediocrity in the quality of products, especially in the engineering industry, as a result of wastage of raw materials, low levels of utilization of plant and a range of products that fails to meet the requirements of the customers, whether they are industries or consumers. There can even be a significant slowing down of technological progress.

In the Soviet Union, as in China, this did not in any way prevent industrialization from undergoing vigorous development. It must be remembered, however, that the principle according to which absolute economic priority had to be given to heavy industry allowed all shortcomings in production to fall back on other sectors – agriculture and light industry. It is therefore difficult to calculate the degree of inefficiency, wastage and delay suffered by industrialization for the reasons mentioned. In any case it is certain that the more serious the phenomenon, the more planning tends to become centralized and to develop a bureaucratic apparatus of control. The efficiency of this bureaucratic apparatus, which is at all events fairly low, depends on the economic possibility of granting privileges to the technicians, on the competence of communist cadres, on their numbers and on the degree of control that the masses themselves are in a position to exercise.

When the communist cadres are cut off among a mass of bourgeois managers, technicians and administrators whom it is difficult to control, and when control by the masses is inadequate, *bureaucratism inevitably develops*. By this I mean a type of political control that inflates the non-productive administrative apparatus and is unable to put production back on its feet and to abolish corruption. It is generally said that **bureaucratism aggravates the disease it claims to cure because it makes** heavier the work of organization and administration; but those who hold this view forget to emphasize that the disease is not static but becomes worse spontaneously. In certain situations bureaucratism is therefore only a lesser evil and is born of a necessity that it would be idealistic to deny.

Centralization and bureaucratism certainly played a more important part during the period of Soviet industralization than in the corresponding period in China. In any event the shortcomings we have pointed out seriously jeopardized economic development only when the construction of socialism switched from the stage of *extensive* economic development – based on an increase in the number of factories and machines – to *intensive* development – based on technological renewal of plant and qualitative improvements in production. If technology remains in the hands of a small number of technicians whose work cannot be adequately controlled, intensive development will be brought to a halt.

For different reasons this is what happened in the Soviet Union and in China round about the 1960s. In China this situation brought home the urgent need for a change in the relations of production in a proletarian direction, but it also brought a radically opposed political line out into the open. In fact if the ownership of technology by a minority is consolidated in the period of construction of socialism, then the project of abandoning the planning system in favour of a system that bestows greater authority on managers and experts is thereby simultaneously strengthened. We shall see later that this solution is a bourgeois solution in defence of particular material interests; the struggle between this line and the proletarian line will be a bitter one, a genuine class struggle.

6 ACCELERATED INDUSTRIALISATION AND THE WORKING CLASS

In order to be able to carry through to the end the political struggle for the development of new relations of production, the Party must be supported by the working class with a high level of proletarian consciousness. In socialist countries that are in the process of industrialization it is therefore of the greatest importance that the working class should develop its skills and technical competence while fully maintaining its adherence to socialism. In fact it must participate in industrialization through production, co-operate with the Party to control the technicians' efficiency at work and develop a sufficiently strong proletarian consciousness to be able to take science and technology into its own hands.

Workers' adherence to socialism depends on a progressive increase in their standard of living, control of work conditions and the ideological action of advanced communist workers.

If, as in China and the Soviet Union, the proletariat lacked sufficient skills to take production and technology into its hands immediately after seizing power, it was perfectly capable of enforcing its control over the conditions of direct labour. It deprived the capitalists of their right to fix work norms, rejected the foremen appointed by the bosses and replaced them with those it had itself elected, and abolished searches on leaving work, dismissals, fines and so on. Finally, it prescribed increases leading to greater egalitarianism.

At the same time the communist vanguard began the task of ideological clarification with the rest of the proletariat: the factories are the property of the people and must produce to satisfy social needs; what is produced by the worker and is not immediately distributed must be used for expansion of production and future improvement in living conditions and so on.

The Party and communist vanguards launched competitive campaigns between the factories and workshops and campaigns for the selection of vanguard workers in production. Communist vanguard workers were directly involved in this socialist-type competition. In fact they must set an example so as to bring the other strata of the working class round to their positions; the task is a difficult one, requiring a spirit of sacrifice because the material incentives are very small, for the workers as well as the vanguard groups.

Accelerated industrialization is not compatible with raising the standard of living. In fact it requires the workers to dedicate their energies to the accelerated construction of basic industries rather than to the production of consumer goods.

But if the whole of the working class was employed in heavy industry the standard of living in the towns would very quickly drop. The production of consumer goods and housing construction would remain at a standstill in the face of an increasing number of workers; individual consumption would have to fall. The planners therefore try to direct some of the new working class into the production of consumer goods to ensure at least a steady standard of living in the towns.

If the process of industrialization does not undergo a serious crisis the majority of the working class continues to adhere to work for the construction of socialism. However major crises easily occur, especially in agriculture, as much through climatic hazards as through the change from family farming to co-operatives.

A crisis in the agricultural sector leads to a reduction in workers' basic consumption and often to rationing. It is sometimes necessary to reduce the number of workers employed. But to avoid checking industrialization an attempt is made to lay off only workers in light industry. The situation thus deteriorates and even the strata with the most highly developed proletarian consciousness tend to become passive because their standard of living continues to fall. Of course as long as they remain in control of working conditions the workers do not oppose socialism; but indiscipline at work, absenteeism, lateness, a fall in output and so on become widespread.

This is what happened in the Soviet Union in the thirties. The agricultural crisis broke out in the third year of the Five-Year-Plan and with it the workers' real wages fell sharply. Indiscipline at work and turnover of employment assumed disastrous proportions, with workers moving from factory to factory, from mine to mine and from town to town. In the Donetz Basin, for example, 432,000 workers left the mines in 1932 and 458,000 were taken on.

The Party therefore had to find other means to gain the support of the masses. The rate of investment could not be reduced, because once it was under way the industrialization plan could not easily be altered. The Party could no longer allow the masses to decide for themselves which sacrifices they were prepared to accept: the construction of socialism would have depended on the workers' will, which is not necessarily favourable to planning.

The Party therefore reacted to the indiscipline and to the fall in productivity by introducing piece-work, wage differentials and penalization of absentee workers (loss of ration cards and accommodation rights; pension reductions; eviction from lodgings; transfers to less well-paid jobs; and dismissals).

During the first six or seven years of industrialization in China (1953–8) there was no agricultural disaster; the workers' standard of living slowly improved and the productivity of industrial output rose. The Party was not compelled to introduce piece-work and with a few exceptions it was thus able to maintain relations of distribution in the factories akin to the socialist principle of, 'to each according to his work'. Manual workers were paid more than white-collar workers, skilled workers were paid approximately the same as staff unconnected with production. But staff connected with production were paid more than all the other categories.

In the second place the workers had the power to elect their shop foremen, to organize the work in the shop themselves, to decide on the allocation of production bonuses and so on. In the third place the Party called meetings to consult the base in order to discuss collectively the particular problems of each enterprise and the solutions proposed by the managing body.

During the stage of industrialization the Chinese working class therefore retained an attitude of support for socialism, a spirit of sacrifice and an acceptance of hard work, and a level of class consciousness that was absent in the Soviet working class. The possibilities for establishing proletarian relations of production were therefore widely preserved.

7 TOWARDS THE UTILIZATION OF ALL THE MATERIAL AND INTELLECTUAL ENERGIES OF THE MASSES

At the beginning of the second Chinese Five-Year Plan (1958) the necessity for a 'great leap forward' in agricultural production made itself felt anew. Many new industrial plants were to come into operation (in the metal working industries in particular) and the number of people in employment therefore had to increase appreciably.

On the other hand even though agriculture still had serious structural weaknesses (lack of mechanization and dependence on climate), it was still necessary to ensure an agricultural supply sufficient for the increasing number of industrial workers, to avoid bringing about a crisis in the process of industrialization itself. It was therefore necessary to economize as much as possible by struggling against wastage and inefficiency, and most of all, by trying to mobilize all the latent energies of the masses (particularly non-utilized working-days), as well as their latent intellectual energies (control of production and mastery of technical development by the workers, and development of small-scale industry in the countryside).

The answer to this series of problems lies at the centre of the 'General Line for the Construction of Socialism in China' (1958). The fundamental principle of this line – in conformity with classical communism – is that the working class is the very foundation of historical development and that economic development must be based on the freeing of its immense material and intellectual forces. The principal task of the Communist Party is to define the forms that will allow these energies to be freed.

According to the 'General Line' it was a question, from a quantitative point of view, of using the huge mass of peasants in the countryside, who were unemployed in the off-seasons, for constructing dams, reservoirs, canals and so on. Hence the forming of communes. On the other hand in the towns it was a question of using female labour in small-scale enterprises producing consumer goods and in the development of social services (crèches, kindergartens, dispensaries, wash-houses, canteens and so on). These are the urban communes.

In order to promote the 'intellectual liberation of the masses' industry was developed in the countryside for making products necessary for agriculture (fertilizers, tools, pumps and so on). This programme contrasted with the tradition of socialist industry based on the concentration of production in large factories, a concentration that makes transport and distribution slow and costly. Local industrialization must no longer take the equipment, skilled workers and technicians it needs from the urban industries. It must rely chiefly on the forces in the countryside (artisans, young people who have finished primary school and display technical abilities, and secondary-school pupils). In other words it was a question of giving latent intellectual abilities an opportunity to reveal themselves and thus of triggering a chain reaction that would rescue the countryside from underdevelopment and would compensate it for lagging behind the towns.

In industrial production the 'great leap forward' can be achieved only if the shortcomings of enterprise management are corrected so as to *secure a vigorous development of 'greater, faster, better and more economical' production*. But as the shortcomings of management spring essentially from the bourgeois division of labour, the programme of radical, though gradual, alteration of the relations of production in the factories must be fully carried out.

We can read about the first practical experiments in the transformation of the relations of production in the *Constitution of the Anshan Iron and Steel Complex* (1960), in which Mao himself established the following five principles– 'Keep politics firmly in command; strengthen Party leadership; launch vigorous mass movements; institute the system of cadre participation in productive labour and worker participation in management, of reform of irrational and outdated rules and regulations; and of close co-operation among workers, cadres and technicians; go full steam ahead with the technical innovations and the technical revolution.'

These basic principles provided the guide lines that were to remain in force later (1960–6), though their subsequent application originated in experiments that enriched them and made them concrete (such as the famous Taching oil-field experiment in proletarian management).

8 SYSTEMS OF PROLETARIAN MANAGEMENT IN THE FACTORIES

As long as the bourgeois division of labour continues to exist economic planning involves two serious shortcomings:

1) 'enterprise particularism' is dominant: enterprise managements take no further interest in the requirements of the economic plan, hence the serious deficiencies in technology and output of production;

2) subjectivism and arbitrariness predominate in the organization of the enterprise plan: drawing up the plan in fact demands a whole range of knowledge that the management alone cannot possess. When a limited group of people take all the decisions relating to a set of questions with which the workers are very familiar and which they could help to solve, decisions are taken on the basis of partial and inaccurate data.

According to the proletarian line all these problems must be solved 'by launching vigorous mass-movements', by mobilizing the masses so that they wholeheartedly express their point of view and their opinions on production and enterprise management. The majority of workers and not only the technicians and managers must draw up the enterprise plan. The workers as a whole must decide whether or not plant is sufficient to achieve the production required; they they must determine the quantities of raw materials and energy necessary to produce the quantities required, and point out wastage that is to be eliminated; finally, it is they who must determine the necessary number of workers and the workrates.

The division between technical and manual labour that characterizes the bourgeois relations of production must be abolished. If we rely on the workers' class-consciousness, that is, on the sense of responsibility of those who are conscious of controlling production, we can ensure production based on the fullest possible knowledge, on economy of raw materials, maintenance of plant, abolition of wastage and extravagance and on concern for the quality of the product.

The atmosphere in the factories will then be stimulating; management will be dominated by democratic centralism, i.e. by the centralization of accurate ideas and not of those of a group of people who give orders.

In order to obtain these results we must 'reform the irrational rules' in order to guarantee to the workers:

1) the possibility of asserting their democratic rights *vis-à-vis* the management – the right to elect cadres from base organizations; the right to hear and discuss the work reports of leading cadres; the right to criticize cadres at any sort of meeting; the right to take part in the economic control of the enterprise; the right to struggle against actions or tendencies that run counter to Party policy; the right to control the way in which the cadres carry out the 'three imperative tests' discussed below;

2) the possibility of asserting their 'five great powers': refusal to operate equipment at a faster rate than the agreed norm; refusal to operate equipment with unskilled personnel; refusal to institute or proceed with building operations if the orders are not clear, if the previous stage has not been completed according to the agreed criteria and if there are not enough materials or they are of poor quality; refusal to work if the safety measures are inadequate; refusal to carry out an order to leave work (dismissal).

In the second place, according to the proletarian line, the bourgeois division of labour prevents technical problems in production from being settled collectively. There must be full confidence in the masses. Because the workers have rich practical experience of technical methods it is possible, by building on this experience, to develop technology according to the criteria of quality, economy and speed.

The rules of the enterprise must be altered in a way that enables the spirit of initiative and the creative capacities of the workers to be mobilized. The system kown as 'three-in-one' must 'ensure close co-operation among cadres, workers and technicians' in special groups to 'energetically lead the technical revolution'. If we rely on the masses and on co-operation between technicians and workers we can promote technical development, smash routine and practise the proletarian principle which says that we must not fear risks, shortcomings and mistakes but must act according to a scientific attitude by developing a knowledge of basic theoretical principles and by learning the best foreign techniques.

In the third place, this revolution in the division of labour requires a radical change in educational systems and an increase in the educational function of the factory. The technicians must acquire their basic training in the factory with the practical experience of manual labour as the starting-point, and getting used to solving increasingly complex technical problems, accompanied by thorough theoretical training at evening courses. The workers who prove to be the most able will be sent to technical colleges and universities; in these colleges of higher education instruction must remain closely linked to problems of production and be relevant to men who have practical experience of machinery and have proven technical ability.

This educational system aims to increase the technicians' skills by getting rid of the shortcomings of the bourgeois educational system which is essentially theoretical and does not prepare technicians for the work they will have to do.

In the fourth place, if the technicians, all of working-class origin, are not to be transformed into a privileged stratum, they must differ from other workers only in the tasks they perform alongside their fellow-workers. They must therefore be workers like the others on the level of wages, and on that of manual labour, which they must continue to perform.

According to the proletarian line, the revolutionary transformation of management methods is also decisive for the revolutionary transformation of the relations of production. The management must adopt the following methods:

1) They must use a system in which leading cadres take part in manual labour so that they have a more accurate knowledge of the work, as well as of the ideas and requirements of the masses (they must keep regular time, obey the work-team leaders, produce material wealth, solve technical problems, specialize in new materials);

2) They must not consider themselves to be a special category (no luxurious buildings or rooms); they must take their meals in the communal canteen and educate their children so that they do not consider themselves to be privileged people;

3) They must behave modestly and honestly.

These are the 'three imperative criteria' that the enterprise managers, Party cadres and technicians must live up to. The way in which they are put into practice is reviewed in general meetings attended by all the employees in the factory. We will not linger here over the three methods of revolutionary transformation of management (the 'two-level' method, 'face-to-face' management and 'first and second line' work).

In short, given the workers' practical experience and concrete technical knowledge it is pure madness to assign control over the production and technology to only a few individuals.

The proletarian cultural revolution tended precisely to transform the spiritual energy latent in the masses into a great material force. It involved an attempt of historical significance: the attempt to offer a field of action to the creative and intellectual power of the working class, and to lead it to take technology and scientific experiments progressively into its own hands, so as to establish collective responsibility and collective concern for production. This enables the energies that sustain economic power to increase a hundredfold.

For the cadres and factory militants in the Party 'to put politics in command' does not mean that they must restrict themselves to propaganda work, but will give rise to a mass movement in the enterprises that establishes workers' control over technology, organization and management. This process demands that the Party should first of all carry out a huge political and ideological task: all sectors (industry, agriculture and commerce) must make a thorough study of the (Taching-type) model experiments in the new system of management.

The Party therefore has the task of preparing the way for criticism. But it is up to the masses to transform the relations of production. Objective and subjective; practice and theory; the construction of socialism and socialist revolution; and the creation of material and spiritual conditions for communism – all are aspects of a single task.

9 INTENSIVE ECONOMIC DEVELOPMENT AND THE RIGHT-WING LINE

Unlike the first Five-Year Plan, this grandiose revolutionary project was not favoured by economic conditions. The harvest in 1958 was enormous, with 200 million tons of grain, but in the next three years agriculture was afflicted by drought and floods. The government had to import food rather than machines. Administration and transport were totally taken up with the struggle against imminent famine. Agricultural produce had to be dispatched to the hardest-hit regions and a system of rationing had to be organized in the towns. If we remember the total withdrawal of Soviet aid (in 1960) it is easy to understand that Chinese industry was hard hit. Owing to the fall in consumption the co-operative movement in the countryside suffered a setback, and in certain areas it regressed.

If the Party had given priority to heavy industry at that time the economic difficulties would have spread to the consumer goods sector (textiles, housing) and to agriculture, where forced collectivization would probably have had to be introduced. The 'great leap forward' had already been banking on parallel development of industry and agriculture; now circumstances led to *agriculture being given priority*. Heavy industry had to produce in a way that gave priority to agriculture and not to the development of heavy industry itself. The latter therefore failed to meet its planned objectives. Planning was suspended and it was decided to make the programme of industrial construction depend on what was available annually from agriculture.

This basic economic choice had important consequences for Chinese domestic policy. In fact, given the shortage of material means, industrial production had to appeal to intensive development (based on efficiency, quality, economy of raw materials and technological innovation) instead of developing extensively (increasing the number of machines and factories). This demanded a radical change in the relations of production. Socialist planning – as we emphasized in section 5 – can develop intensively only if the working class takes technology into its own hands and assumes responsibility for the technical and qualitative aspects of production; if instead intensive economic development is entrusted to a group of technicians, this economic development can be seriously hindered.

Thus while the proletarian line became more difficult as a result of the economic crisis, the change-over to intensive development made its implementation urgent. In fact the right-wing line had been strengthening from this period (1960–2). It denounced the principles of the 'great leap forward' and the communes and attributed the agricultural and industrial crisis to poor organization of the economy. It even attacked planning, reproaching the planners for subjecting the management of the factories to extra-economic criteria that were incompatible with the principles of healthy management (quality, full utilization of plant, technological development and so on). According to the right-wing line the proletarian solution was idealistic and adventurist. Instead of giving responsibilities for management to the masses, the management should take full responsibility not only for production but also for the very existence of the enterprise. The life of each enterprise should therefore again depend on its competitive ability. The central economic organization should be relieved from the duty of supplying every enterprise, selling its products and paying its wages. Every enterprise should be financially self-sufficient. 'A more sensitive' indicator can then be introduced 'to measure good or bad enterprise management and to judge its efficiency: profit'. Thus 'the enterprises which freely dispose of their profits and face up to their own losses should be multiplied: a factory should make money or be closed'.

If the existence of enterprises depends on profit realized on the market, everything should be subordinated to profit and the managers should have greater powers than the Party committees and the vanguard workers. 'The experience of capitalist management of enterprises, in particular of monopoly enterprises, should be studied.' The 'one-man management system' and the principle according to which 'in economic construction one must rely on the experts, the manager, the engineers and technicians who give the orders should be relied on', while the workers are only the labour force that should carry out the orders, must be established.

Rules in the factories should become more rigid. Work norms should be raised again by introducing piece-work and further wage differentials; the management should be able to use the weapon of dismissals to combat indiscipline and inefficiency among workers.

This applies equally to cadres in the factory and to technicians, whose work efficiency should be controlled by the managing director and stimulated by bonuses and material advantages. Because the autonomy of the enterprise in the market demands more competent and responsible management managers and technicians should be able to obtain compensation – material advantages proportional to the growth of the profits obtained.

The right-wing line was not successful in enforcing its general economic ideas, which remained at the level of theoretical discussion. But certain practical results were obtained: a) in the domain of management many Party committees in the enterprises reduced their work to a simple propaganda task and entrusted all economic affairs to the manager; the factory rules became stricter; b) in the domain of education many school and university Party committees went back to the bourgeois educational system that was in use before the 'great leap forward'.

10 THE CLASS ORIGINS OF REVISIONISM

From about 1960 onwards an increasingly clear conflict developed in China between the proletarian line and the right-wing line. Until then the proletarian line had restricted itself to combating the right-wing line as a manifestation of opportunist bourgeois ideology, without for all that accusing it of expressing the material interests of the class enemy. But from 1962 the proletarian line declared that a dangerous revisionist ideology existed in China and stressed that the class struggle must never be forgotten, that the expropriation of the capitalists and the development of the socialist economy do not by themselves guarantee the power of the proletariat, and that proletarian relations of production must be strengthened in order to avoid a strengthening of the bourgeoisie and the restoration of capitalism.

Facing the advent of revisionism in the Soviet Union, the proletarian line had from 1960 onwards come to the conclusion that the latter indicated the seizure of power by a new bourgeoisie and that the Chinese revolution was threatened by the same degeneration.

During the construction of socialism the Stalinist leadership had not been able to avoid the bourgeois division of labour in the service of the planned economy. It is true that at the same time as a switch from private to public ownership, the relations between men must be transformed into relations of equality and co-operation; the only difference between the cadres and the masses in the Party must arise from the division of labour; and the cadres must act like ordinary workers and have no special privileges. But the transformation of ownership does not by itself establish new relations of production. The old systems of management cannot be replaced immediately. They create obstacles that slow down the establishment of new relations of production. Now Stalin, creating and strengthening a new bourgeoisie by objective necessity, had not tried to develop proletarian relations of production to replace the bourgeois division of labour.

The theoreticians of the Chinese proletarian line write on this subject:

Do classes and the class struggle last for a long time after the seizure of power by the proletariat? Lenin replies positively to this question. He says: 'The abolition of classes requires a long, difficult and stubborn class struggle'. He emphasizes that the bourgeoisie that has been overthrown retains its power of resistance for a long time; it remains even stronger than the proletariat. He says: 'Skill in administering the

State and military and economic skill give the exploiters a very marked superiority; their importance is therefore incomparably greater than their numerical proportion in the population. . . .

After socialist industrialization and collectivization of agriculture had been carried out in the Soviet Union . . . Stalin delivered a report . . . in which he correctly drew up a balance-sheet of the great successes that had been achieved . . . but at the same time he made theoretical errors: he did not recognize that classes and the class struggle persist in society throughout the historical period of the dictatorship of the proletariat. He wrote: 'All the exploiting classes have been abolished. . . . The dividing line between the working class and the peasantry, and between these classes and the intelligentsia, is being obliterated. This means that the distance between these social groups is steadily diminishing. . . .' On the theoretical level Stalin did not wish to acknowledge that one problem that is still unresolved is precisely that of knowing 'who will win the revolution'; and this problem must be resolved throughout the historical period of the dictatorship of the proletariat; in other words, if we are not careful there is a possibility that the bourgeoisie will regain power.

Should we speak of the 'dictatorship of the proletariat' for this historical period? Yes, because it is not the bourgeoisie who compelled the Stalinist leadership to uphold the bourgeois division of labour but the Stalinist leadership that upheld the bourgeois division of labour to ensure the development of socialist industrialization, i.e. the economic foundations of proletarian power.

Stalin prevented the new bourgeoisie from seizing the principal levers of the State and from adapting the domestic and foreign policy of the Soviet Union to its class interests. For more than thirty years this class was forced to serve proletarian policy. It did not manage to appropriate the social wealth or to use production for its own interests; in other words, it did not manage to enforce a different type of development from accelerated industrialization. On several occasions the Stalinist leadership had recourse to violence against all the leading strata of the country: technicians, economic leaders, officers, intellectuals, scientists and even Party members.

In fact for want of reliable cadres the Party had opened its ranks to any technician who said he was prepared to serve it. Although occasionally removed by purges, these intermediate cadres were strengthened as the tasks of organization and control increased. Thus the formation of a class of technicians objectively linked by its privileges to the new technical and administrative bourgeoisie took place within the Party.

During the last years of his life Stalin understood this problem. The industrialization of the Soviet Union was being completed. It was becoming necessary to replace extensive development by intensive development based on the technological revolution. A large skilled working class had been formed. The objective bases for a radical change in the relations of production were therefore available. There was no longer any reason to uphold relations based on domination rather than on co-operation, equality and reciprocal aid.

But broad strata of the new bourgeoisie had their vanguard in the very midst of the Party, where after Stalin's death, an anti-proletarian revisionist clique managed to seize an important share of power and subsequently to adapt the domestic and foreign policy of the Soviet Union to its own class interests. In the field of domestic policy this meant decentralization of enterprises, restoration of the market and profit and differentiation of incomes; in foreign policy it meant peaceful co-existence with imperialism, and a cut-back in military production, which enabled industry to meet the consumer needs of the privileged few more satisfactorily.

In fact the new bourgeois class that possesses technology and runs the enterprises does not see the problems of economic development from the point of view of its disappearance as a class but from the point of view of a strengthening of its functions and therefore of its privileges. In other words, according to the technicians economic efficiency depends on the efficiency of their work; in order to obtain this efficiency they should be given more power in the factory (they can then secure maximum output from the workers). They suggest that their work efficiency should be measured by the profit of the enterprise and demand material privileges proportional to their work efficiency.

11 REACTIVATING THE CLASS STRUGGLE

On the basis of the Chinese interpretation of the degeneration of socialism in the Soviet Union, the right-wing line in China must be interpreted as a revisionist line in view of the formation, in China as well, of a privileged social stratum of bourgeois specialists seeking power. According to the proletarian line, lessons must be drawn from the degeneration of power in the Soviet Union. The bourgeois division of labour must be abolished during the stage of socialist construction if a degeneration of the Communist Party and the advent of a new bourgeoisie are to be avoided. The proletariat can remain in power only if its political vanguard progressively strengthens the proletarian relations of production. The proletarian line can no longer simply rely on the strength of enthusiasm for new management systems tested in certain advanced proletarian sectors (like Taching) and then publicized by all the news media — for the revisionist leaders in the Party and the intermediary cadres who come under their influence oppose changes with passive resistance and even introduce bourgeois systems, more or less disguised, in factory management. Simple appeals to the proletarian consciousness will not triumph over bourgeois and revisionist ideology and deeply entrenched systems for organizing social relations. The methods of struggle must be changed.

IL MANIFESTO

Challenging the Role of Technical Experts*

The first question is to find out what exactly is meant by 'scientific and technical staff' (*techniciens*). This is not merely semantic quibbling – misuse of the expression often conceals dangerous political confusion. In fact in both trade-union and student debates the expression tends to be used to refer to white-collar workers (*employés*) in general. This kind of usage, however, apart from being theoretically imprecise, is also bad politics, since it fails to make an important distinction. Recent trade-union activity in Italy has been based essentially upon a conjectured process of 'proletarianization of scientific and technical staff'. We prefer, however, in relation to this proletarianization, to refer to 'employees'. For as we shall see, those who have some measure of power on the basis of technical or scientific qualifications (i.e. scientific and technical staff in a restricted sense) are in a very different situation.

To talk about *proletarianization of employees or white-collar workers* implies that as a result of changes in the nature of their work, status and modes of payment, the position of the administrative, managerial and clerical staff in the hierarchy of production increasingly tends to become closer to that of the shop-floor workers. It follows that distinctions between shop-floor workers and these white-collar employees (payment by wages rather than salaries, security of employment and so on) no longer tend to correspond to a social and political differentiation. It is extremely important to take note of these changes, not only because of their serious implications for trade-union activity but above all because of their political consequences. (It is sufficient to recall the part played by the petty-bourgeois stratum of the white-collar workers in the rise of fascism in Italy to press this point home.)

In the earlier, premonopolistic phase of capitalism the white-collar worker, whatever his qualification and skills, was a kind of representative of the owner. The entrepreneur delegated some of his authority to him.

*This essay is the outcome of collective work conducted by groups of left-wing clerical, technical and administrative workers in Italy. It appeared originally in *Il Manifesto* (October-November 1969). A revised French version, on which this translation is based, first appeared in *Les Temps Modernes* (April 1970), as 'Division du travail et technique du pouvoir'. Translated by M. D.

Whereas the manual worker only carried out orders and actually produced the goods – an activity in which the owner did not participate – the white-collar worker belonged to the sphere of those who were in control. At this earlier stage of capitalism management was not subject to strict rules. It consisted in taking the right decision at the right moment, and for this the manager needed reliable information much more than specialised knowledge. Since those who were responsible for taking decisions and supplying information were difficult to control the main quality the entrepreneur expected of them was loyalty. As a matter of fact the present Italian Civil Code defines loyalty as a legal duty of the employee (*impiegato*).

Because of this special relationship of loyalty white-collar workers enjoyed certain privileges. The *structural basis* for the political and trade union inertia of white-collar workers consists in the fact that they were not, by and large, workers from whom surplus-value was extracted. At the *subjective* level they were regarded as being in the enviable position of doing less onerous work for better rewards, both monetary and in terms of other privileges. In addition the nature of their work was subjectively taken to be of the same kind as that of the "upper classes".

The fundamental changes which modern capitalism is undergoing are resulting in the proletarianization of white-collar workers. Industrial concentration is the key factor. It is evident that there is an enormous growth not only in the volume of production but also in the amount of administrative and technical information which needs to be supplied, transmitted, classified and selected. In addition there is a continual increase in the market-research each firm must carry out.

As a result of these developments a significant part of the production process is shifted to tertiary activities. In order to produce large quantities of goods at low prices one must have machine production of information, a factor of production just as important as any other. All the operations involved in the sales activities of the firm will also be multiplied. (Interestingly enough, it is no coincidence that in Italian commercial terminology 'to sell' and 'salesman' are synonomous with 'to produce' and 'producer'.)

Thus clerical and technical staff no longer exercise power and become instead producers of a number of non-material, but economically important 'products'. It is within this context that we can begin to analyse the nature and causes of the processes that lead to the proletarianization of employees and technicians. The most important determinant of this process is a division of labour chosen by capitalism in order to obtain, within each enterprise, the maximum productivity with the maximum amount of control. This, in effect, has meant an all-pervasive extension of the Taylorism of the shop floor to include all the operations undertaken within the enterprise.

Taylorism can be defined as the detailed ordering of the simplest possible operations and their distribution according to a planned sequence. Thus the need for individual skills is minimized, as the mechanical and repetitive nature of the operations helps both to accelerate output and to economize on training. The fragmented, simplified and repetitive nature of assembly-line work is well known, but many people will be surprised to learn that about 80 per cent of administrative employees also do nothing but repeat strictly predetermined tasks that, in the majority of cases, preclude any personal initiative; that among white-collar workers in production departments about 60 per cent of all personnel follow a rigidly defined procedure; and, finally, that in sales departments about 60 per cent of the salesmen operate according to a pre-arranged sales schedule, which lays down all the details for interviews, including what to say, and even what vocabulary to use.

The great majority of employees have become passive participants in a thoroughly rationalized economic process. *Capital has less and less need of a stratum of trustworthy representatives to whom it can delegate some of its authority. Under modern conditions it organizes the labour process primarily by objectifying all existing tasks and functions.* The great majority of employees no longer exercise power on behalf of the owners.

These changes mean that it is no longer necessary for capital to maintain the traditionally higher payments to employees. Like the workers, they can be paid according to the difficulty of their job and the specialized training required. Wherever job-evaluation surveys show such factors as 'trustworthiness' or 'responsibility' to be of great importance, you can bet that the job in question will be reorganized and transformed to make it more restrictive.

The majority of employees tend to be exploited in the same way as workers, with whom they also share a total indifference to their work. As a result employees are objectively more open and amenable than in the past to trade-union organization and working-class politics. But there are obstacles. They continue to be restrained by a powerful sense of status and social superiority and, most of all, by recognition of the undeniable advantages to be gained from their status as salaried employees (in relation to sickness, pensions, security of employment, annual increments and so on). The anti-union effects of this formal differentiation are the main reason why it is not abolished by employers.

Considerable possibilities exist for mobilizing employees, although the question of the platform on which this should be done remains. A platform can arise only out of an analysis of the mechanics of capitalist power and the various models by which the system is managed. Improvements in salaries or increased bargaining power can no longer compensate for their psychological downgrading and their professional dequalification which tend to transform employees into passive objects in the production process.

PROFESSIONAL AUTONOMY

We have discussed the process of proletarianizing large groups of clerical and administrative personnel. But a closer scrutiny will reveal that a sizeable fraction of white collar workers find themselves in an altogether different situation. The planner, the systems analyst, the production analyst and so on, not to mention supervisors of all sorts – all these must be distinguished from proletarianized employees. This is tacitly recognized by the occupational classification. Several other factors, such as the type and amount of remuneration and levels of academic and technical training distinguish these functionaries from the employees and the shop-floor workers. However the most critical distinction, indeed the fundamental criterion that defines their specific status, is *the degree of autonomy arising from the nature of their jobs and the influence that this exerts over the processes of production.*

To argue that they are merely representatives of the capitalists, or simply to maintain that in carrying out their delegated functions they automatically identify with or aspire to capitalist ownership, confuses the issue and explains next to nothing. The reality is a great deal more complex, and it is important to go beyond this superficial analysis and to grasp the objective and subjective factors determining the real positions occupied by the technical and scientific staff. This is of the greatest importance, because in their functions lies the real nature of the power of modern capitalism as it is exercised within the factories. To elaborate this point we must return to the model of capitalism referred to above. The capitalist enterprise has become increasingly like a complex machine. Job-content and the workers' relations with objects or with one another are not of daily or immediate concern to top management; they are not defined by the arbitrary exercise of hierarchical authority. Instead they are 'objectively' defined and fixed once and for all, by the norms and organizational structures of the enterprise.

Yet the question of who designs, modifies and directs this complex machine remains. The trade-union response, vague and almost bordering on the mythical, is simply 'the boss'. And when, as is often the case, a boss figure no longer exists or cannot be physically located, the unions tend to fall back on the idea that it is 'those who carry out the will of the owners'. Directors, managers, administrators, clerical and technical staff are lumped together as the mere executors of the will of capitalism. Thus promoted and branded, the technicians are isolated by an imaginary barrier from the mass of the workers below.

We shall deal with the criteria that distinguish the technicians from the rest of the working class at a later stage. First we must clarify why technicians regard themselves as distinct from top management, and in fact are distinct from it. We must distinguish here between two groups of scientific and technical personnel; the researchers producing technical or organizational innovations; and the operators, who execute and use these schemes.

The majority of jobs in a capitalist firm are repetitive and involve no creativity or initiative. At the same time the firm must constantly adapt to an ever-changing economic and social situation. There is always, therefore, an in-built need for innovations and modifications – for new products, new technologies, new sales techniques, new data processing systems and organizational forms whose production requires a certain degree of independence. All these innovative activities are complex and require high levels of competence and specialization. Skilled operators are needed to execute them, although admittedly it is 'the boss' who co-ordinates all innovation and ultimately benefits from it. Technological progress constantly modifies fundamentally the structures and processes of production according to its own laws and momentum. An autonomous new form of power, which is no longer strictly identifiable with the decision-making power of ownership, has emerged. For example working out an aircraft project, investigating the properties of a mathematical function or of new materials, creating new data-processing systems, conducting market research, optimizing stocks – none of these can be classified as a job to be performed by the managers or owners.

These considerations, neglected or ignored in trade-union writings on the subject, are of the utmost importance in shaping the way in which the scientific and technical workers think about themselves. Technical and scientific staff imagine that they have freedom and independence, because within their specialized domains they do not take any orders from an immediately recognizable 'boss'. This sense of autonomy is reinforced by constant reference to Science, and to Technology, which current ideology places above and beyond any company or social system. University and technical training stresses the specialized nature of all knowledge and it is true that in research the education and specialized skill of the researcher are important factors in the success or otherwise of his work.

We will discuss later not only how capitalism gives direction to the results of research and puts them to use but also how science and technology themselves bear the imprint of the ideology and needs of capitalist ideology. But in spite of all this it would be incorrect to depict scientific and technical workers simply as loyal representatives of the bosses, even though they so clearly work on their behalf.

THE MANAGERS

We must now consider the jobs performed by owners and their agents: organization, co-ordination and decision-making. The group performing these tasks exercise power over the activities of other people, but are in turn subordinate to others. Their functions slot the managers and administrators into a hierarchical pyramid, at the top of which is to be found the 'big boss' (whether owner or president of the company) and the board of directors, controlling all the operations and making the most important decisions. These decisions are passed down the chain of command to cover all sectors and levels of the pyramid. In so far as they are instrumental in carrying out the decisions handed down from above, the managers and administrators can be said to represent the interests of ownership. And this is certainly true of some sectors of top and middle management groups placed in key organizational posts. But a considerable number of people in similar positions of responsibility do not identify with the top brass.

A number of important cultural factors determine the different way in which each group perceive their own role. The most important factor is that none of these groups *challenges the existing division of labour*. Thus although some managers may not directly identify with the top échelons, they nevertheless regard their own functions as vital and indispensable within any social system. The content of managerial functions (planning, production and sales) are thought of as essential to the fulfilment of the general objectives of any industrial system and, what is worse, the workers themselves are encouraged to see things in the same way. It is interesting to note the connection between these attitudes and a certain type of moderately progressive bourgeois ideology, which accepts these management functions as good in themselves, while lashing out verbally against the misuse of profit, misery and social injustice. The solutions to these problems, it is claimed, are to be found in a different domain altogether, and have nothing to do with the structure of the capitalist enterprise itself.

Today, however, the nature of management is rapidly changing. It can now be carried out with more rigorous means and instruments: operational research, systems dynamics, standard costing, the use of computers, the 'science' of industrial psychology, time-and-motion studies, planning and so on – all these require important numbers of specialized technicians and almost make management a new profession.

To summarize: neither the top directorship nor the owners were ever capable of producing technological innovations. At present they are no longer even capable of devising systems of management. These 'commodities' have, therefore, to be purchased from the specialists and the scientists. These specialists have come to acquire a certain type of power, which may be described as the power *to reduce the degree of uncertainty in the process of decision-making*. That is, to the extent that decision-making at the top of the enterprise becomes more complex and dependent upon a constellation of technical variables, the crucial importance of furnishing and evaluating data and information increases. To enable top management to take all vital decisions (which, in fact, tend to be essentially policy decisions on which depend the control of the labour force and the growth of profits) the data that are gathered must be properly analysed and presented by the specialized services.

March and Simon state: 'Anyone who receives information ... must have confidence on the way [this] has been processed. The people engaged in the verification, evaluation and transmission of facts and information constitute an important link between the fact and the organizational actions which depend on this ... and it is hardly possible to check all the facts thus communicated.' Thus the research methods used in economic forecasting, systems analysis, econometrics and so on, which all tend to reduce the degree of uncertainty, consciously or unconsciously become means of obtaining and exercising power within the factory hierarchy. An empiricist culture that makes a fetish of factual statements (particularly when they do not contradict 'common-sense' perceptions) encourages the illusion that all decisions are made according to 'neutral' or 'objective' facts and criteria. Whoever the authority formally entitled to take decisions may be, *a large part of effective executive power now resides in those who gather, compute or synthesize facts and data, and who thus integrate the computation of probabilities with the process of decision-making.*

As yet there has been no detailed study of the effects of this technical power on the workings of the firm. But there is no doubt that the behaviour of the firm is greatly influenced by the technical staff: they increase its 'solidity', integration and functional efficiency, and above all give an appearance of objectivity to the functioning and structure of the firm.

We have tried to show that the new forms developed under modern capitalism appear as the inevitable result of scientific principles of organization and management. We have tried to understand the class position of the technicians and the possibilities of mobilizing them in anti-authoritarian struggles. But we want to emphasize that in the shop-floor struggle against capitalism it is not enough to challenge orders from above, which are handed down the chain of command until they reach the base of the hierarchical pyramid. Above all the workers must question the capitalist division of labour and *these new systems of 'objectified' management and control* and the very 'roles' and 'functions' they define and which give a scientific appearance to the captalist power structure. If we do not accept this, we are in effect denying to the managers of a future socialist system the means of behaving differently from the managers of capitalism.

CAPITALIST AUTHORITARIANISM

Thus the intermediate stratum of technicians and management specialists, the 'generalists', as Meynaud calls them, do not regard themselves as the representatives of the head of the firm – which, objectively, they are not. On the other hand, in contrast to the workers and proletarianized employees, they wield technological power and have a degree of influence on the development of the system of the production. It must be realized, however, that given the present structure of production relations, their professionalism and expertise inevitably reinforce and further develop the capitalist system. In order to survive, the huge oligopolistic conglomorates that constitute the pillars of modern capitalism must effectively concentrate and maintain power in the hands of a small group of people. Yet this is in direct contradiction to the scale and complexity of these organizations.

To resolve this problem the large capitalist firm resorts to two basic devices. The first and most widespread means of controlling the various phases of the production process is the hierarchical pyramid. The chain of command descending from the top assigns the degrees of power and responsibility to each person, and goes with a system of financial rewards or sanctions for ensuring total compliance. The other methods, necessitated by the inadequacies of the first, is to diminish the importance of individual decisions. In a manner designed and predetermined by the top échelons, the functioning of the system is rendered more and more automatic and the phases of the operations are standardized by narrowly specifying the *objective functions* of each operation and by making each clearly distinct from all others.

That is why individuals, whether they possess a degree of latitude or perform an absolutely predetermined and fixed task, can no longer consciously intervene in the dialectic of the firm. In this way, the perpetuation of the system is assured not only by the hierarchical chain of command and controls, but also by the functioning of the machine-like organization. Trapped by the very logic that separates roles and functions, an individual activity is geared to servicing and improving the mechanism. Individuals can cause disruptions only be refusing to work, but the transformation of the mechanism requires a collective struggle as a result of which alternative structures will emerge.

The process of objectifying the power of capitalism goes through three fundamental stages. The first is the rigid compartmentalization of the activities within the firm. The activities of an integrated firm involve the *designing* of new products, *producing* them and *marketing* them. These three fields of activity can be separated operationally, technologically and also in their timing, but they must be seen as a whole if we want to understand as well as to run the enterprise.

In the artisan's workshop (or for that matter in a small firm) the three activities are concentrated in the hands of a single person. The artisan knew what to produce, and his ingenuity and intimate knowledge of the market enabled him to introduce innovations. Production was carefully judged according to the technological capacities available. And if confronted with rising costs, he had to attempt to meet this problem by modifying his technology. Finally the product was marketed, with or without the use of intermediaries, by the artisan himself. At this point the production cycle started again.

This example illustrates a model of production that has now become almost obsolete. The complexity of the products themselves and of technology, together with marketing and increases in the volume of production no longer allows one man on his own to master the whole cycle. On the other hand the model does illustrate a situation where the aritsan can exercise control over the real objects of his labour, i.e. over his economic activity, by virtue of the fact that he can understand the interconnections between its various components.

It must be borne in mind, however, that the limited scope of individual activity (working, for example, in the planning sections of the firm rather than in marketing) does not inevitably lead to a total inability to understand the more general relevance of one's specialized functions. And it does not necessarily mean that individuals can no longer consciously influence other spheres of work and activity, because each individual function is indissolubly interconnected with the others. Yet the process of objectification, characteristic of capitalism, not only limits and curtails the scope of work, but also sets up prohibitive barriers preventing workers from grasping the interrelations and dialectic of the whole – and thus the decisions and policies of the enterprise as a whole.

How is this achieved in concrete practice? Quite simply by planning and predetermining every function down to the minutest detail, as in the case of assembly-line workers. Wherever certain jobs call for or necessitate initiative, a flexible margin of action is granted both to individuals and to organizational units. But the *means of communication* and the *outcome of consultation* between individuals and units are fixed in such a way as to be completely functional to the system. The individuals are inserted into a microcosm and can no longer perceive the totality and thus the interconnections of the system. A whole scale of sanctions and incentives is set up to ensure that the results obtained correspond to goals fixed in advance. Of course there are frequent instances of communication between those who perform the different functions. So long as they serve to achieve fixed targets, these incursions are resentfully tolerated. At any rate means and channels of communication are rigorously systematized, and anyway one of the functions of top management is to control and resolve demarcation disputes between departments. Finally, such is the degree of objectification of relations between the various organizational units that further units dealing specifically with liaison and communication problems have to be set up (for example the 'engineering' service that links design with manufacturing). These not only perform a number of specialized jobs but develop into autonomous, self-justifying entities. Technical and scientific research, like the production process itself, become increasingly distorted, narrow and incomprehensible, except to those who control the whole enterprise from the summit.

The second main phase in the process of objectification that develops under capitalism consists of the fact that the function of developing and designing new products or processes on the one hand, and that of actually putting these into practice on the other, are kept separate. These two functions are always present to some degree in any non-reified human activity. Capitalism reifies them and separates them out as distinct functions. Capitalism is characterized by a culture in which there is a permanent separation between theory and practice, between idea and execution, between thought and action. This does not mean, of course, that the capitalist organization is free from the dialectic that governs all collective work, or that it could function in any other manner. But within the capitalist enterprise the *dialectical synthesis is determined from above* and does not occur where the two moments of the dialectic actually come into being. In other words capitalism increases the abstract character of labour (in the Marxist sense). In reducing the power of those operating within the system it prevents their autonomous understanding of the reality of the system and their ability to transform it.

To understand capitalism one has to grasp its economic activity as a whole. But this understanding is precisely what is denied to individuals who are limited either to theorizing divorced from action, or to actions devoid of conscious thought.

THE POLITICAL FUNCTION OF ROLES

We must guard against the facile radicalism that rejects outright any necessity for a division of labour. No single individual can master the vast fields of knowledge opened up by modern science and technology. What characterizes capitalism, however, is the nature and political function of the division of labour specific to it.

The objection is not that there should be, for example, an engineer mainly responsible for designing new products, or a technician controlling the production line, or sales managers or manual workers. In fact three kinds of objections can be raised.

1) There is no real rotation between different roles except for nominal, almost ficticious changes between rigidly determined strata. The engineer never changes places with the manual worker and the worker still less with the engineer, or else the worker becomes something other than what he or she is. This lack of mobility and interchange reinforces social stratification and actively encourages identification with one's own particular function and status.

2) Those who actually carry out a project have no say or control over the innovators or designers of the project. When a design engineer fails to take into account certain shop-floor conditions, neither the workers nor the foremen have the right to challenge him directly. Any criticism must go through pre-established, hierarchical channels (worker–foreman–head of department–production manager) and functional channels (production–technical department–project planning–project direction). Needless to say, any grounds for criticism that are not directly related to the output of a person or a unit fall by the wayside. But as the output or work-load of each individual or unit is fixed from above, it is easy to understand how this fragmented structure enables communication to take place only when it is functional with regard to the system.

3) The managerial staff have no opportunities for conceptualizing the real conditions of work, and so are in no position to bring about relevant modifications. The same applies to the innovators and project designers: they cannot experience or control the effects of their work in all the relevant spheres (technological, scientific, human or economic).

Every day the foremen or the workers deal with thousands of facts that, if rationally ordered and thought out, could give rise to numerous innovations and modifications worked out collectively. Yet they are not authorized to take such initiatives; their time, and especially their training, limit them; and any new ideas coming from the shop-floor are restricted to routine details, in the 'suggestion-box' manner. They are taught only what is of immediate relevance to their allotted tasks, and are induced to disregard anything that does not fit in with the required performance by which they are judged.

The designer or engineer, on the other hand, has to create a machine according to certain specifications. The reasons for these specifications – the purpose of the machine, its place in the economic planning of the company, its cultural and economic value for society in general, the effect on those who will use and produce it and so on – are hidden in decisions made in other departments or sections of the company. Once the design is completed all that its creator can determine is whether the machine works or not. He cannot investigate, for example, whether it will make the worker's job harder, or whether it will furnish society with yet another useless or dangerous product. Yet such effects are produced by the designer himself, who implements decisions made over his head and considered to be outside his sphere of professional responsibility.

THE 'NEUTRALITY OF SCIENCE'

What helps to produce such blind acquiescence on the part of the technicians to impersonal directives from above is, paradoxically, their education. They are trained in an *instrumentalist ideology* that is inculcated into them, first at school and later in their jobs. According to this ideology, which permeates the teaching of all the natural and applied sciences, science is a technique for gathering data, or merely a method for quantifying individual phenomena, the syntheses of which are considered to be outside its province. It does not involve elaborating concepts for the dialectical analysis of qualitative facts. Thus, in spite of Galileo, science begins once again with Aristotelian categories: reality is divided into myriads of phenomena classified according to their characteristics rather than their origin. Irregular or unquantifiable phenomena are either totally excluded from the field of science or expressed in simplistic models that are functional to the system. There is no point in discussing at length the anti-authoritarian movement that has shaken science to its very foundations and has led to a profound crisis, or, obviously, in reopening the debate on the 'neutrality' of science and technology – if we can still use the term 'science' for disciplines that appear to be trapped in the vicious circle of self-verifying hypotheses acclaimed once and for all as absolute truths.

The servile acceptance of utilitarianism and the cult of efficiency (the typical characteristics of the world of technology); the fragmentation of science and the rejection of dialectics; the suspicious attitude towards those who discuss the social and political implications of the prevalent conception of technology; the refusal to include these implications within the scope of one's professional preoccupations – for science students, and subsequently for technicians, all these factors constitute the most obvious reasons for accepting the fragmented functions they are called upon to fulfil.

The third stage in the process of the capitalist concentration of power is the *structure of internal stratification* within the firm.

We have seen how capitalism separates the different activities within a firm so that their relationships can be understood and directed only from the top of the hierarchical pyramid. We have also seen how separating planning from execution diminishes the unity and meaning of work, subordinating all activity not only to a hierarchical chain of command, but also to a machine-like system that conditions and pre-establishes all professional behaviour. But all these ramifications of the system are not enough if, even in this alienated context, a large number of people are still needed to make decisions. Here the importance of Taylorism in determining the division of labour becomes absolutely clear. All decisions affecting production are taken away from the mass of the workers. They are not allowed to have any say in the running of the firm, even in relation to the practical matters that concern them in relation to their work. Technicians and middle management are admittedly allowed a degree of control over their respective jobs. Yet these functions are inherently encapsulated in fixed positions within a hierarchy of command. And those who perform them are ultimately accountable to a small clique of directors who are ideologically committed to the system.

AUTONOMY AND REAL POWER

Workers and proletarianized employees are subject to these three types of objectification. Firstly, they are compartmentalized within a narrow section of the company, with no possibility of obtaining a broader view of the processes in which they are caught up. Secondly, as we have seen, creativity and initiative are either discouraged or not permitted. Thirdly, the fragmented and rigidly predetermined content of their work deprives them of any influence on or say in the running of the firm; and they cannot acquire the requisite knowledge and experience that might enable them to transcend this isolation and think up alternatives to the existing system.

Under these circumstances, the actual power of the workers is totally external to the labour process as such. It develops from an awareness of exploitation to become a potentially radical rejection of the system as a whole. But this is more a rejection of the capitalist appropriation of surplus-value, and of the capitalist division of labour and the class power exercised in the hierarchical pyramid of command, than aspiration towards different forms of management, methods of production and organization of men and their work. A genuinely revolutionary alternative, if it is to involve something more than simply replacing the élite at the top of the pyramid, will have to give back to the workers the power to make independent decisions, and to use their initiative. This clearly implies that in order to get rid of capitalist objectification and division of labour the working class as a whole must seize and control both political power and the means of production of scientific knowledge.

We therefore think that the best way of revealing and explaining the distribution of power within an enterprise is to map out to what extent people have the power to make decisions affecting their work and the work process generally, rather than any other descriptive model such as the chain of command within the hierarchical pyramid. Every autonomous act of decision is an act of power, and consequently any absence of the possibility of decision-making implies a lack or absence of power. If we cling to the conception that the internal structure of any capitalist enterprise is exclusively determined by its hierarchical structure, this throws no light on the fundamental factors that deprive workers and proletarianized employees of power and limit the reduced, but still considerable, power of technical and scientific workers. Above all the pyramid model helps to support the illusion that the overthrow of the propertied class (i.e. changes and replacements at the top of the pyramid) is sufficient in itself to abolish the authoritarian structure of the factories and of society in general.

Yet in what way does autonomy in decision-making constitute real power? An extremely superficial view maintains that the only meaningful autonomy is located within top management, as their decisions command unopposed obedience; the lower échelons deal with what are essentially fictitious choices or alternatives. An ultra-empirical view, and one that is dear to the hearts of American sociologists, affirms that, on the contrary, some real autonomy in decision-making resides even with piece-workers, who can adapt methods of work according to their personal requirements (i.e. by distributing work over a period and so on). However what we understand by power through autonomy in decision-making is power to make decisions that influence the overall policies of the enterprise, and its possibilities for survival, growth and development. It is here that the fundamental contradiction in the role of technicians becomes acutely apparent.

Some recent studies have asserted that this contradiction consists of the private appropriation of a resource (i.e. technology) that is the common possession of all. But in fact dominated by capital, technology differs from what it might otherwise have been; it can never be neutral. Moreover this assertion sheds no light on the mechanisms of the exploitation of technicians. And it does not in any way reveal the possibilities that can be seized upon to mobilize and radically alter their present degree of politicization.

In our opinion, the fundamental contradiction concerning technicians lies elsewhere. It lies in the disproportion between on the one hand the increasing importance of technicians within the production process, and on the other, the imposition from outside of what his function is to be. Hence their alienation from the ends that their indispensable contribution helps to attain. In other words the technician has complete responsibility within his own specific field. But has absolutely no responsibility in the general running either of the firm or of society at large. The matter does not rest here, however: technological work does admittedly necessitate non-technical choices, involving value judgements and an awareness of how society functions. Although they are absolved from such responsibilities, the technicians are nevertheless constantly confronted with them at every level of their work. The question of social responsibility therefore has to be posed at the level of the nature of their occupation and function.

The technicians are becoming increasingly aware of this contradiction in their position and role. But the confrontation and disputes this has led to are still technocratic and corporative. On the other hand we can say with certainty that *the power they wield as innovators and as experts in the decision-making process belongs exclusively to the technicians only because capitalism, in order to control this power better, has taken it away from the overwhelming mass of the workers*. The problem of the alienation and objectification of the powers and capacities of technicians is therefore rooted in the general problem of the capitalist division of labour. This alienation is not a special problem whose solution can be found within the experience of this stratum alone. It can be overcome only in a struggle that eliminates its causes (the present division of labour) by uniting with the working class, i.e. with the social force that the division of labour was designed to fight in the first place.

DISSATISFACTION AMONG TECHNICIANS

The purposes served by the objectification of capitalist power are rarely intelligible to those who suffer its effects. The reasons for this suffering, which renders the gilded cage of the technician a great deal less comfortable than one might expect, are far from being homogenous.

If questioned about the reasons for their dissatisfaction with their work, nine times out of ten technicians (including those who do have some degree of independence and power) will say that their superiors are either lacking in competence in the field concerned; or that they make judgements on unfamiliar, non-technical criteria; that decisions made independently at the top do not conform to technical rationality or planning; (in short an accusation of managerial incompetence); that they are assigned specific tasks whose purpose, context and ultimate application they do not know; and that their own products (inventions, apparatuses and so on) are put to uses of which they are kept in ignorance.

One common, technocratically oriented interpretation of these difficulties – one that is dear to the technicians' hearts and is also shared by top management – refers to the lack of rationalisation and streamlining in European companies – the persistence of archaic forms of organization, the lack of managerial training, the inadequacy of channels of communication and so on – in contrast, it is said, to the wonderful organization in American companies.

It is undoubtedly true that even the most modern Italian companies are not streamlined enough. But what we have said above shows clearly that the technicians' dissatisfaction stems from structural causes related to the capitalist division of labour. Let us look more carefully at the technicians' complaints.

Incompetence

The use of non-technical criteria in judging technicians' work stems from the need to co-ordinate the different departments and functions politically and organize hierarchical control. Those who perform these tasks carry out their functions according to the general requisites of the system. Their background, training and ideological conformity to the system and their degree of involvement with it commend them for these tasks. Within the structure of command the 'supervisors' are channels for the transmission of orders from above. They set into motion and co-ordinate the various planned operations, and transmit and supervise any policy changes decreed by the directors.

Thus what is at stake here is not a matter of incompetence but the permanent separation of creativity, scientific knowledge and technical skill from the uses made of them by management.

Irrationality

Decisions seem irrational because, for capitalists, rationality is not a 'value' in itself but only a tool to help them control the forces of production better. That is why rationality – on whose altar the technician would naively sacrifice everything else – is continually violated by those who hold administrative power. A manager is not discredited when he behaves irrationally but when he fails to realize the expected profits. The moral is *princeps omnibus legibus solutus* – the prince is not bound to respect the law, as laws are made not for the powerful but to curb the multitude.

Compartmentalization

The isolation and unrelatedness of technical functions are integral to the structure of the modern corporation, not merely an incidental inconvenience. We can now see in retrospect why the process of compartmentalization is central to our analysis. This is regarded by the technicians as the most resented of all professional constraints even though they often misinterpret its real significance. The most frequent instances of 'disobedience' among technicians are related to professional conflicts, interference in one another's work, refusal to obey instructions based on inoperative norms and rejection of low work standards. Though some roles and positions may be better or worse than others in these respects it would be wrong to draw the conclusion, as technocrats do, that all problems that arise are simply problems of organization.

THE HUMAN COSTS

Even *frustrations of an apparently personal nature* are linked to the way the capitalist division of labour compartmentalizes technical functions. Here are some examples.

Lack of mobility

During the recent troubles at SNAM and at Siemens the issue of upward mobility was one of the most hotly debated. By using organizational devices some firms actually manage to 'invent' new echelons. In fact these functions are always so specialized and so restricted that they do not allow staff to develop skills and creativity. Attempts to escape from this trap by moving on to different firms usually prove to be hopeless. At most they can hope to finish up doing the same kind of work with perhaps a rise in pay and new office furnishings.

It is usually stated that the 'generalists' (i.e. technicians who co-ordinate plans and projects) are free from such constraints. Yet the norms of a job in one firm are often so specialized (scale, climate, kind of organization, regional peculiarities and so on) that experience cannot be transferred to other firms.

The obsolescence of technical skills is another index of the technician's subordinate position. A computer programmer trained seven years ago with the machines of that time is no longer employable. Once past the age of 35-40, both the specialists and the generalists find it hard to get a job; at best they reach a 'ceiling' in their company, after which their pay and responsibility, and the interest of their work remain basically the same. Because of the limited nature of their training, specialists very rarely retain their creativity past this age; as for the generalists, the daily conflicts and tensions of their work usually wear them out, draining all creative energy. The only ones to escape this fate are those who manage to make the leap into upper management.

Inadequate in-service training

This inadequacy is not only qualitative (in the sense that one learns only the knowledge required by one's specific function) but also quantitative (opportunities to study are few and far between). Retraining diminishes the labour time available and hence affects profits. Even when retraining does occur (and it is encouraged by the larger companies nowadays), the instruction is always aimed at fulfilling immediate tasks and needs. Its purpose is not human, cultural enrichment or even preparation for long-term changes within the company. The very nature of the career militates against further training. Besides, many people refuse to attend courses for fear of being replaced during their temporary absence.

The careerist ideology and its human costs

The careerist ideology can be summed up in a nutshell – the strongest rise to the top, and the weaker succumb. There are thousands of stories to illustrate the supposed virtues of the competitive system. Firstly, therefore, the myth of the survival of the fittest fostered by this system must be destroyed. Anyone who has worked in a company knows that the criteria for promotion are completely non-objective. Even where promotion is not completely arbitrary and indiscriminate, careers are dependent on two fundamental criteria: on the one hand on a number of personal attributes such as sociability, adaptability, aggressiveness, personal authority and above all practical and operational aptitudes; on the other hand conformity to the system, obedience to the hierarchy, the ability to innovate without altering pre-established norms and plans, 'loyalty' and 'discretion' in relaying information to the top, and legitimate ambition.

Secondly, what does this competitive system cost in terms of people's lives, and how does it affect them? A brief list would include: an almost chronic sense of frustration and humiliation caused by failures at work, which are felt to be indications of personal inadequacy; the devaluation of other areas of personal fulfilment – the impoverishment not only of political and cultural life but of family life, friendships and all social life; and nervous tension provoked by the competitive relations at work and giving rise not only to anxiety but to heart trouble, ulcers and so on.

POLITICAL IMPLICATIONS
So far the complex system of rewards and punishment has worked in that it has sublimated the frustrations of the technicians. We must look beyond moralistic or psychological simplifications involving the technicians' capacity for corruption or their servile nature. The fundamental problem lies in the technician's predisposition to think of the present mode of production and organization as an unchangeable objective fact. They have been so conditioned by the cultural and professional values inculcated into them from school, college or university onwards.

We must ask ourselves why, after such a lengthy period during which not the slightest sign of collective dissatisfaction was seen, the technicians have now become restless. The reasons are complex and interrelated. Cultural patterns and norms are in the process of changing. The student protest movement is producing individuals who are sensitive to the most subtle manifestations of authoritarianism and who are far less responsive to the rewards the system offers – consumption, prestige and social success.

But this is only one factor among many others. In the first place the contradictions of the system are becoming more acute, and the reasons for dissatisfaction among technicians are becoming more overt and immediate. In the second place strong anti-authoritarian tendencies are developing within the working class. The movement is no longer exclusively limited to wage demands (it was difficult to draw in the technicians on these grounds alone), but dramatically confronts the inadequacies of the system as a whole. Thus a basis for mass debates on the possibility of alternative methods of management and control, indeed for alternative structures in organizing production and society, has been created. For the first time since the war the sharpening class struggle creates a situation in which people are confronted with the necessity of making decisions, of choosing their loyalties.

More than ever before mobilization of the technicians is both possible and necessary today. The guiding theme of a technician's movement must be the call for the abolition of the present division of labour, which distinguishes them from the rest of the working class but nevertheless remains the source of their oppression. Since the present division of labour is the concrete manifestion of corporate capitalist domination, this theme will inevitably guide working-class strategy as well.

The implication for political practice arising from this analysis is that *each person must question and challenge his or her allotted job, function and role within the capitalist system of production and domination.*

For technicians this means rejecting an abstract commitment that relegates politics to one's 'spare time' and fails to link political activity with the content and experience of work. This sort of élitist commitment, which is usually widespread among intellectuals, usually amounts to authoritarian sermonizing to those who are regarded as less 'cultivated', and is based on a supposed distinction between those who are in the know and those who are not. We naturally do not underestimate the importance of joining revolutionary organizations. But we want to draw attention to less 'lofty' ways of making a political contribution. The technicians must enter trade-union activity as fellow-victims of capitalist exploitation and oppression. In consciously questioning their position under capitalism they must also come to reject élitist assumptions of leadership within trade-union organizations.

We want to elaborate on what exactly it means to challenge and to call into question one's allotted tasks, and hence one's role within the capitalist system of division of labour. This questioning must start with an analysis of the political significance of particular roles and functions, and of their specific importance within the power structures that produce them. We have become used to analyses that are highly abstract and non-specific but have no explanatory value whatsoever. Maoist student organizations, for example, are particularly prone to such sloganizing. They announce: 'Technical workers are lackeys in the service of capital' and 'Technology is not neutral' and so on. And while all this may be true, assertions like these can scarcely be said to throw any light on how things work in detail, on the concrete level, or to be helpful in showing technical workers what they can do about their situation. What we need is concrete case studies – what exactly is the content of the roles of, say, a computer programmer or a machine designer? Ony on this basis can we understand the political function of such roles and define a strategy for struggling to change them.

A challenge to the functions that people have to perform may take off from an individual refusal to accept without criticism orders and tasks assigned from on high – perhaps some new project, or a particular mathematical model, or a request to re-evaluate the work rates on an assembly line, or to design a new work routine. But at this personalized level, what we have is a defiance that normally goes no further than creating a scandal: 'I'm not going to do what you ask because I don't understand its presuppositions or its consequences. I refuse to do work that doesn't make any sense to me.' A more sophisticated refusal would be to reject the full implications, causes and consequences of the order. But it is easy for management to deal with this type of challenge. They have far more information available, and anyway the task concerned will usually be uncontestable given the technical criteria on which the argument will be based.

The second phase of protest will involved the *development of new norms and criteria that are alien to capitalist rationality*. The technician will come to assume responsibility for all the direct and indirect consequences of his activities. Beginning with twinges of moral responsibility, he will start to judge his functions in the light of a new political rationality, based upon an awareness of alternatives to existing values and forms of management.

CHALLENGING THE ROLE OF TECHNICAL AND SCIENTIFIC WORKERS

The challenge to capitalist rationality must simultaneously involve demands for the reformulation of science and technology. The rejection of roles and functions will also mean a refusal to be duped by methods of work and the assumptions inherent in this work. For example operations research and time-and-motion studies become 'scientific' once their basic, implicit assumptions concerning human beings are accepted as facts – i.e. the assumption that men are extremely simple productive mechanisms, composed wholly of motion and memory, who start and stop to command. We are not suggesting that technicians should take time off from work to discuss the philosophical and psychological implications of the works of Frederick Taylor, but rather that they should start from a totally different conception of human nature and should challenge, necessarily by means of the most careful and thorough study, the nature and content of technology and of organizational 'science' every time they conflict with this alternative view of human nature.

Let us be firm on one point – we should beware of using over-generalized and abstract slogans in trying to analyse the content and function of technical and scientific work. Such generalities simply lead to interminable wrangles about theoretical differences and the splits in the international working-class movement, ultimately destroying any possibility of political mobilization. When calling one's own role into question one must proceed in such a way as to practically demonstrate the existence and soundness of alternative criteria and methods. It is strategically essential, therefore, to engage in a series of concrete actions from which partial but lasting victories can be won. In every case this has led to a break in the chain of command and a challenge to the norms and criteria of management invoked by the hierarchy. Such a strategy cannot achieve its results in one almighty push or through a grandiose overall rejection of capitalism. And revolutionary consciousness cannot be achieved through an implacably destructive attitude designed to bring the enterprise to a complete standstill in the hope that something better will emerge from its smouldering ruins. Instead it will come about through a struggle with rigorously defined aims, in which every battle will produce new cultural patterns and put forward alternative forms of organization.

The detailed content of such campaigns will to a large extent be determined by the general strategy. Obviously roles cannot be challenged by one individual alone, though a confrontation might be sparked off by one particular instance. If an individual is isolated he is at the mercy of those with power; thus if we are to resist disciplinary pressures, to assume the offensive, to hope to gain meaningful concessions, the challenge must be a collective one. Initial efforts can be made by small groups, but they will have to attempt to encompass ever-larger sectors of the technicians and to link up with the struggles of other employees and workers.

But why not attempt mobilization on a more overtly general political basis? Because it is of the utmost importance that all existing experiences and concepts of organization and management should be *concretely criticized in detail*. Only on this basis will it be possible to expand the struggle and to develop new criteria and norms, new ideas for socialist alternatives for managing production. In this sense the challenging of one's role is also a prelude to having it judged by the working-class. And at this stage a method of struggle is transformed into a struggle with a definite objective: 'I won't do this work until it has been evaluated and redefined by those who depend on it – myself, my colleagues and other employees and workers, society at large. . . .' This is the beginning of a process of democratizing technical knowledge, of creative experimentation. We must repeat again that all the new concepts for defining the role of management in production, and the new sets of relationships envisaged, must be produced and judged by the only class capable of such vision – the working class.

We must avoid the mistake, so typical of the technocratic mentality, with its naive faith in analytical reasoning, of seeing what we have described as a straight redefinition or adjustment of functions by the independent action of the technicians themselves. In this context we need only point to the number of so-called technical and supervisory positions that would become totally redundant if the capitalist division of labour were to be genuinely abolished to realize how wrong it is to talk about a mere redefinition of technical roles.

Without this clarification, our proposals may run the risk of becoming a strategy for the development of technocracy and could be regarded as an appeal of the type 'all power to the technicians'. If there is any appeal in the position we have developed it is rather 'all power to the masses'.

The technicians' struggle is for us a phase, a moment in the class struggle, and the relationship between technicians and workers is an organic and permanent relationship at all levels of productive and political activity.

Our whole analysis assumes that the working class will go beyond the struggle for wages and better conditions of work and resolutely put forward demands for control over the productive process. One problem, however, still remains. In spite of the fact that there have been more and more struggles about conditions of work and protests about the nature of work a full and clear awareness that the fundamental problem lies in the division of labour has not yet developed. The trade-union struggles we have so far witnessed have not been based on a fully developed analysis or detailed interpretation of the nature of shop-floor work. There are no explicit ideas about a *new type of labour that would enable the individual's potential to be fully realized, that would be worth while and would enable the workers to exercise control over the factories.*

Unless the working class, together with its political and union organizations, conducts its struggle on this level and in this light, it is obvious that the technicians cannot question their roles, except from a technocratic standpoint. And this means stagnation and defeat. We must be bold enough to work in this direction, even if a number of fundamental conditions for success are missing today. The strategy we have put forward can incite the working class to progress from what is often an unconsciously guided rebellion against the division of labour to the creation of new forms of co-operative management within an enterprise.

It is the capacity to advance in this direction that will decide not only whether the dominant class can be replaced but also whether institutions, forms of management and a culture can be created that could ensure that the revolution will retain its character as a process of liberation.

ANTONIO LETTIERI
Factory and Education*

The scope of the workers' movement has become considerably broader in recent years as a result of worker and student struggles. These struggles have posed in an acute and concrete way problems that only a few years ago would have seemed completely abstract. But it is a feature of the present situation that there is a potential for struggles with more advanced objectives than those the movement sets itself. The struggles of May 1968 in France and of student and (to some extent) worker movements in Italy and other capitalist countries have all manifested an absence of strategy and an absence of well-defined, progressive objectives. As an obvious example of this we have only to consider the problem of the relationship between the factory and the educational system, and between workers and students, that is to say the relationship between the most explosive social forces of this phase in the development of capitalism.

The central problem is that of the interrelationship between the different levels of social protest, between the different forms of social struggle and between the agents of these various processes. The following remarks attempt to analyse some of these interrelationships on the basis of a study of certain features of recent struggles, of their strategy and objectives. Four kinds of issue are discussed:

1) the issue of defining workers' qualifications and skills and the associated problem of job classification; this is illustrated by reference to the recent agreements at Italsider, which eliminated the system of job evaluation and associated wage scales;

2) the problem of the relationship between work organization and the

* This article originally appeared in *Problemi del Socialismo*, XLIX as 'Note su qualifiche, scuola e orari di lavoro'. A revised version, from which this translation has been prepared, appeared first in *Les Temps Modernes*, (August-September 1971). The author is a leader of the FIOM-CGIL and was responsible for drawing up the statement of demands made by the striking Italsider steelworkers to which he refers at several points in this article. Translated by John Mepham.

[The Italian steel industry comprises a privately owned sector, which accounts for about one quarter of production, and Italsider, a rapidly expanding sector under public control. The latter is run by a public holding corporation, IRI (which also controls shipyards, heavy engineering industries and so on), and its various factories (with an aggregate capacity of over 40 million tons of steel and cast iron in 1974) are operated as branches of one large national trust. *Trans.*]

educational system; and of the possibility of finding a different way to organize work;

3) aspects of the crisis in the educational system, and the relationship between workers' control of work organization and the need for a fundamental change in the educational system;

4) the relationship between work organization and education on the one hand, and the length of the working day and the working week on the other.

These remarks do not add up to a definitive treatment of each of these problems. Certain themes are developed as a basis for discussion about general strategic objectives. In our view the central problem for the Left is that of unifying the diverse social forces and the struggles they are waging.

THE ELIMINATION OF WAGE SCALES BASED ON JOB EVALUATION

The elimination of work 'analysis and evaluation' and of associated wage scales, which was a feature of the recent agreement at Italsider on a new system of classification in a way represents the end of an era. Work analysis and evaluation was the most refined and complex extension of 'scientific' work organization. It was, moreover, the aspect of the work situation which workers had the least possibility of influencing. [1]

Job evaluation claimed to be able to establish a strict correlation between level of payment and the nature of the work (analysed in terms of prerequisite training, degree of responsibility, risks and so on). It was really applicable only to fragmented, repetitive and simple tasks. It was therefore not only a reflection of the fact that work was divided into measurable tasks (and the correlated differentiation in wages); it actually accentuated these tendencies.

When Italsider workers mounted a campaign in the first half of 1970, to do away with the system of job classification that was then in use, this involved them in the task of collectively elaborating a new system to replace the old one. In fact neither the Italian steel industry nor the steel industries in other capitalist countries offered a model on which they could build, a model that really expressed their ideas and their demands. Even in systems of classification apparently based on training and qualifications wage levels are in fact always determined by other conditions as well (danger, heat, physical strain and so on). The workers wanted to disregard such conditions in defining their job classification, so as to avoid all 'monetization' of dangerous and unhealthy working conditions.*

Given this fact, how can a job be evaluated in relation to the level of training and skills required for its execution? What do such 'qualifications' amount to when abstracted from the real conditions in which the work is

---

* [One of the constant themes of the Italian Unions is the assertion that health is not for sale whatever the price. The rejection of 'monetization' means: the boss may buy our labour power, but we won't sell him our bodies and lives. *Trans.*]

actually done? How are we to define the abstract level of qualification of the foundry worker or the rolling-mill worker, leaving aside considerations of the heat, dust, noise and so on in which they work? How are we to establish comparisons between the training and skills of the various trades, for example of those who strictly speaking work outside the steelmaking process itself (turners, fitters and so on)? Answers to these questions had to be found, not only because they were bound to crop up in responding to the management line in negotiations, but also because they were questions that troubled the workers themselves. No armchair solutions would have carried conviction.

The method adopted at Italsider was collective discussion. This discussion had a completely new aim; it involved deciding in relation to this concrete case how many 'levels' were needed for a satisfactory classification of more than forty thousand workers, leaving aside both the management's method of approach ('job analysis and evaluation') and the system of classification actually built into existing agreements and contracts. The most important aspect of this collective labour of analysing and reflecting on work organization was that it was conducted by the workers themselves, first on the level of work teams and workshops and then, after comparison of results and discussion, on the level of the factory, and ultimately on the level of the entire nation wide steel trust.

The workers thereby developed their own views on the problem of classification. One non-union group put forward the view that there should be a single class for all workers, but this did not prevail. The workers defined their own scale of qualifications, but reduced their number to a minimum. The old system had divided blue-collar workers into twenty-four categories; the proposed system had six categories in all, for both blue-collar and white-collar workers. There were to be no more than four blue-collar classes, the lowest of which was to be a transitional one for new workers. The other interesting aspect of the discussion concerned the criteria for promotion from one class to another by means of individual or collective acquisition of the knowledge and skill necessary to increase the number of points within the production process at which the individual or team could perform the necessary work.

The outcome, after one of the hardest struggles of that autumn (1970), was not too far removed from the spirit of the demands. Agreement was reached on a system of eight categories, covering both shop-floor and office workers. But the number of categories was not in itself the important thing. What was important was the process by which it had been arrived at. As we have seen, the initial demand for six categories was the outcome of a process of collective inquiry and discussion among the workers. The agreement on eight categories was simply the expression of the balance of forces as between the workers, who wanted to fix the number of categories at a lower limit,[2] and the management, who wanted to minimize the reduction in the number of classes (they proposed fourteen to begin with, then ten) so as to preserve their power of manoeuvre in relation both to work organization and to wage scales.

This experiment is described here not just for its incidental interest but because it helps to demonstrate a general truth: systems of classification may appear to be 'objective', but they are actually conventional. They are based not on objective criteria but on a balance of forces. The question is, who decides on the system of classification and on the ends it is to serve? In reality the classification of workers within a firm, even if it is arrived at by negotiated agreement, has always been an aspect of work organization that is beyond the control of the workers and the unions.

CLASSIFICATION: THE EXPRESSION OF A BALANCE OF FORCES

In practice workers with equal skills and doing comparable jobs are divided into two or three different categories. Moreover there is no fixed correlation between the class a worker is assigned to and the wages he is paid. Even where workers within each category do earn roughly the same average wage in the various different plants of a big firm, this is in fact only a formal equality. In reality 'the criteria of classification are so different that in the last analysis a worker is assigned to a category on the basis of the wage it is decided he is to be paid, and not the reverse' (report of the ENI-IRI* inquiry on wages, 1968).

It has sometimes been pointed out that each wage rate on the scale fluctuates round an average that is allegedly determined by the state of the labour market. For example the inquiry showed that the average wages actually paid to welders, turners, fitters and tool-makers were the same to within 2 or 3 per cent. We could conclude from this that the state of the labour market was roughly the same for each trade. But in fact in most of the firms studied the deviation of wages from this average was of the order of 50-80 per cent. However we look at it, it is clear that classification and wage scales were in fact the result of labour policy within each firm, and not of objective criteria. This must be the starting-point for the workers' response to job-classification policies. Their objective must be workers' control over the system of classification, and self-determination of the criteria on which it is to be based.

A new classification policy cannot, however, be limited solely to the question of wages. It must be integrated into the general strategy that aims to extend the scope of social control by the workers over the conditions of work. If the problem of classification is posed solely in terms of wage scales any solution will be purely illusory.

---

* [ENI (Ente Nazionale Idrocarburi) is the publicly controlled oil and natural gas corporation which also produces petrochemicals and drilling equipment; IRI is the publicly controlled holding of state participation in industry. Together they represent the equivalent of the nationalized sector. *Trans.*]

THE DEFINITION OF SKILLS AND THE ORGANIZATION OF WORK

Fundamentally the problem of classification is the problem of the organization of work. The qualifications of a worker, his trade or professional skills, are not objective and static quantities. They are the temporary and changeable outcome of his relationship with a certain technology, a technology that tends in fact to under-employ the worker's general abilities to such an extent that the result is individual and collective mutilation. This situation is not a technical necessity. It is open to collective transformation. That is why the problem cannot be reduced to a demand for a 'fair' system of classification. The essential task is to allow the workers once again to do forms of work in which they can grow and develop by actually employing their abilities and skills, i.e. to enable them to master, to take over and to change the process of production by putting science and technology in the service of their own human development.

Obviously this is not a matter of going back to some traditional notion of 'crafts' and 'trades', with their associated corporatist ideologies. Nor is it simply a matter of adapting the idea of trade qualifications accepted today to a situation in which workers have to retrain continually to cope with the demands of a rapidly changing technology. This line can certainly be profitably adopted in the context of particular negotiations within a factory or firm, but there is always the risk that this will keep the more fundamental issue hidden. It is the transformation of the organization of work that workers must insist on, not some purely formal recognition of, and payment for, their potential abilities which in fact they will never be allowed to bring into play at work. To be reclassified into a higher category without the nature of one's work, which remains fragmented and monotonous, being in any way improved is simply to get oneself paid more for one's daily dose of stupefaction and exhaustion, and to miss the central problem – that of the workers acquiring control over the organization of work.

The old idea of 'scientific work organization' has been in doubt for many years, and traditional conceptions of the various trades have been gradually eroded. As a result an army of psychologists, sociologists and economists have been mobilized and have been active for the last thirty years in the United States in the service of capital, attempting to discover methods of organization that are more effective than the old ones worked out by Taylor and Ford. Recomposition of jobs and job enrichment have been experimented with and adopted by some large corporations such as Philips and IBM. But these new techniques of work organization in no way alter the underlying ideology of exploitation and profit; on the contrary, they are designed with these objectives in mind. The 'development of the worker's personality and abilities' has been a mere device designed to attract people, to gain their alliegance, to fight absenteeism and to prevent conflict. To the extent that these new techniques of work organization are designed and introduced by management in the context of cultural and political subordination on the part of the workers, they function in effect as ways of 'integrating' the worker, of 'personalizing work' while depersonalizing the worker. Moreover these experiments have so far been attempted only on a very restricted scale, within a few selected plants.

But the fact that these techniques exist (recomposition of jobs, autonomy of work teams, collective promotion and so on) does illustrate some significant facts: a) managers and owners often shake off cultural prejudices more rapidly than the working class; b) there are alternatives to the present technical division of labour; and c) these alternatives are politically ambiguous. There should be no question of trying mechanically to impose limits on them, or of rejecting them altogether simply because they are introduced by the bosses, and rarely at that. We must remember that techniques are not simply objectively given facts. Technology controlled by the bosses is a solution to bosses' problems. It can solve workers' problems only if it is controlled collectively by the working class with a full awareness of its technical and political significance.

A new policy concerning job classification must therefore be integrated with the struggle against wage differentials and the struggle for a new system of work organization, as the first steps toward the *social* control by the workers of the production process. These are complementary aspects of the struggle because wage differentials will inevitably reappear as long as work organization remains as it is. If management retain the initiative in experimenting with new methods of work organization they will use this as an opportunity for consolidating their power both over the division of labour and over wage scales. If the initiative is taken by the workers, if they struggle to change wages and work organization simultaneously, then they must often start by campaigning against the hierarchization of wages in order to use the ensuing deadlock as the opportunity for launching a struggle on more fundamental issues.

In other words an assembly-line worker who repeats the same simple movements every few seconds might obtain reclassification. But this promotion will do nothing for him except give him a few more pence per hour. The decisive problem remains that of work organization. What is needed is recomposition of jobs so that his work involves more extensive and complex functions, and job rotation to break down the divorce between production, control, tool-making, regulation and so on. But such a transformation cannot be achieved all at once, and the first step towards it must be the abolition of arbitrary systems of classification that restrict masses of workers to repetitive, stupefying and degrading work with no hope of escape.

We need a definition of concrete demands integrated with a long-term strategy. And this means that we must aim to reclassify workers into only two categories, which, for the sake of convenience, we can call 'skilled' and 'unskilled'. The objective of this policy is to design work so that it continuously provides opportunities for developing both theoretical and practical abilities, so that each worker can develop his faculties to the full. Moreover the worker's 'career' should not be conceived in terms of training in traditional trades – in fact the pace of technical development makes the distinctions between the trades artificial and useless. And how can we justify such distinctions as that between a wage-earning blue-collar technical worker and a salaried white-collar technical worker? To abolish such distinctions of classification and pay must be one of our aims.

FACTORY AND SCHOOL

It is impossible to pose the problem of qualifications and classifications correctly without at the same time calling the division of labour into question. But it is impossible to contest the division of labour without at the same time raising the question of *education*.

Workers' attempts to take control of the labour process come up against the problem of the rapid obsolescence of their technical knowledge and the inadequacy of the information available to them. Hence the necessity for the workers' movement to control science and education and to transform the social functions they perform. The fact that there are nearly a million workers in Italy taking evening classes is an indication of how widespread is the aspiration to escape from the lot of the ordinary worker by going back to school. But such efforts nearly always end in failure because there is no connection between education and factory, between the need to change the nature and organization of work on the one hand and what is actually taught in schools and colleges on the other. A survey in Turin revealed that workers usually thought of education as a means of avoiding the worker's lot, of getting 'higher-grade' jobs, though these might in fact be no less alienating.[3]

The problem must be posed in a more radical manner: the right of every worker, young or old, not only to make use of the educational system but to transform it, revolutionize it and run it must be recognized. I know that it is easy to dismiss such demands as 'unrealistic' because they go against deeply entrenched habits of thought. Capitalism has allowed us to get used to living under a system in which intellectual and manual work tend to be incompatible with one another. This mutual exclusion is, moreover, a characteristic feature of petty bourgeois ideology, which is horrified by the idea of manual work, and especially of factory work.

If this isolation of the factories could never be overcome the aspirations of growing numbers of workers would be Utopian. We would have to give up our struggle to change methods of work organization and to unite the struggles of students and workers, who at present, in all the capitalist countries, fight and are defeated in isolation from one another.

Conversely there is a direct connection between the crisis in educational institutions and their separation from the world of productive labour. The present educational system is a class system not only because it discriminates against *workers' children,* but chiefly because it discriminates against *the workers themselves.* We are warned that the class bias of the system will persist and worsen if higher education were open to everyone. This is because the class element in the educational system really stems from the divorce between 'culture' and production, between science and technology, between intellectual and manual work. In fact present-day capitalism no longer denies people access to education. But it does not allow a change in the social function of education.

The United States offers a good illustration of this. There the educational system has become an important element in the hypertrophied tertiary sector, a development typical of a society characterized by its waste and its sterilisation of potentially productive energies. Education is no longer something to be freely chosen as an aspect of individual or collective development. It is imposed on young people as the only alternative to unemployment or the army.

Education, according to an analysis made by some American sociologists, is a means of slowing down the entry of the majority of young people into the adult world of work. By means of the educational system millions of young people have to submit to work which Baran and Sweezy see as the only way of preventing the American economy from being suffocated by its massive surplus. In 1965 52.1 per cent of United States citizens between 17 and 24 years of age were students, soldiers or unemployed; 37.4 per cent were university students.[4]

This is one of the most catastrophic features of the most advanced of all capitalist societies. For the majority of young people between 17 and 24 education is the only escape from the army or unemployment. In the last five years the situation has become considerably worse. At the end of 1970 over 6 per cent of the workforce were unemployed and almost 18 per cent of young people had been unable to get their first job. The educational system has thus taken on the function of absorbing a superfluous labour force and putting to unproductive work the energies and potentialities for which the capitalist system has no use. According to the Council of Economic Advisors to the President young people who are excluded from the productive system represent a loss of income of the order of 30,000 million dollars a year. Education is, therefore, *unpaid, forced unproductive labour*. It is one of the most flexible, but also one of the most alienating, forms of exploitation.

These facts are significant. In the first place they reveal the inadequacies of the traditional type of analysis, which restricts itself to condemning the educational system on the grounds that it is 'functional' to capitalist production. This was true only up to a certain point. Beyond that point education became 'functional' to non-production, to waste, to keeping young people out of work and out of the adult world. This monstrous and sterile growth of education corresponds to the fact that educational qualifications are counting for less and less. The fact that entry into education becomes less and less selective no longer contradicts the needs of capitalism. Schools and colleges can happily get on with the job of turning out 'sophisticated' young people, just as the 'consumer society' produces overfed people. A growing proportion of these products of educational institutions have no choice but to return to them as teachers. The selection of higher technical personnel is no longer performed at this level, but takes place in the universities or specialized institutions of higher education, firmly under the control of the capitalist institutions whose needs they serve.

The education crisis in present-day capitalist society consists less of any limitation on *the right to study* than of the denial of *the right to work*, to perform freely chosen productive labour. Schools are increasingly open to masses of young people, but only in order to keep them incarcerated within their deformed structures. In fact they play a part in stabilizing the system.

EDUCATION AS FORCED UNPRODUCTIVE LABOUR

Italian studies on the probable future development of the relationship between education and employment reveal tendencies similar to those observed in the United States. ISRIL predicts that in 1980 the number of those leaving full-time education with exam passes and other qualifications will be far higher than the number of available jobs.[5] On the other hand Censis[6] estimates that at least until 1975 there will be a deficit of trained and qualified people. But it is significant, given what we have already said, that of these trained people almost 60 per cent will be needed in the teaching profession. In other words education will be the only industry capable in the near future of absorbing manpower, whether in the form of students, for whom the prospects of productive employment are decreasing, or in the form of teachers, who have no choice but to remain within the educational sector. It is no accident that 'Project 80' predicts for 1980 about 1,150,000 teachers, compared with 265,000 in 1965. While employment opportunities in industry will level off employment in education will more than quadruple over a period of 15 years.[7]

Thus from the point of view of both students and teachers, education is a safety-valve for the labour market, a means of disguising the growing number of unemployed produced by the development of capitalism. But even more fundamental is the institutional separation of education from the world of work. The capitalist development of education institutionalizes the divorce between productive and unproductive labour. Its tendency is to render useless immense resources of intellectual and physical energy in keeping them separated from production. The function of the school, in a sense, becomes essentially one of self-perpetuation. In this context of isolation the collective control of *present* educational institutions, as proposed by the Left, could be just another means of making this functional isolation even more complete and of implicitly endorsing its stabilizing role within capitalism.

The education crisis is in this respect one aspect of the general crisis of the system. The important thing is not to control *this* kind of education, but to subvert its function. It must be reintegrated with the world of productive labour and social development. It is important to reunify theory with practice, and culture with politics. This is the only way of reunifying *socially*, and not in a purely abstract way, educational institution and factory, and the forces that are struggling within them. The implication of all this is that we must aim to reconstruct education on the basis of social control in such a way as to change the content and manner of it, not merely the methods by which it is run.

There is therefore a dual relationship between education and factory. On the one hand the problem of education is connected with the problem of training and of the social control of work organization; on the other hand only a transformation of work organization and a different way of using science and technology can prevent educational institutions from fulfilling their present function of institutionalizing *forced unproductive labour*.

THE RIGHT TO STUDY AND THE RIGHT TO WORK

The workers' movement must therefore demand both *the right to study* for all workers and at the same time *the right to work* for all students. This means releasing workers and students from the ghettos to which they are now confined, and liberating the immense energies that are at present being wasted. But in making these demands we must be perfectly clear that they would involve a complete rupture of the traditional relationship between education and qualification, in favour of a more immediately political approach that would include the problems of work organization, industrial development and forms of employment. Any attempt to overcome the separation between factory and educational institution must be based on an analysis of the problem of the duration of work. The average duration of work has at present two mutually reinforcing consequences: it keeps workers out of education, and students out of productive employment. The 40-hour week (won in the 1969-70 agreements) divided into 5 working days of 8 hours each prevents workers from doing any serious studying. Those workers who do study after work, making enormous sacrifices, cannot really study properly. On the other hand the 40-hour week, given present-day technical and productivity norms, prevents young people from doing productive work and 'condemns' them to continue their education.

In a recent article Garavini insists on the need for unions to adopt the objective of a 36-hour working week and at the same time a continuous working day of 6 hours. The unbroken working day, together with the reduction of the working week, is, given present-day scientific and technological development, the prerequisite for the reunification of practical and intellectual work, production and study, so that educational institutions should no longer be divorced from industry but should become a permanent vehicle for growth and development. [8]

Somebody is bound to object that this is necessarily a long-term aim, even a Utopian one. But I insist that it is in fact already a practical, concrete possibility today. In the first place, so far as Italy is concerned (and this is also true of the most advanced capitalist society, the United

States), it is the only concrete way of posing the problem of unemployment. The reduction of the working week to 36 hours would make room for 500,000 additional production workers. It is no accident that the compulsory shortening of the average working week has been responsible for an increase of nearly 2 per cent in the number of industrial jobs.

There is another objection to adopting these demands – that Italian industry would have to carry the burden of extra labour costs compared with other European capitalist countries. But this argument is unsound for two reasons. In the first place we always have to choose between different objectives. The reduction of the working week to 36 hours without a reduction in pay would mean an increase in costs for each firm of the same order of magnitude as that involved in the introduction of the 'fourteenth month' (the 'thirteenth month' having already been won in Italy).* The unions must decide on their objectives in the light of a clear, carefully worked-out strategy that is capable of unifying the movement.

As for the competitiveness of industry, it should be obvious that, given the increased organic composition of capital, a firm's profits are determined more by the proportion of each day that its industrial plant is in operation (hence by the number of daily and weekly shifts) than by the absolute cost of labour. For example negotiations could be conducted in which a correlation is made between the reduction of the working week to 36 hours and some way of increasing plant utilization. This is not a purely hypothetical possibility. In 1970 these problems of a shorter working week and plant utilization were already being discussed in Italy in relation to one another, and in particular in relation to the possibility of drastically reducing overtime.

The management line in these negotiations was to demand both overtime and a larger number of shifts. The union varied its response to suit local conditions. In regions of low unemployment, where there was no question of bringing in extra workers, the union went for demands that would result in fewer weekly shifts (for instance no more Saturday-evening or Sunday working), and less night work and overtime. In regions where there was considerable unemployment a more flexible approach was adopted and an increase in the number of jobs was tied to more intensive plant utilization and thus to an increase in the number of shifts. This allowed them to forge solidarity between workers and the unemployed and the social and political gain balanced the sacrifice of putting up with Saturday work and the night shift.

DURATION OF WORK AND A NEW EDUCATIONAL SYSTEM

If the 36-hour week has to go together with the introduction of a second or third shift, so as to keep the machines turning for 12 or 18 hours a day instead of 8 or 16 hours as at present, production will increase in the

* ['The thirteenth month' is an annual bonus payment equivalent to a month's wages paid, on certain conditions, at the end of each year. *Trans.*]

developed regions without any increase in investment (to the extent that local manpower is available, which it usually is – young people and women are in effect at present excluded from production). The bulk of new investment can therefore be concentrated in the under-developed regions.

All of which brings us back to the problem we started with: the relationship between education and production, between time at work and time available for study. In the context of a 6-hour day the idea of part-time work could take on new meaning. It could mean 4 hours at work, with plenty of time left over for study or for any other social activity. As for pay, there are several possibilities. In the beginning 4 hours' work might be paid *pro rata*, i.e. a weekly pay of two thirds of the norm. Later it might be possible to consider hours of study on the same basis as hours at work, to be paid as a whole (for example via some fund that all firms would contribute to). The reduction of the working day to 6 hours in itself implies a different relationship between working time and free time, between practical and intellectual work. The parallel reduction of the working day to 4 hours would allow young people to divide their time between educational institution and factory. This would imply a coming together of these two institutions, which the capitalist system tends to keep strictly apart.

At the same time the reduction of the normal working week from 40 to 36 hours and the introduction of a working week of 24 hours for young people and women who could not or did not wish to work full time, would enable hundreds of thousands of new jobs to be created and would reverse the present tendency towards a pathological contraction of the workforce.

To sum up: the relationship between factory and educational institutions is clearly illustrated not only by the problem of qualifications and training and the struggle for social control of work organization, but also by that of the length of the working week, which is the key to any solution to the problem of the separation of factory and educational institution. This separation is present in the lived experience of every worker: first he goes to a school or college which is cut off from the real world of production, which is experienced as an enclosed and *unreal* world, and then he lives the reality of productive work, which is cut off from scientific and cultural development.

Are the options outlined here risky or Utopian? We can answer this only by reference to an analysis of new tendencies within the workers' movement. The workers are refusing to submit to the phoney objectivity of technology; 'scientific' work organization is being called into question; systems of job classification have reached a state of crisis. Confronted with these developing contradictions, and with a crisis in education, capitalism hesitates between two apparently incompatible, but in fact complementary, ways out – reform and repression. It is no accident that in Italy 1970 ended with a call for an end to worker and student struggles, and with an attack on the new spectre that is haunting Europe, the spectre of protesting 'minorities'. These minorities are in fact the great mass of workers and students. Repression and reform have a single aim – to keep these explosive social forces apart, to keep the site of production separate from that of education. They are united only for the élite who wield economic and political power.

The workers' movement must not respond to this dual crisis with demands for piecemeal reforms that do not tackle the fundamental problems. The response must be a unifying one and must bring together what capitalism tends to keep apart – workers with one another; the world of production with that of culture, factory and education; workers and students.

NOTES

1 Job evaluation implies, by definition, a wide range of wage rates. At Italsider there were twenty-four categories for the shop-floor workers and sixteen for office workers and special categories. The artificial character of this hierarchical structure contrasted sharply with the increasingly egalitarian mood of the workers.

2 The six classes (or pay categories) were as follows: one for new entrants; three graded classes covering both shop-floor and office workers; and two classes for administrative and higher-grade technical staff. When the demands were more closely studied, during the struggle, by a larger number of administrative and technical staff, it was found that it implied too great a contraction of pay differentials to be realistic. This is how the union arrived at the eight pay categories that featured in the eventual settlement.

3 There is a summary of this survey in G. Lévi Arian, G. Alasia, A. Chiesa, P. Bergoglio and L. Benigni, *I lavatori studenti. Testimonianze raccolte a Torino*, with an introduction by V. Foa (Turin: Einaudi 1969).

4 Cf. John and Margaret Rowntree, 'Youth as class' *International Socialist Journal*, XXVIII-XXIX.

5 N. Cacace and M. D'Ambrosio (ISRIL), *Domanda e offerta d i Laureati in Italia, a* supplement to *Futuribili*, II.

6 Censis, *Le strutture formative al 1975* (Rome 1966).

7 Duplicated report delivered to a conference in Rome by A. Asor Rosa, *Formation de la force de travail et les débouchés professionnels* (May 1970).

8 S. Garavini, 'Le nuove strutture democratiche in fabbrica e la politica rivendicativa', *Problemi del Socialismo*, XLIV.

ANDRÉ GORZ

Technology, Technicians and Class Struggle*

The man of knowledge and the productive labourer come to be widely divided from each other, and knowledge, instead of remaining the handmaid of labour in the hand of the labourer to increase his productive powers . . . has almost everywhere arrayed itself against labour . . . systematically deluding and leading them [the labourers] astray in order to render their muscular powers entirely mechanical and obedient.

W. Thompson, *An Inquiry into the Principles of the Distribution of Wealth* (1824), quoted in Marx, *Capital* [1]

I

Until recently most Marxists still thought of forces of production – in particular science and technology – as ideologically neutral, and they considered the development of these forces of production to be inherently positive. They usually held the view that as it matured capitalism was producing a material base on which socialism could be constructed, and it was thought that the more the forces of production developed under capitalism the easier it would be to build socialism. Such productive forces as technology, science, human skills and knowledge and abundant dead labour (fixed capital) were considered to be assets that would greatly facilitate the transition to socialism.

These views were based on a rather mechanistic interpretation of the Marxian thesis that the forces of production, as they develop, stand in ever greater contradiction with capitalist social relations of production. Most European communist parties supported the view that capitalist relations of production were acting as fetters on the development of the forces of production and that socialism, by tearing down the superstructures of the capitalist state and capitalist social relations, would be able to release at a stroke the tremendous potential for socio-economic development and growth that had until then been fettered.

In conformity with this thesis the European communist parties usually consider all available productive capacity and all available manual, technical, professional and intellectual skills to be forces that will be valuable and useful during the period of transition to socialism, and therefore believe that it is important that they should be preserved. Socialism, they claim, will be able to employ all these productive capacities

*This article originally appeared in *Les Temps Modernes* (August-September 1971) Translated by John Mepham.

for the benefit of the whole of society and all these forms of skilled work will be granted their appropriate rewards, whereas capitalism makes use of them only in a destructive or parasitic manner, or even fails to use them at all.

Such a thesis, which is an *ideological* analysis of the growing integration of science and technology with the processes of production, a development foreseen by Marx, is intimately bound up with a *political* analysis. The fundamental political thesis is that the transition to socialism must proceed in a peaceful manner, and in stages, and must in no way involve overthrowing the organization of work and the division of labour, or the technological basis of material production on which they are founded. Rather these must be preserved, but put to use for social goals of a 'democratic' character. In other words the whole collection of professions, skills and abilities involved in capitalist production, together with the way in which they are integrated and their hierarchical structure, are considered to be suitable for preservation in a society in transition to socialism, without any need for a thorough ideological change or a 'cultural revolution', or a professional, intellectual and moral upheaval. Everything that is productive from the point of view of capital, within the framework of the capitalist mode of production, is supposed to be able to remain productive (or even to become yet more productive) during the period of transition to socialism. This transition must be based politically on an 'anti-monopoly alliance', an alliance of all those workers who, under monopoly capitalism, constitute the 'collective productive worker' (*Gesamtarbeiter* is Marx's term for it), i.e. those whose individual labour 'combines to form the overall productive machine' when socially combined. This group comprises manual workers, foremen and supervisors as well as the 'engineers, managers, technologists etc.' who, according to certain passages in Marx, 'are to be included in the group of productive workers directly exploited by capital and subordinated to its processes of production and realisation'.[2] The real conjuring trick happens when all these people, including the 'NCOs of production', are incorporated, as a result of a selective reading of Marx, into the 'collective productive worker' and are hence thought of as an integral part of the working class, because according to this view the working class includes just about everybody, and has lost its characteristic ruggedness and its ideological and cultural distinctiveness. It includes more or less the whole hierarchy in the factory and can be seen only as a force for order. Political power, exercised in the name of this working class, would be feared only by the monopolists – and by the proletariat.

That is why we must attempt a critical analysis of the forces of production and of capitalist development. Of course in certain respects there is nothing new about this idea. For example it is not new in as much as it is a matter of showing the following:

1) that capitalism develops the forces of production in such a way as to destroy, disguise or deny their liberating potential. The development of

forces of production is indissolubly linked to that of forces of destruction; that which is productive at the level of particular capitals can be destructive at the level of the capitalist economy as a whole, and above all destructive of the possibilities for going beyond capitalism that develop within capitalism itself;[3]

2) that an increasing proportion of the labour-power put to work under capitalism performs labour that is unproductive and parasitic. Such labour requires particular skills and capacities and confers social status, of a kind that should disappear along with the capitalist system. But this status, while making the irrationality of the capitalist system obvious, does at the same time provide it with a fairly broad social base, notably among the parasitic 'new middle classes';[4]

3) that capitalist development takes place overall in such a way that the contradiction between forces and relations of production, far from making itself felt *spontaneously*, can be contained and masked. Productive forces, including people's abilities and skills, are developed in a deformed way, so that they are, if we consider them from the point of view of social needs, useless. But they are functional within the system and are subject to its logic precisely because of the deformed character that it gives them. So we cannot subject this deformation to critical analysis from a standpoint *within* this system, from a standpoint that presupposes the value of these existing skills and productive forces. We must try to see things from a point of view *beyond* the system, and to see that it is *possible* to go beyond the system. This possibility is maturing in the development of the system itself, but it is continually being buried and hidden from view. That is why we must break away from all manifestations, at all levels, of capitalist ideology, subvert them and engage in head-on battle with them.[5]

But all this is so far nothing but generalities. The critique of the capitalist development of the forces of production has up to now concentrated mainly on the ways in which the processes whereby capital is reproduced in fact involve a continual destruction of productive capital and render so much potentially available labour-power socially useless. But one vital question has been left unasked; what are the implications of this critique for our view of science and technology? How are we to analyse the means of production in which science and technology are incorporated, and the forms and division of labour that have come about as a result of the 'technification' and 'scientization' of production? Can it be shown – as was concretely indicated by the Chinese Cultural Revolution – that *capitalist* relations of production and *capitalist* division of labour leave their imprint on science and technology themselves, on their fragmentation and specialization, on the directions in which they develop, on their practical applications and even on their language?[6] If this can be shown the implication would be that any attempt to revolutionize the relations of production would necessarily also involve a simultaneous radical transformation of the means and techniques of production, and not only of the uses to which they are put. Unchanged means and techniques of production, and hence an unchanged, capitalist division of labour, would involve the reappearance of capitalist relations of production.[7] This analysis would also imply that scientific and technical workers, in performing their technical functions, are also performing the function of reproducing *the conditions and the forms of the domination of labour by capital*.

I shall discuss these problems by raising the following three questions:

1) Is it the process of material production as such that requires scientific and technical workers to perform this function, or does this requirement stem rather from the concern of capital to dominate and control living labour in such a way as to extract from it the maximum of surplus labour?

2) Is the function performed by scientific and technical workers determined by the need to discover the most efficient techniques of material production, or is the search for technical efficiency and of organization of labour itself limited by, and in contradiction with, the concern (necessity even) of capital to guarantee for itself uncontested power over labour by means of the hierarchical division of the 'collective labourer'?

3) Is the present definition of technical skills and qualifications required primarily by the technical division of labour and thereby based upon scientific, ideologically neutral facts, or is the definition of technical skills and qualifications primarily social and ideological, designed to preserve and consolidate the social division of labour?

II

Let us try to examine these questions. And to start with let us focus on one problem that, in certain respects, underlies them all. What is the purpose of accelerating technological innovation, which necessitates an increasing proportion of technical and scientific labour in the fields of research and development *in industry* or *on behalf of industry?*

In fact the expansion of research does not primarily concern 'fundamental' or 'pure' research, but research directly or indirectly connected with the production process. Research conducted in universities and other 'independent' institutions that, in France, have been subjected to technocratic attacks in the last ten years ('industrialization' and 'technocratization' of the universities), is no longer, in the developed capitalist world at large, anything more than an appendage to industrial research. In the United States applied research – research on the potential industrial applications of the results of fundamental research – has been more or less the only form of research since about 1870. The United States has imported, mostly from Great Britain, the results of fundamental research. American 'pioneers' of science often became 'pioneers' of industry, i.e. capitalist entrepreneurs. Nowadays most university research in the United States is financed by industry or by the 'military-industrial complex'. It is, as it were, subcontracted.

In Germany the industrialization of research was introduced in about

1880 by Carl Duisberg at the Bayer company. Research work was organized and subjected to a division of labour in a manner appropriate to capitalist industry. Research was oriented and evaluated in the light of the aim of producing knowledge and techniques that would be directly usable in the production process, and would be likely to lower costs and to guarantee the company a technical monopoly and super-profits.

The main aim of fundamental research is to produce knowledge, not money. It is unproductive from the point of view of capital. Nevertheless it survived. But it was influenced indirectly by the priorities of capitalist production and became ever more closely dependent on it. The amount of public money poured into fundamental research varied according to the likelihood of its results having a profitable application; or, which amounts to the same thing, it depended on the fact that the monopolies needed to extend and deepen their theroretical knowledge in those fields where they could hope for some 'great leap forward' in technology. Because of this the development of scientific knowledge has become more and more uneven. Sciences capable of being 'capitalized', or being 'realized as capital' in the production process, have developed very much faster than those concerned with health, for example, or people's general physical well-being, or the best ways of making knowledge accessible to all, or the improvement of working conditions and so on. (More remarks relevant to this point will be found in note 10.)

Up the the beginning of the Second World War by far the most important aim of research and technical innovation was to counteract by *a reduction in production costs* the tendency of the rate of profit to fall. Innovations were made mainly on the level of the production process, by the introduction of techniques and machines that were able to increase the productivity of living labour, i.e. to replace living labour (variable capital) by dead labour (fixed capital), to speed up the turnover of circulating capital, to produce the same quantity of commodities with a reduced quantity of social labour. Throughout the 1930s these innovations, in the production process rather than in the nature of the products, reflected the stagnation of an economy in the process of developing monopolistic concentration, in which the big companies attempted to maintain their rates of profit by means of technical efficiency. Their monopoly of these technical processes enabled them, at least for a time, to make super-profits, and to earn additional income from rent or the sale of patents.

While innovations in production *processes* are still of decisive importance, they have developed *relatively* less rapidly since the beginning of the 1950s, than innovations in the nature, style and presentation of consumer *products*. Instead of products evolving more slowly than the processes involved in their production, the situation is now often reversed. The reason for this change is clear. In an economy in which monopolistic concentration has been more or less accomplished, increasing productivity must sooner or later come up against a limit, in other words the limited capacity of the market to absorb the goods produced. If the market

becomes saturated for a given range of commodities at given prices then the production of these commodities cannot be increased unless there is a fall in prices. Such a fall in prices, however, would only have the anticipated effect (of expanding the market) and would be profitable only given the following conditions: 1) That there are no *physical* limits to
1) That there are no *physical* limits to the absorption by the market of increased production of commodities of a given type;
2) that there is enough growth in the productivity of labour to allow increased profits in spite of the reduction in unit price.

The first of these conditions is obviously not met. There is a physical limit to the capacity of the market to absorb equivalent products whatever their price, at any rate in so far as these products are offered for sale on the basis of their use-value. As for the second condition: the higher the productivity of labour (i.e. the lower the price of living labour as a proportion of the cost-price), the less profitable it is *for capital* to seek new gains in productivity through innovation. [8]

That is why, in a virtually saturated market, innovation is more and more directed to the products and no longer primarily to the production process. Innovation in production techniques tends to slow down once the first stage in automation has been accomplished, [9] and monopoly competition (the search for super-profits in an effort to defeat the tendency for the rate of profit to fall) takes place in the field of product innovation rather than in the development of the productive forces. The main problem for the monopolies is to prevent the saturation of the market and to engineer an on-going or, if possible, an expanding demand for commodities that they can manufacture at maximum profit. There is only one way in which they can achieve this: by means of constant innovation in the field of consumer goods, whereby commodities for which the market is close to saturation-point are constantly made obsolete and are replaced by new, different, more sophisticated products with the same functions. Scientific and technical research therefore has the increasingly important function of accelerating the obsolescence and 'moral depreciation' of commodities, and of replacing them by new ones, in such a way as to speed up the turnover of capital and to create new opportunities for profitable investment of the growing mass of profits. [10] In a word: *the main purpose of research and innovation is to counteract the tendency of the rate of profit to fall and to create new opportunities for profitable investment.* [11]

As a result, in the United States, and tendentially in Western Europe, monopolistic production is growing much more rapidly 'in value' than in terms of physical quantities. Monopolistic expansion relies less on increasing the volume of goods produced than on substituting for relatively simple goods more elaborate and costly goods the use-value of which is, however, no greater, and may even in fact be less. This type of growth obviously cannot eliminate poverty and satisfy social and cultural needs. Instead it creates new types of poverty because it destroys the environment and leads to deterioration in the cities, and to acute inadequacies in the fields of housing, medical services, public health, public transport and so on.

In other words a significant proportion of the productive forces put to work by the capitalist mode of production, and in particular a significant proportion of scientific and technical knowledge and research, are functional and 'productive' only in relation to the orientation and priorities of monopolistic growth. To a large extent this type of scientific and technical labour and this type of research would be of little use in a society in which priority was given to satisfying the social and cultural needs of the masses. Much of this knowledge and skill would be of no interest in a communist society. In fact such a society would at first be hindered by the lack of the kinds of knowledge, skill and technique that would be needed for improving the quality of life, for placing science at the service of the people, for reducing the physical and mental stress caused by industrial work, and for changing the nature of work so that it could be adapted to the physical and mental needs of an intellectually and psychologically developed people.

It is therefore a *conservative* political line that focuses on the defence of the immediate professional interests of scientific and technical workers, or on their unconditional right to work in jobs in which they can use their *present* skills. Such a line cannot result in deep politicization. If scientific and technical workers are to be politically radicalized we must call into question and contest the content and orientation of their professional activities and skills, and thus also contest the capitalist ideology with which science and technology are thoroughly infected.

For science and technology cannot be considered to be ideologically 'neutral'. They are conditioned by the purposes to which they are put by the bourgeoisie and by the constraints within which they perform their functions within the capitalist system. A system poses only such problems as it can resolve; or, more precisely, it tends to pose problems in such a way that they can be resolved without endangering the stability or the logic of the system. Science and technology develop their overall priorities and direction in response to demands made on them by industry and by the State, demands that are obviously not the same in capitalist society as they would be in a 'liberated society'.

Science and technology are thus not independent of the dominant ideology or immunized against it. Subordinated to the production process and integrated within it, they are, as forces of production, indelibly marked by the capitalist relations of production. In fact, of course, this integration is never complete. Scientific research, which is a form of work designed to produce knowledge, has, *just like any other kind of work,* a degree of irreducible autonomy. This autonomy is located in the worker himself considered as sovereign *praxis.*[12] Science can be placed at the service of predetermined ends, can be developed in one direction at the expense of others, can be forced to answer problems set for it by the bourgeois State and ideology. But scientific workers cannot be prevented from raising different questions from those they are supposed to be asking, or from coming up with solutions to problems never posed by the bourgeoisie. When scientists work to produce the solutions that are demanded of them, solutions to problems that are set for them, they always find that they can pose and solve these problems in a different way. But they know that such possibilities are prohibited. It is in this that they recognize their submission to a culture and to an ideology. As a result they learn that the content and orientation of scientific research could be other than it is, but that this would be possible only with a different technology and in a different society. As a result they know that scientific work is not a force for revolution, but that it could be. And, finally, as a result it is neither voluntarist nor Utopian to challenge them to struggle, to criticize and to repudiate the orientation and content of their skills and knowledge, and the illusory neutrality and unassailability of their scientific work.

A number of objective difficulties stand in the way of such a critique. It is as if the bourgeoisie were aware of this dangerous possibility and to guard against it had imposed a thorough ideological imprint upon scientific and technical education. Technical and scientific knowledge is not only divorced to a large extent from the needs and the life of the masses. It is also culturally and semantically divorced from the general culture and the language of everyday life. It is divided into narrow specialities, each of which is esoteric in its language and difficult to communicate to non-specialists. This fragmentation of science and technology into narrow 'sub-cultures' is a consequence of the capitalist division of labour, and is at the same time one of the conditions that enables it to continue. It places strict limits on the knowledge and power of technical and scientific workers and tends to make them into what the Germans call *Fachidioten* ('specialized imbeciles'). They are restricted to their specialized fields, and each of them is called upon to produce purely technical solutions to problems posed in purely technical terms. They are thus prevented from viewing their specialized concerns in a broader perspective and from producing a comprehensive technical-scientific culture broad enough to challenge the false universality of bourgeois ideology. Hence the paradox that the most widespread intellectual activity of advanced capitalist societies should remain sterile as regards the development of a popular culture (i.e. of a culture really belonging to the masses), and that technical-scientific ideologies are no more than disguised forms of bourgeois ideology.

But there is really nothing surprising about this. The sub-cultures of science and technology remain narrow, fragmented and divorced from general life and culture because their subject-matter, the means and processes of production, are themselves separated and alienated from the people. In a society where the means and processes of production are estranged from the people and are raised to the status of 'autonomous powers', independent of men and their will, it is not surprising that knowledge about the means and processes of production should also be alienated and 'reified',[13] and should take the form of many limited and partial kinds of knowledge suitable for the partial and limited work that scientists and technicians perform as members of the 'collective worker'.

Technical and scientific culture and skills thus clearly bear the mark of the capitalist relations of production – autonomization and alienation of the means and forces of production as 'independent powers' – and of the capitalist division of labour that separates intellectual from manual work, combines only in an *external* way the various kinds of work that together create the 'social product', denies the workers any possibility of voluntary co-operation, makes it impossible for them to understand and control the production process and its overall objectives, divorces decision-making from productive work and separates the ability to produce knowledge from responsibility for the uses to which it is put.

But, even though it seems legitimate to consider that industrial scientific and technical workers belong to the category of productive, exploited and alienated workers, it does not seem correct to consider them to be purely and simply an integral part of the working class. Although it is certainly true that the science and the technology they produce are alienated from them, are at the service of capital and confront them as an alien power over which they have no control, it is also true (as Marx noted in the passages mentioned above) that from the point of view of the working class science and technology are means of exploitation and of extraction of surplus-value. In other words whereas scientific and technical workers have the same *relation to capital* as the working class they do not stand in the same relation to *one another*. As long as technical-scientific work and manual work are performed in parallel but separately, it must remain true that technical and scientific workers produce the means by which other workers are exploited and oppressed, and will necessarily be perceived by them as being the agents of capital. Manual workers, on the other hand, do not produce the means whereby technical and scientific workers are exploited. At the point where the relationship between the two is direct it is not a reciprocal one, but a hierarchical one.

It is therefore not adequate, in characterizing the position of scientific and technical workers in the production process, to examine it solely from the point of view of the relationship between capital and labour. It is just as important to consider it from the point of view of their relationship to other workers, and this will have an important bearing on the way in which scientific and technical workers consider their own class membership; it thus has an effect on their class-consciousness. We therefore need to distinguish:

1) situations where technical workers supervise, organize, control and command groups of production workers who, whatever their skills, have an inferior position in the industrial hierarchy and are subordinated to the former;

2) situations where the process is predominantly carried out by technical workers doing routine or repetitive work, with no authority or

hierarchical privilege over other workers in the same production unit.

A large number of misunderstandings have arisen from the fact that some sociologists (Serge Mallet and Radovan Richta in particular) have focused attention on the second kind of situation, whereas in fact the first is much more widespread, and will remain so in the foreseeable future. I shall therefore start by examining briefly the position of technical workers in this first kind of situation. I shall then try to throw some light on the ambiguities of protest movements among technical workers in the second situation, movements that cannot be understood except in relation to a general evolution that is progressively shifting technical workers from a supervisory to a directly productive function.

III

To understand the function of technical workers in manufacturing industry we must appreciate that their role is both technical and ideological. They are entrusted not only with planning the labour process and with keeping production up to pre-established technical standards, but also, and mainly, with maintaining the hierarchical structure of the labour force and with perpetuating capitalist social relations, that is with keeping the producers separated (alienated) from the product of their collective labour and from the production process.

Usually this second aspect of their role takes precedence over the first. But this fact has rarely received attention in capitalist societies and it is only since the Chinese Cultural Revolution that militants in the West have attempted to draw attention to it. Until recently it has been generally assumed that the division, specialization and separation of jobs in industrial production was not a prerequisite of the *capitalist* division of labour but was necessitated by the *technical* imperatives of large-scale mechanized production. It has been assumed that minutely fragmented and repetitive jobs are a consequence of the rationalization of the technical division of labour. It has moreover seemed that this unskilled and repetitive labour needed to be co-ordinated, supervised, planned and timed by technical experts responsible for overseeing all or part of the complex final product, for all or part of the overall work process. These experts, it seemed, needed to have both superior technical skills and intellectual and hierarchical authority.

But if we look into it more closely, we must ask: why must labour be minutely fragmented? Why must the narrowly specialized jobs be performed separately by different workers? The reasons usually given are: 1) narrow specialization requires less skill and less training; 2) repetitive tasks enable the workers to work faster and thus to increase output. In other words the fragmentation of work enables each individual worker and the labour force considered overall to become more productive.

In fact these seemingly objective reasons have only limited validity. Even within the framework of the capitalist exploitation of alienated labour they do not hold good universally. In fact it was not the development of the technical basis of production that caused the fragmentation of work. It was quite the other way round.[14] From the very beginning what the capitalist bosses were after was to maximize their power and control over wage labour. The work process was organized with this aim in mind, and this was effective in determining the forms of production technology. It might be argued that the maximization of control was a precondition for the maximization of exploitation and *therefore* of the maximization of the physical productivity of labour. In fact, however, while the first of these assertions is obviously true, the second can be shown to be false. *The kinds of discipline and control that enable the amount of surplus-labour that can be forced out of the worker to be maximized are almost never compatible with the kind of work organization that would enable the quantity of goods produced to be maximized with the minimum of human wear and tear.* In other words productivity *from the point of view of capital* is not automatically the same thing as productive efficiency (or physical productivity).

As a matter of fact – and we'll be looking at this more closely later on – looking for maximum physical productivity is exactly the same as looking for the conditions that allow workers to produce the greatest possible quantity of a given kind of product while using the optimal amount of energy in the most rational and effective manner. It is not a matter of reducing the amount of energy used to a *minimum*; a rhythm of work that is too slow or a job that is too easy or too monotonous is more exhausting than a rhythm and a degree of difficulty and complexity that keep the individual physically and intellectually alert. So the conditions for the maximum productive efficiency of labour can be worked out only collectively, by the workers themselves. This means that they must participate collectively of their own free will and be free to organize and regulate the work processes, and to modify, or even design for themselves, their tools and machines. And all this is incompatible with the power of the capitalist boss.

Productivity from the point of view of capital is something completely different. It is obtained by looking for the conditions that enable the greatest possible quantity of a given product to be produced *by the use of the maximum amount of human energy that can be obtained for the minimum of wages* (variable capital). The difference between this and the former definition is obvious. From the point of view of the worker the productivity of his labour does not increase unless he can produce more without becoming increasingly tired. From the point of view of capital the productivity of labour goes up whenever it can impose on the worker *an increased amount of work without a proportionate increase in his wages*. The ideas of 'technical progress' and of 'increased productivity' therefore have quite different meanings for the worker and for the capitalist. For the former they mean that improvements in 'machines' cause his labour to be more effective without any increase in the amount of work involved; for the latter they mean over and above this (and sometimes *only*) that improvements in 'machines' force the worker to expend a greater amount of physical and mental labour. In fact only the first definition captures the idea of increased productivity in a logically coherent way. It measures it by an increase in output without a proportional increase in input. The second definition, by contrast, is clearly incoherent because it takes into account only the increase in output and ignores the increase in input in as much as this takes the form of human energy.

These clarifications make it easier for us to understand the rationality, from the point of view of capital, of the hierarchical and fragmented division of labour and the necessity for it. It is not technical progress in the true sense of the word that makes this necessary, but the search for maximum exploitation. And this is not in general compatible with the most efficient (in the true sense of the word) organization and techniques of production.[15] That is why it is reasonable to suppose that production techniques and models of work organization and division of labour would have been – and could be – quite different if their overall aim were not the maximum exploitation, and hence the maximum hierarchical control, of labour, but – as we can see in the case of the Chinese Cultural Revolution – the maximum of *collective* initiative designed to make a given amount of work as effective as possible. This collective initiative obviously presupposes the suppression of hierarchical obstacles and of the separation between intellectual and manual labour, a new way of dividing up work into different jobs, a redefinition of professional 'qualifications' and 'career ladders' in such a way as to allow every worker to be continually enriching his practical and theoretical knowledge. Factory and education, productive labour and the acquisition of knowledge would need to be integrated so that from adolescence to retirement everybody would be at one and the same time productive worker, student and (often) teacher. We would have to avoid condemning anyone to spend their whole life doing monotonous, unskilled work, which would either be eliminated altogether by the permanent enrichment and transformation of the labour process, or would be performed on some rota basis. Although the aims of this kind of revolution of labour in China have been predominantly political and ideological, it has also been based on the implicit hypothesis that the collective initiative of the workers would permit optimal utilization of human and material resources and therefore a significant increase in productivity as well.

This basic postulate of the Chinese Cultural Revolution has been viewed sceptically in Europe and seen as wrong in principle. It is said that the Cultural Revolution must inevitably cause a decrease in the productivity of labour (in the true sense). We do not have sufficient data to refute this view. But experiments performed in the United States, although there have been few of these and they were limited in scope, do show that this basic scepticism is not justified. Indeed these experiments were conducted because it had become clear, in relation both to machine-based piece-work and to assembly-line work, that the division of labour in these types of work, and the technology on which it is based, cannot result in the maximization of technical efficiency.

These two types of work have one feature in common; in both cases the time required for performing a repetitive job is worked out 'scientifically'. The time required for each movement is worked out to a tenth or even hundredth of a second and a standard time is calculated for the performance of a succession of movements. Usually the length of time is of the order of 1 minute (between 30 and 120 seconds). If time and motion are to be studied 'scientifically' certain conditions must be fulfilled.

1) The nature of each movement must be 'standardized' in advance. It must not be left to the discretion of the worker, and it must not depend on his individual skill or agility. This standardization is possible because a number of standard variables that can be combined in the definition of each individual job are laid down. In other words the nature and duration of each movement can be defined and calculated on the basis of a grid, without any need to resort to observing and measuring any individual worker.

2) Clearly such 'scientific' study of time and motion can be applied only to jobs that are simple in the extreme, and from which all unpredictable human fluctuations have been eliminated. The movements of the worker must be made as mechanical as those of the mechanism to which he is the appendage. If the task was complicated and required initiative, thought and intelligence, the worker would retain, within certain limits, the power to determine for himself his way of working, the speed of his movements and the intensity of his effort. He would never expend the maximum energy of which he was capable. He would find his own 'cruising speed' and would invent ways of going about his work, short cuts and so on. It is by no means certain that he would produce less. What is certain is that the boss would have no sure means of knowing whether or not he was giving as much labour as he was capable of, and no sure means of forcing him to give the same amount of labour the whole year round.

These brief remarks should be enough to make it clear that the infinitesimal fragmentation of jobs is not the consequence of a technology that has developed according to its own laws, independently of the social and political context, but of a technology that is designed to function as a weapon in the class-struggle and to enable the amount of labour demanded from each worker to be 'scientifically' determined to prevent the worker from 'stealing' from the boss the time to smoke a cigarette, to read a newspaper or to put his feet up for a while. Work has not been made idiotic because the workers are idiots, or because you can increase the efficient expenditure of a given amount of human energy by turning them into idiots. Work has been made idiotic *because the workers cannot be trusted*. As long as they retain any control over their own work they are liable to use this against their exploiters. 'Scientific' work organization is above all the scientific destruction of any possibility of workers' control. [16]

Science, then, has helped to turn work into a straitjacket. But the other side of the coin has been the predictable development by the workers of new forms of resistance, notably absenteeism, sabotage and various forms of work-stoppage. Moreover scientific studies have shown that the more monotonous and repetitive work becomes the more exhausting it is, and that it is therefore less productive at a given level of expended energy than complex work involving a broad range of manual and intellectual faculties.

In a small number of British and American enterprises facing difficulties caused by work-stoppages, strikes over work rates, continual sabotage and chronic wastage, the bosses have therefore allowed themselves to be persuaded by the psychologists to give up imposing work norms, and to give the workforce responsibility for organizing the labour process, for determining the rhythm and pace of work and for modifying the design of the technical equipment. Clocking in and out of work has been abolished. The works canteen is shared by shop-floor and white-collar workers. Foremen, supervisors and factory cops and other 'NCOs of production' are dispensed with. The number and length of breaks are left to the discretion of the workers themselves. Jobs that had been fragmented are reorganized so that each individual and each group are responsible for a complex product and for quality control of their own products. The management are obliged to consider all modifications and technical and organizational innovations put forward by the work groups, and these are all discussed at workshop assemblies. No suggestion that the workforce judges, after discussion, to be worth while can be rejected. Technical workers and engineers are no longer in command. Their function is to make their technical and scientific knowledge available to the workers and thereby to help them to resolve technical problems. They are at the workers' disposal, and not the other way round. Finally, wages increase in proportion to productivity.[17]

In the dozen or so companies where this system has been tried out (most of them middle-sized but at least one, ICI in Britain, a giant international corporation) it has always resulted, after an initial period of adjustment, in spectacular rises in productivity, of the order of 20 per cent per annum over several consecutive years, *at the same time allowing workers to become less exhausted* while searching for the optimal work effort. In all cases absenteeism disappeared. Quality rejects dropped drastically, or even, in the case of certain high-precision products, were eliminated altogether. Breakdowns and the destruction of tools and equipment diminished on a spectacular scale. Wage differentials were sharply reduced. A flood of ideas for innovations and technical changes swept through the workshops.

In other words workers' control of the work process has exposed the technical irrationality and the politico-cultural bias of the capitalist division of labour. These experiments show that there is no *technical* need to turn workers into unskilled robots. Indeed the work process can be so organized that it is simultaneously a process of continuous apprenticeship. It is possible to integrate productive labour and the continuous acquisition of knowledge and skill. There is no reason why anyone should be restricted to unskilled, mindless and subordinate work. People's working lives can develop so that their work becomes progressively richer and they can show ever-greater skill and inventiveness.

The advantages of this kind of system are so striking that some people, including some of those involved in initiating the experiments mentioned above, naively wonder why it has not caught on more than it has. We can guess at some of the reasons for this.

1) This system is based on workers' control of technology and work organization. The workers would not be willing to exercise their initiative and creativity unless they could be sure that the bosses would not attempt to grab the results of their labours for themselves and to exploit them even more. The whole experiment would collapse if the increases in wages did not keep up with the growth in productivity or if the results of increased production could not be sold and resulted in redundancies. But job security and indexation of wages to productivity can be agreed to under capitalism only by some select companies and then only for limited periods. Some of these companies in the United States were able to avoid sacking workers during a recession only by asking for, and getting, an exceptional effort from their workers in order to beat the competition and to monopolize their sector of the market. The workforce of such a company, therefore, saved their own jobs only by destroying the capital of competing companies and condemning their workers to unemployment. Thus even if the majority of capitalist managers became convinced of the advantages of technical workers' control, its general introduction would still not be compatible with the capitalist system. Job security and a guarantee that the workers themselves would benefit from increased productivity (either directly through wage increases or indirectly through social services or increased leisure time and so on) presuppose social control of the whole of social production. It is only within the framework of workers' control of social production as a whole that technical workers' control can spread and become an effective norm.[18] It is incompatible both with capitalist management and with bureaucratic management, whether centralized or not. Both forms of management involve the same kind of hierarchical division of labour and form obstacles to the search for optimum physical productivity because they both subordinate labour to capital, and in separating labour from the means of production constantly reproduce capitalist relations of production.

2) Part of the increase in productivity obtained in the examples mentioned above was the result of the elimination of the numerous supervisors, foremen and inspectors whose job in a 'normal' capitalist firm is to keep the workers at their jobs, to combine the various bits of work from outside to form a whole, to control work rates and product quality, and so on. When the workers themselves take over the management of the labour process they discover (contrary to what Marx believed) that these 'NCOs of production' are parasites. Tiny parasites of course. But why not

attack the big ones as well? That is precisely the question raised by a shop steward at ICI's Gloucester nylon-spinning plant when he said, two years after the introduction of technical workers' control: 'The sociologists were right: we do enjoy our work more. But that's not going far enough. You can't open peoples' eyes and then tell them where to draw the line. They know there are still plenty of layabouts and parasites to be got rid of if we had half a chance. We know we're capable of running this factory. Our next step is to get a bigger say in making decisions.'[19]

3) Technical workers' control always involves destroying hierarchy and authority. First of all it comes up against resistance from the 'little bosses'. Then, if the hierarchical structure of wages and salaries is called into question, it comes up against resistance from the technicians and administrative staff – which can go as far as rebellion and sabotage. Think about it: workers who can get almost as much (and sometimes even more) as technical workers, lower-ranking engineers and junior technical sales staff. Throughout the hierarchy class relations are being contested, and thereby the power of the bosses and the power of the bourgeois owners is being called into question. If productivity and profits go up that's one thing; but is the whole game worth it if the representatives of the ruling class can no longer guarantee their power in the factories, or be sure that they are working for their own success? Fundamentally they are as interested in status as in money, and in the power of which money is the symbol as much as in money for its own sake.

We are now back at our starting-point. The capitalist division of labour, with its separation of manual and intellectual work, of execution and decision, of production and management, is a technique of domination as much as a technique of production. It is claimed that domination is necessary if production is to be maximized. But this is not true. Domination is necessary to maximize exploitation, to maximize the extent to which work serves the interests of capital and not those of the workers. The aim of capital is accumulation, and the pursuit of this aim involves the separation of the producers from the product of their labour, from the means of production and from work itself, which must be imposed on them from outside as a predetermined quantity, fixed by the inhuman necessities of the labour process. Hence there is a vicious circle:

1) since the purpose of production is not the satisfaction of the producers' needs, but the extortion of surplus labour, capitalist production cannot rely upon the workers' willingness to work;

2) the less capitalist management wishes to rely upon the willingness of the workers to work, the more extraneous, regimented and idiotic work has to become;

3) the more extraneous, regimented and idiotic work becomes, the less capitalist management can rely upon the workers' willingness.

Thus because relations at the workplace are established right from the word go on the basis of antagonistic class relations, hierarchical work organization and control always appear to capital to be the necessary preconditions for production and an end in themselves. [20] They are built into the very methods and tools used in production and they appear to be technical necessities of the production process itself.

That is why all those whose job it is, because of their technical qualifications, to supervise the smooth running of production in fact work to reproduce the hierarchical division of labour and capitalist relations of production. This applies just as much to the lower-ranking technicians (time-and-motion men, quality-control inspectors and so on) as to the engineers and higher-grade technical workers, and others who perform the functions of authority and supervision. Their role, in manufacturing industry, is to secure the subordination of living labour to machinery (dead labour) and thus to capital. [21] They have a monopoly of the technical and intellectual skills required by the production process and they *deny* these skills to the workers. Their role is to dequalify workers and to reduce work to manual work pure and simple. They represent the skill and knowledge of which workers have been robbed, the separation between intellectual and manual work, between conception and execution. They enjoy significant financial, social and cultural privileges. They are the workers' most immediate enemy. In a machine-tool shop every technician hired may turn ten or twenty hitherto skilled workers into unskilled underdogs (providing, of course, that semi-automatic machines are installed at the same time).

As an illustration of the role of technicans in the dequalification of skilled workers and in the arbitrary separation of manual work, reduced to simple execution, from the technical work of supervision and control, I give here an extract from a conversation I had with a young technician (who thought of himself as a 'Maoist') in a machine-tool factory. He had done three years of technical studies and was very proud of his knowledge. He earned twice as much as the workers he was supervising. When I asked him what he knew that the workers did not he replied: 'I have studied calculus and mechanics, and I'm a very good industrial draughtsman.'

'Do you ever use calculus in your work?'

'No. But I'm glad I've learned it. It's a good training for the mind.'

'What about the draughtsmanship? Is that very useful?'

'Of course. You can't possibly make anything unless you can read a blueprint. Its like the ABC.'

'Well then, if all the workers in your workshop know how to read a blueprint what do you know that they don't, apart from calculus?'

'I've got a more comprehensive insight into what it's all about. These blokes have all got their noses stuck in their own machines. I know about all the machines. I prepare and organize their work and when a problem crops up I show them how to sort it out.'

'Could the workers know as much as you do without having studied at a technical college?'

'There are some old blokes in my workshop who know a hell of a lot. But it takes time.'

'How much time?'

'Oh, at least five or six years.'

This technician had been to a technical college for three years. You will have noticed that it was his knowledge of calculus that, more than anything else, gave him a sense of superiority. His hierarchical and social privileges were based on this 'mental training'. But the calculus was of no use to him at all in his work. Calculus was the cultural status symbol that elevated him above the workers: it was the one thing he knew that the others could not learn from their practical experience.

This is a perfect illustration of the way in which the educational system is instrumental in building up the social hierarchy. This young technician's place on the social ladder, his sense of being worth more than an ordinary worker, did not stem from any superiority of *useful* knowledge. As he himself said, any useful knowledge he had could be acquired by workers with no academic training as a result of five or six years of practical experience on the job. His hierarchical superiority stemmed from superiority of *useless* knowledge. He had not been trained in calculus to become more *efficient* (more productive) than untrained workers, but to become *superior* to them. And the workers had not failed to learn calculus because they were too stupid to learn it, but because they were intended to remain culturally, and therefore hierarchically, inferior, whatever their skill.

But what the young technician said also shows us that these socio-cultural differences between the directly productive workers and the low-ranking technical cadres are not *class* differences. Marx was correct when he claimed that these cadres are objectively members of the working class. Although they are in a hierarchically oppressive position with respect to the workers they are themselves oppressed, exploited and alienated in their own work. Their position in relation to those above them in the hierarchy and to the representatives of capital is just the same as that of the workers in relation to them. But this objective class position must be understood correctly: these low-ranking technical cadres are not *bound* to owe allegiance to any other than the working class; they *can* feel themselves to be an integral part of this class, for that is what they are objectively. If Marxist analysis in terms of classes is to have any meaning they cannot be excluded *a priori* from the working class. But equally, they cannot be included in it without qualification, because while it is true that they belong objectively to no other class, it is also true that they are conditioned by their technical training to think of themselves as *not* belonging to the working class. We could say that they are workers who have been mystified, and that their hierarchical privileges sustain this mystification.

But mystification can be overcome. In situations of acute conflict an ideological breakthrough is possible. This can happen in periods of revolutionary crisis, or during a mass factory occupation or 'work-in' and so on. When, during a bitter struggle, the workers attack the capitalist division of labour and demand or set up a different way of doing things, without hierarchies and with equal pay for all (or demand some non-hierarchical system of pay increases), they may sometimes win over technical staff to their way of thinking. In the infectious atmosphere of a strike some of these technicians may even be found in the forefront of the struggle. Cases of this were to be seen in France in May 1968 and in the long 'hot autumn' of 1969 in Italy.

But the fact that this kind of ideological conversion is possible does not mean that it is inevitable. And it certainly does not mean that technical workers are destined to form the vanguard. The nature of their role in production does not prepare them for class confrontations, let alone for assuming positions of leadership. How they behave in a period of confrontation will depend mostly on their previous political and ideological education; and they don't get education like this in technical college. They get it from the politically radicalized workers in the course of the struggle when they come to understand that they stand to win more than they would lose by the abolition of the hierarchical division of labour. This is the thesis of Edoarda Masi,[22] who points out that they cannot be expected to adopt working-class viewpoints, or to struggle for the proletarian revolution until they can question *themselves,* and can make clear to everyone, including the workers, that their *apparently* purely technical functions are in reality political and ideological. Which means that they must:

1) endeavour to distinguish between their particular technical and scientific skills on the one hand, and their role in the hierarchical division of labour on the other hand;

2) endeavour to 'socialize' their technical skills; this means that they must search for ways and means whereby technical skills can be exercised collectively, and cease to be *professionally* monopolized by the few at the expense of everyone else,[23] this requires a struggle against unnecessary specialized jargon, a new definition of skills, a radical transformation of education and technical training and of the division of labour;

3) refuse the social privileges and the hierachical position of power attached to the *professional* exercise of technical and intellectual skills in the capitalist division of labour.

In other words the sharpest possible distinction must be made between specialization, professionalism and privilege. Whereas specialization cannot be abolished in the immediate future, privilege and professionalism can be. (This is one of the innovations made by the Chinese Cultural Revolution.) There is no inherent need, for example, to professionalize some of the skills and social functions of engineers or teachers. There is no intrinsic need to grant privileges of status, power and money to certain skills. The existence of these privileges cannot be accounted for by the scarcity of intellectual or technical skills, or of the ability to acquire them. It is questionable whether there ever was any such scarcity, and if there

was it has certainly virtually ceased to exist now. Instead there is a
potential over-abundance of intellectual skills. Scarcities that can still be
observed cannot be ascribed to a scarcity of talent or a lack of the ability to
learn. They are the result of the class character of the educational system.
As we have seen in the example of the young technician, so proud of his
mathematical skill, education aims at persuading a minority that they are
an élite, and it thereby reproduces the hierarchical stratification of labour
required by capitalist social relations. This result is achieved by abstract
teaching methods that make the acquisition of intellectual skills difficult
for children of less educated parents, and by identifying good school marks
with a right to privilege and to social promotion. The educational system is
thus the key instrument of social hierarchization: the differences of skill
and aptitude it claims to be able to *assess* are in fact *produced* by the
system itself.[24]

IV

It might seem at first sight that the hierarchical and social privileges
discussed above are not possessed by the growing stratum of technical and
scientific personnel who work in big engineering firms, in the 'scientific'
industries and research centres, and are themselves subjected to the
capitalist division of labour. In recent years we have seen mass-rebellions
and strikes by draughtsmen and engineering, technical and research staff
in the scientific industries, computer firms and research institutes. In many
cases such rebellion was motivated by the frustration and humiliation that
these workers experienced when they were subjected to the same
job-evaluation, fragmentation and hierarchical control of work as manual
workers. When intellectual workers cease to exercise hierarchical authority
over manual workers, and are themselves reduced to being producers of
immaterial commodities – projects, programmes, systems, information – or
to being supervisors of automated processes, they in their turn can come to
seem proletarianized and alienated from the stupefying specialization of
their work.

But we must be careful not to jump to the conclusion that their rebellion
is the sign of a leap to proletarian class-consciousness. This conclusion
would be justified only if these workers showed, or attempted to show,
solidarity with manual workers, and if they joined forces with them on a
class basis to fight for common objectives. This has happened – notably in
the chemical and electronics industries – but only as the exception to the
rule. More often than not the rebellion of intellectual workers is
profoundly ambiguous: they rebel not *as* proletarians, but *against* being
treated as proletarians. They rebel against the hierarchical organization,
fragmentation and meaninglessness of their work, and against the loss of
all or part of their social privileges.

It might be argued that there is no difference here, since the proletarian
who is aware of his position also fights against being a proletarian. And of
course this is true. But what counts is how he struggles and what he

struggles for. The class-conscious member of the proletariat can conceive of his liberation only in the context of the liberation of the whole class and the transformation of the whole system of social relations. But in most cases rebellious intellectual workers do not have this as their aim. Their struggle against hierarchy and authority is usually part and parcel of their demand for the reinstatement of the privileges they once enjoyed as members of the professional 'middle class'. They refuse proletarianization for themselves (but only for themselves), and assume that they can avoid it because they think of themselves as distinct from the workers. Hence the ambiguity of their struggles, which are in fact anti-monopolist rather than anti-capitalist in character.

To understand this ambiguity we must go back to the problem of the kind of training that most technical workers go through, and their motivations in putting up with it.

Further education in almost all capitalist countries is sharply divided into two distinct branches: the more traditional liberal univeristy education on the one hand, and that of the technical and engineering colleges on the other.[25] The content and methods of education differ significantly in these two branches. While teaching in the universities is by and large liberal/informal, in the technical and engineering colleges it is strict and disciplinarian, almost para-military. While the universities as a rule aim to convey knowledge, and to train students to become intellectually self-reliant, technical and engineering colleges aim to convey both knowledge and practical skills, and to shape the personality of the students so as to make them fit readily into the hierarchical and authoritarian regime in the factories, the laboratories and the bureaucracy. University students are supposed to acquire and develop a critical intelligence that should enable them to work in an independent manner, in the professions, as research workers, as private entrepreneurs or as teachers. Their degrees do not prepare them for definite jobs, and graduates often spend time looking round for what they could do, or even doing nothing much at all. Technicians and engineers, in contrast, are trained for particular jobs and to occupy a definite place in the social hierarchy and in the division of labour. They have chosen this particular kind of training and employment for two reasons:

1) their social origin leaves them little hope of becoming anything other than salaried employees; they do not have enough time or money to attempt an independent career or to run the risk of not finding a job as soon as they have finished their studies;

2) they have social ambitions; they aim for a salaried position 'above' that of the ordinary workers and employees, but without any hope of going right to the top, to positions of real power.

Such ambitions can be realized only within the established order of things, if they accept its scale of values, which implies that they should not aim too high and that they should respect those who are in control. And this is precisely the lesson they learn at the technical and engineering colleges. They are trained in specialized technical fields in which they learn how to solve the technical problems of designing means to predetermined ends without calling the actual ends in question. These schools dispense an essentially subordinate 'culture' that, unlike the 'culture' of the liberal universities, is not concerned with goals and values or with the meaning of things, but with ways of dealing effectively with the means to hand in the service of values decided upon elsewhere. This divorce between so-called higher culture – the humanities, the liberal arts – and technical skill and knowledge is fundamental to the reproduction of the social division of labour.[26]

Thus technical colleges and similar institutions are instrumental in producing a particular type of 'adapted' individual. Or, to put it the other way round, those who will put up with the regimentation, repression, discipline and deliberately unattractive programmes of the technical colleges are exactly the kind of people that capitalist industry needs. They are a hand-picked minority selected from the mass of young workers (the majority, according to some studies) who dream of improving their qualifications in order to escape from the tension and boredom of mindless, repetitive work. It *should* be possible for them to get a balanced practical and theoretical training, if teaching methods and educational programmes were made attractive enough. But these methods and programmes are deliberately designed in such a way as to discourage, repel and eliminate somewhere between a half and three-quarters of the students (who themselves represent only a small fraction on the number of those who would like to learn).

There is an obvious social function in the fact that these colleges are highly selective and that such a high percentage of the students do not last out the course. As long as a large amount of manual and unskilled work remains to be done the colleges must produce a high enough number of 'failures', who will have no choice but to accept these jobs. For the reproduction of hierarchical social relations it is just as important to produce rejects as it is to produce graduates. A definite proportion of adolescents must be persuaded by the *seemingly* objective processes of educational selection that they are good for nothing but unskilled work. They must be persuaded that their educational failure is not *the schools' failure* to educate them but the result of their own social and individual shortcomings, that they have 'no gift for learning'. Conversely, those who do well at school and college must be convinced that they are the gifted ones whose talent, application and ambition deserve to be rewarded with social superiority. Technical colleges must make sure that their successful graduates will feel condescending towards workers and respectful to those above them. What we have here, then, is the operation of a system that divides the working class into quite distinct, and if possible separate, strata, and persuades the technically qualified stratum to identify themselves more with the 'middle classes' than with the proletariat.

This attempt to upgrade the technical worker socially is not merely a hangover from earlier days, when technicians had a supervisory role rather than a subordinate and directly productive one. It also meets the capitalists' need to be able to entrust the supervision of highly automated plant to staff who are ideologically reliable, who will not be tempted to use their technical knowledge to their own political advantage or, even worse, to put it at the disposal of the working class. People who actually control the more or less automatic processes involved in key sectors of production must, by some means or other, be integrated into the system's privileged strata, and be made blind as to their own class position.

The effectiveness of this strategy of integration is, however, dependent on the reality of the privileges that the system can confer. It meets no insurmountable obstacles here as long as the stratum of technical workers remains only a small minority. But when the proportion of technically skilled to unskilled jobs is reversed the contradictions become explosive. The situation now potentially exists in the United States and, for the time being to a lesser extent, in Western Europe.

Advanced capitalist economies are, from a technological point of view, in a transition period (the 'third industrial revolution') between assembly-line production and automation. The schools and colleges must keep producing a proportion of failures so as to provide non-qualified personnel for industry (and 'services'). But it is already clear that the percentage of unskilled jobs is rapidly decreasing and that further education is becoming a prerequisite for finding a job, however narrowly specialized and dehumanizing it may be. The arbitrariness of the education system's selectiveness is thus becoming manifest. A clear proportion of adolescents is prohibited from pursuing further education – about two-thirds in Western Europe, about one-third in the United States – not because they couldn't be educated but because this is judged to be undesirable. Education would render them 'unfit' for the lowest-grade jobs.

On the other hand, as more and more jobs do require further education *the link between such training and the privileges that it used to confer can no longer be maintained.* According to recent American statistics [27] the expected lifetime earnings of youngsters with one to three years of college or university education is only 6.25 per cent higher than that of youngsters who have only a secondary-school education ($119,000 as against $112,000). Hence the following contradiction: further education remains selective and competitive, and continues to inculcate the conformist attitudes that are expected of those who wish to 'succeed' socially and to rise in the world; but the jobs for which the technical colleges and polytechnics (and, in France and Italy, the first university degree) prepare people no longer confer many social, professional or financial privileges. The majority of trainees are destined to become the low-grade labourers of the technically advanced industries and 'services' (which are themselves industrialized) and to perform the ungratifying and frustrating work of the 'post-industrial society'. [28] Such jobs, it might be argued, are less intolerable than those in the assembly-line industries. This may be obvious to workers in these industries, but it hardly offers consolation to the young technical workers of the 'post-industrial society'.

For these workers there are two possibilities:

1) Having put up with the regimentation and competitiveness of the educational institutions in the hope of privilege and promotion, they rebel when they find out that the low-grade and stupefying jobs they end up with don't match up to the promises offered by the system and frustrate their desire for responsibility and respectability and initiative. Such rebellion is politically ambiguous and is as likely to become fascist as reformist in character.

2) Or they can find out before they even finish their training that the values and the promises offered by the educational system are a big swindle, in which case they rebel against regimentation at school first and against regimentation at work later. Why should they put up with the disciplinarian and authoritarian methods of training when this training cannot either enable them to rise socially or get them work that is interesting and helps them to develop their faculties? If success at school does you no good, well fuck the schools and fuck the system. You might as well decide for yourself what to do and what to learn.

Only this second attitude is potentially revolutionary. It exposes the objective bankruptcy of the ideas that can lead an adolescent to put up with barrack-like educational institutions and the barrack-like factories or offices for which they are a preparation. It points to the connection between protest and crisis in the educational system and protest and crisis in the social system, with its hierarchical division of labour. It goes beyond the inherent ambiguity of the first attitude, which rebels against the alienation and proletarianization of technical work, but from the standpoint of a petit-bourgeois view of hierarchy, a view that is upheld by the system in spite of its being in contradiction with its technico-productive development.

When Serge Mallet and others wrote about the 'new working class' ten years ago they missed this ambiguity. They distinguished (correctly at the time) between the 'old' working class, whose demands were essentially limited to 'quantitative' matters, wages and the like, and the 'new working class', which struggles for more 'qualitative' goals. As technical or further education and the technicization (or 'intellectualization') of work becomes more and more widespread, the distinction between the 'old' and 'new' working class is becoming obsolete, at least as far as younger workers are concerned. They know or sense that the technical worker is the proletarian of the 'technological society'. They have learned from their experience at school and college that the system channels towards technical studies and jobs those it considers to be 'unfit for anything better'. They have learned that their teachers are on the same side of the fence as the cops and the bosses who will be assaulting and exploiting them. Their rebellion against repression and stupidity in the schools and colleges is a foretaste of their rebellion against repressive and hierarchical organization at work. They know that their technical skills, which become obsolete within five years anyhow, are worth no more than traditional manual skills and offer no hope of escape from boredom and oppression at work.

There is, therefore, an objective basis, in their common attack on the capitalist division of labour, for the political and ideological unification of technical and manual workers. But the objective possibility of this unification needs to be worked out in more detail in relation to the objectives and the location of the struggle. The objectives must necessarily be those of a 'cultural revolution': the destruction of inequalities, of hierarchy, of the separation between intellectual and manual work and between conception and execution; the liberation of the creative capacities of all workers. The location is necessarily simultaneously the factories, where the workers are oppressed and intellectually mutilated, and the educational institutions, which produce the 'human material' the factories need.

A crisis must be created in the capitalist system's reproduction of its social relations and its hierarchical division of labour by a concerted attack on hierarchy in the factories and on the educational system that makes it possible.[29] Instruction and production, training and work, have been kept separate because theoretical knowledge is kept separate from practical experience, because the worker is separated from the means of production and from general cultural and social life. That is why, if communism is our goal, the reunification of education and production, and of work and culture, is absolutely essential.

NOTES

1 K. Marx, *Capital*, I (Moscow: Progress Publishers; London: Lawrence & Wishart 1961), ch. 14, p. 361.

2 The passages from Marx to which I am referring may seem to offer support to reformist or 'revisionist' theoretical views. It is essential to remember that the distinction between productive and unproductive labour in these passages is always made from the point of view of capital. To call an activity 'productive' implies no value judgement as to its intrinsic interest or its utility from some standpoint other than that of capital; it can tell us nothing about how one would define 'productive labour' in relation to some other mode of production.

For Marx labour is productive if it produces surplus-value, and thus contributes directly to the reproduction of the capital with which its own reproduction is paid for (in the form of wages). Any labour, however much it may be wage-labour and oppressive, is unproductive if it produces no surplus-value – even if it is essential to the realization of surplus-value (sales and publicity staff and so on) or to the circulation of capital (bank staff), and even if it helps to create the conditions that make capitalist production possible (as with education and private research, for example).

On the subject of the 'collective productive worker' Marx says:

Given that, with the progressive development of real subordination of labour to capital, i.e. of the specifically capitalist mode of production, it is no longer the individual worker but, increasingly, socially combined labour that becomes the real agent of the process of collective labour; and that the various kinds of collective labour that combine to form the overall collective productive machine participate in quite different ways in the direct process of production of commodities, one mainly with his hands, another mainly with his head, one as a manager or engineer or technician etc, another as a supervisor, yet another as a direct manual worker or perhaps just as an assistant – a growing number of different labour functions are included under the concept of productive labour and their agents under the concept of productive labourer, directly exploited by capital and subordinated to its processes of production and realization. If we consider the collective worker who makes up a factory, his combined activity is materially realized in the form of a collective product that is at the same time a sum of commodities, and it is totally irrelevant whether the function performed by some individual worker, who is no more than a member of this collective worker, is more or less distinct from direct manual labour ['Results of the direct process of production', from a chapter of *Capital* that Marx left out of published editions and that is not as yet available in English. It has been published in Germany by EVA of Frankfurt and in France in the 10/18 paperback collection].

Consider also the following passage:

For example the unskilled labourers in a factory . . . have nothing directly to do with the working up of the raw material. The workmen who function as overseers of those directly engaged in working up the raw material are one step further away; the works engineer has yet another relation and in the main works only with his brain, and so on. But the *totality of these labourers*, who possess labour-power of different value . . . , are the living production machine of these *products* : just as, taking the production process as a whole, they exchange their labour for capital and reproduce the capitalist's money as capital. . . . *It is indeed the characteristic feature of the capitalist mode of production that it separates the various kinds of labour from each other, therefore also mental and manual labour . . . and distributes them among different people. This however does not prevent the material product from being the common product of these persons* [Marx, *Theories of Surplus-Value* (Moscow: Progress Publishers; London: Lawrence & Wishart 1969), pt I, p. 411, my italics].

It should be noted that these last two sentences, which I have emphasized, very much restrict the possibilities for a 'revisionist' interpretation of the analyses that precede them.

3 This is one of the central claims of Herbert Marcuse. I believe it to be fundamentally correct, although I do not go along with all the analyses that Marcuse offers in support of it, or with some of the political conclusions he draws from it.

4 This is one of the central themes of Paul Baran and Paul Sweezy, *Monopoly Capitalism* (Harmondsworth: Penguin Books 1968).

5 All the different branches of the revolutionary Left agree on this point, although they emphasize different levels of struggle: 'practice of Utopian living', counter-culture, 'change of life-style'; ideological war, armed struggle; programme of transitional demands; communist programme.

6 The ambiguity on this point of Marcuse's *One-Dimensional Man* lies in the fact that he jumps straight from a *historical* critique of technification to a *general* critique of technology and of the scientific-technical attitude *per se*. He gives an account of the development of capitalism and technology and thereby of the dominance of the ideology of means, but evades what is, in my opinion, the basic problem: is indifference to ends a *general and inherent* feature of technology and science, arising from the specific attitude of 'objectivity' or 'value-neutrality' (*Wertfreiheit*)? Or is this indifference to ends a consequence within scientific-technical activity (and not *only* there) of the separation, within the capitalist division of labour, between activity, means and ends, theory and practice, science and the people; and of the systematic production (by upbringing and selection) of the kind of individual who is 'indifferent to ends', who corresponds more closely to the *idea* that capital

has of scientific-technical activity than to its real internal logic?

7 This conclusion is suggested by Charles Bettelheim in *Economic Calculation and Forms of Property* (London: Routledge & Kegan Paul, forthcoming). See also Bettelheim, *The Transition to Socialist Economy* (Hassocks: Harvester 1975) and *Industrial Organisation and Cultural Revolution in China* (New York: Monthly Review Press 1975) and Jean Daubier, *Histoire de la Révolution Culturelle Chinoise* (Paris: Maspero 1970), Introduction.

8 Marx demonstrates this in the *Grundrisse* (Harmondsworth: Penguin Books 1973) with the following argument: 'If *necessary labour* had already been reduced to 1/1,000, then the total surplus-value would be = 999/1,000. Now if the productive force increased a thousandfold, then *necessary labour* would decline to 1/1,000,000 working day and the total surplus-value would amount to 999,999/1,000,000 of a working day; . . . it would thus have grown by 999/1,000,000 . . . i.e. the thousandfold increase in productive force would have increased the total surplus by not even 1/1,000 (p. 338). NB Marx write 1/11, which was an obvious miscalculation.

9 See Karl Heinz Roth, in K. H. Roth and Eckhard Kanzow, *Unwissen als Ohnmacht, (Berlin: Voltaire* 1970) ch. 1.

10 The pharmaceutical industry is entirely typical in this respect. When a new product is launched the firm holding the patent can make super-profits for a certain length of time (for as long as it has a monopoly on that type of product). These profits can be of the order of 1000 per cent of the production cost. New special drugs, the therapeutic effectiveness of which is *often no greater* than that of drugs already available – it is often simply a matter of new combinations or new preparations of existing drugs or of new drugs therapeutically equivalent to existing ones – but the cost of which is much higher, are made the objects of such intense propaganda to the doctors that they are progressively substituted for the old drugs, which in the end become unobtainable. Part of the super-profits made as a result of these new products are then reinvested in research for yet more new products, and so on.

11 According to a United States Senate Anti-Trust Committee Report (1965), research expenditure in the United States is divided among the different kinds of research in the following proportions: 1 per cent for fundamental research (i.e. for the acquisition of scientific knowledge in the true sense of the term); 3 per cent for applied research, (i.e. for investigation into possible industrial applications of new scientific knowledge); 26 per cent for technological research, (i.e. for the study of new processes and products that applied research had shown to be possible); 70 per cent for development (i.e. for the development and improvement of industrial products and production processes).

12 It is because he neglects or underestimates the dimension of *praxis* that underlies all technology, science and the production of commodities that Marcuse (unlike Marx) can paint a picture of 'technological society' as a stable system and of its workers as integrated into it.

13 Cf. Marx, *Grundrisse:* 'The science which compels the inanimate limbs of the machinery, by their construction, to act purposefully, as an automaton, does not exist in the worker's consciousness, but rather acts upon him through the machine as an alien power, as the power of the machine itself' (p. 693). And in the unpublished chapter 6 of book I of *Capital* (see note 2 above) Marx wrote that science is thoroughly separated

> . . . from the skills and knowledge of the individual workers – and although it is itself produced by labour it appears, wherever it is an aspect of the labour process, as an element of capital . . . All of its applications, although based on *social labour*, appear as *means of exploitation of labour* . . . *therefore as the strength of capital in its relation to labour* . . . *And this is how it comes about that the development of the forces of social production and the conditions that make this development possible, appear to be the products of capital;* the worker's relation to them is not merely passive, they stand over

and *against* him [EVA ed, p. 81].

14 Stephen Marglin, 'What do bosses do? The origins and function of hierarchy in capitalist production' (appears in this edition as the second chapter, pages 13-54. The French edition contains only an extract).

15 Stephen Marglin has shown, in the essay referred to above, that the search for maximum technical efficiency was never the first concern of the capitalist bosses. Industry did not develop on the basis of new and more efficient technology; rather new technologies (steam engines, machinery) could be introduced only in the wake of a concentration of artisanal production in manufacturing establishments. The reason for this concentration was not the technical superiority of manufacture – weaving techniques remained unchanged – but the desire of the capitalist bosses to:

   1 take into their own hands control of the whole of what the weavers produced; if they were not supervised in the manufacturing workshops the weavers would pilfer goods and sell them for themselves;

   2 force the weavers to work longer hours and at greater intensity than they would have chosen to do had they remained masters of their own tools;

   3 appropriate all technical innovations for their own benefit, to maximize their profits;

   4 finally, and most importantly, to organize production in such a way that the direct producers became entirely dependent on the bosses.

16 Cf. the essay by Antonio Lettieri in this book. He shows that work organization and the classification of skills are the result of the balance of forces as between workers and bosses and not of 'objective' technical requirements.

17 I have described the principal characteristics of these experiments. They are present to a varying extent and combined in different ways in various different 'recipes'. These recipes are usually worked out by 'consultants' with a background in psychology or sociology, and because their careers depend on the success they show they tend to emphasize the uniqueness of their own recipes (and of their 'philosophy') rather than the features that are common to all the variants. Still, there is general agreement that the prerequisites for success are the destruction of hierarchical scales, despecialization of jobs, abolition of relations of authority, self-organization of production teams and clear (or at least apparent) common objectives and means of attaining them; all of these are scarcely compatible with 'managerial prerogatives'.

18 This is clearly yet another argument *for*, and not against, experimenting with forms of technical workers' control *as methods of struggle* (workers' takeover of machinery, control of the work process, of pace of work and so on).

19 *Business Week* (17 October 1970), p. 59. It goes without saying – and this workers' spokesman probably had no illusions on this score – that this fight cannot be won at the level of a single factory, or even of a whole corporation.

20 William Foote White describes the insurmountable resistance put up by workers in a large machine-tool workshop to the imposition of work-rates: 'Here it seems that management is so preoccupied with its efforts to establish control over the workers that it loses sight of the presumed purpose of the organisation. A casual visitor to the plant might indeed be surprised to learn that its purpose was *to get out production*. Certainly, if it had been possible to enforce some of the rules described (above), the result would have been a slowing down of production' (*Money and Motivation* (New York: Harper & Row 1955), p. 65).

21 It should be remembered that in this section I am discussing only industries in which technical workers and manual workers are in a hierarchical relation, and not automated industries in which technical workers supervise ony complex machines and processes.

22 'Sur l'autocontestation des intellectuels', *Les Temps Modernes*, ccxcv (February 1971).

23 The term 'professional' is used here, as in Edoarda Masi's article, in the following sense; a qualification is a 'professional' one when the holder of it has a special status, and when no one is recognized as having this status unless he has the requisite institutionalized educational or professional title to it.

24 Cf. Pierre Bourdieu and Jean-Claude Passeron, *La Reproduction* (Paris: Editions de Minuit 1970).

25 The engineering colleges (including, in Britain, the polytechnics) must not be confused with the technical universities (or, in Britain, the science and engineering departments of the universities), which are élite institutions with a highly selective intake that turn out high-level personnel destined for posts in the 'high command'. In France the *'Grandes écoles'* are functionally similar to the universities; they have rigorous selection, protracted courses, an élitist ethos. It is for contingent historical reasons, and not because of any functional difference, that they are not part of the university system. By 'engineering colleges' I mean the technical colleges and polytechnics and other vocational and professional training institutions in as much as they are characterized by relatively short courses, leading up to qualifications less highly regarded than university degrees, and where the training programmes are usually (in France) under the control of industrialists and their representatives.

26 Eckhard Kanzow gives the following description of German engineering schools, which is equally applicable to schools in other countries: up to 40 hours compulsory tuition per week; very high pace of course work; large amount of homework; in order to do everything asked of him the student would need more than 24 hours in a day; rigid discipline, frequent exams, authoritarian demeanour of teachers, all contributing to a standardization of performance and behaviour among the students. In such a system 'success' and 'survival' are the same thing.

Their studies actually consist of a mish-mash of heterogeneous kinds of training quite unconnected with each other. No coherent programme has ever been developed. It is almost entirely a matter of learning facts and formulae by heart, and of learning how to assimilate fragmentary and disconnected bits of information rapidly. The result of all this is that students cannot gain any understanding beyond the scope of their special subjects; cannot develop the ability to learn for themselves; complete lack of any critical perspective on their own special subjects; lack of independence in making decisions, or in developing for themselves their own concepts or ways of thinking within their subjects.

This type of training inculcates in the individual the style of behaviour expected of him by the firms ... Result: an uncritical, narrow-minded 'NCO of production', tailor-made for the job, capable of fitting in and of obeying whatever orders he may get from the officers above him in the chain of command.

Engineering school students come mostly from social strata that are under-represented in the universities. If the ruling class had abolished the present privileged pattern of recruitment to the universities, to the benefit of the under-privileged classes, while stressing the vocational and disciplinary character of universities, they would have exposed their social function. They could not allow themselves to do so. The universities would have become centres of social protest. The expansion of the engineering schools therefore represents a compromise solution; cultural privilege was extended to a field over which the ruling class have firm control (classes not too large, students kept isolated from any experience of other forms of higher education). Moreover engineering school students were to be easily corrupted by the promise of rapid social promotion.'

Elsewhere Kanzow has described the adult technical training colleges whose role is to 'equalize opportunity' by making available better career prospects to those workers who demonstrate some 'gift for applied science'. These colleges are controlled by the Employers' Federation (BDA) in West Germany. Kanzow gives the following quote from an ideologist of the employers:

The improved training that is required by the rationalization of production is always designed in such a way as to keep intact the hierarchy of the firm. If the hierarchy of the firm changes under the impact of technological progress it must be stablised by having a promotion ladder such that each rung gives access to certain positions in the firm . . . The abolition of classes implies equality and this is only possible if, over and above the elimination of the few remaining social differences, ideological differences are also removed [Roth and Kanzow, *op. cit.*, pp. 224–6, 171].

27 Given in Samuel Bowles, 'Contradictions in U.S. higher education', mimeo. A French translation appeared in *Tempes Modernes* (August-September 1971).

28 Cf. Antonio Lettieri's claim that higher education is *forced unproductive labour* with the function (among others) of disguising unemployment among young people.

29 From this point of view students in the professional, technical and engineering schools are in a better position than students in the *lycées* (French grammar schools) and universities to stimulate the formation of a mass revolutionary *avant-garde*. For a long time they have been regarded by university students as sheep-like. It is true that political radicalization started in the *lycées* and universities and only later spread to the higher technical and professional schools. This time-lag is not surprising. The ideological formation of a new radicalism never begins within the strata that suffer most severe oppression and insecurity. It always appears first among those who have some intellectual and material independence (among the smallholders rather than the agricultural wage-labourers; among the relatively skilled rather than the unskilled workers and so on).

But this time-lag does not mean that those who radicalize later radicalize less rapidly or profoundly once the process has begun. In the educational sector the best illustration of this is provided by the West German professional and engineering-school students. Their main union, the SVI (*Studentenverband deutscher Ingenieurschulen*) twice went into action, in March 1968 and April 1969, when the university student rebellion was at its height. On both occasions their movement was far more extensive (between 70 and 90 per cent of all students) and more outspoken than that of the university students. It involved indefinite strike from classes, boycott of exams, occupation of public buildings, expulsion of a bureaucratic leadership, collective attempts to design new training methods and programmes, organization of 'anti-schools' and, most important of all, something that university students managed to do only rarely, penetration into the factories to explain their strike to the workers and discuss objectives with them.

The manifesto of the spring 1969 general strike opened with a resolution in which the SVI declared in particular:

The economy is run by a reactionary handful of capitalists whose aim is the accumulation of capital and the maximization of profits . . . Subtle forms of domination have been developed to perpetuate this economic system – such as the hierarchical structure of factories, fixed scales of qualifications, the deliberate production of specialized imbeciles (*Fachidioten*) . . . Training is designed to meet the requirements of rationalization in industry, and has the job of producing as efficiently as possible, for delivery to the factories, the required 'human material', narrowly specialized, an investment on which the returns can be calculated in advance . . . Hence the objectives of this strike. It is not enough to demand reformist improvements that will only prop up or even rationalize the bankrupt social system . . . This is why, in interrupting this semester, we are escaping from the limits of this training. We are on strike because we refuse to give ourselves to this economic system . . . and this means that we must take our protests into the factories.

Just how dangerous this was for the system was shown by the brutality of its reaction: withdrawal of grants from those on strike, strikers called up for military service, attempts to blacklist the strikers to prevent them from ever gaining employment, police brutality (especially in Berlin, where the students were politically more isolated) and so on. From now on, wrote Kanzow, 'Students know that future demonstrations and strikes will need to confront the full range of repressive forces and methods at the disposal of those in power, and that it will be impossible to win a struggle on those terms. The struggle against the ruling class and its repressive power cannot be won unless it can be integrated with the coming struggles of the working class'. (Roth and Kanzow, *op. cit.*, pp. 237–44).

Marxist Theory and Contemporary Capitalism Series

Charles BETTELHEIM

The Transition to Socialist Economy

This book is devoted to the development of the economic theory of the transition to socialism.

Studies in this area are still very rare, in spite of the ever-growing practical and theoretical importance of the subject. Bettelheim provides a fundamental critical study of the complex problems which are inadequately summed up in the expression 'the transition to socialism'. This expression suggests a leap forward in a unilinear historical movement from capitalism, through a transitional stage, to socialism, as if the tendencies and forces of the 'transitional period' could only be in one direction. But there is no such guaranteed unilinear movement to socialism. The economic structure of a transitional society must be understood in its own terms and without evasive presuppositions about its future. Such a society might, indeed, be in transition to socialism, or it might alternatively develop new forms of capitalism, notably State capitalism.

Bettelheim, one of the most important Marxist economists in the world, lays the foundations for a critical reflection on the concepts 'socialist economy', 'socialist planning' and 'socialist property relations', etc.; and he prepares the way for an analysis of transitional social formations, an analysis which will also need to take account of the political and ideological domains and of the relations between these and the structure of economic relations. This book is essential reading for all those engaged in the struggle for socialism.

Michel BOSQUET

Capitalism in Crisis and Everyday Life

Starting from the everyday scandals of capitalism, and from the facts and events which turn up in the news, these essays reveal a system in crisis, and analyse the logic and contradictions of this system. The author aims to show how the system operates concretely, to expose its faults and to challenge it in the name of all those urgent human needs that it is incapable of satisfying.

The workers' movement struggles to discover the strategy and forms of organisation which will enable it successfully to wage a political fight for socialism and to discover the force and imagination necessary to go beyond the anarchy of capitalism and the servitude of Stalinism.

The essays in this book, now published in English translation, originally appeared in the influential French socialist weekly *Le Nouvel Observateur* of which Michel Bosquet has been editor for economic and social affairs since 1964.

Claudie BROYELLE

Women's Liberation in China

The emancipation of women in the context of Mao's revolution in China is the subject of this book, which will be of enormous interest to women both within and outside the women's movement. The picture that Claudie Broyelle draws of Chinese society in the 1970s will also be of consequence to Marxists, non-Marxists concerned with China and South East Asia, and to anybody concerned with the oppression of women and children, or, indeed, with revolutionary politics as a whole.

Claudie Broyelle, at present working in Peking, is a French journalist and author, who visited China in 1971 with a group of eleven other women. They went to more closely investigate the situation of women in China's revolution. One of the results was this book, which is both a delightful narrative of Chinese life but also Claudie Broyelle's reflections on and analysis of the women's movement in the West — in the light of her Chinese experience. Her approach is unconventional. Many of her ideas are refreshingly provocative. She makes use of a host of anecdotes and the actual experiences of many Chinese women and men — workers and peasants alike. Of all the many books on China, this is a study quite out of the ordinary.

Lucien SÈVE

Man in Marxist Theory: Towards a Marxist Psychology

This book is about the Marxist answer to the question, 'What is man?' As Marx says in his famous sixth thesis on Feuerbach: "The essence of man is no abstraction inhering in each single individual. It is the ensemble of social relationships."

What are the implications of historical materialism for the scientific understanding of the human individual, his needs and personality? Lucien Sève provides an analysis of the general Marxist conception of man, and on this basis he makes a fundamental contribution to the development of the psychological sciences, in particular to a science of human personality based on historical materialism.

This is a rigorous, scientific and very brilliantly argued book whose specific purpose is to provide a basis for Marxist psychology. It has no rivals in its range and coverage.